W9-ASH-537

GLOBAL SOUTH ASIA

Padma Kaimal
K. Sivaramakrishnan
Anand A. Yang
SERIES EDITORS

Marrying for a Future

Transnational Sri Lankan Tamil Marriages in the Shadow of War

SIDHARTHAN MAUNAGURU

UNIVERSITY OF WASHINGTON PRESS

Seattle

Marrying for a Future was made possible in part by support from the Faculty of Arts and Social Sciences at the National University of Singapore.

Copyright © 2019 by the University of Washington Press
Printed and bound in the United States of America

Composed in Minion Pro, typeface designed by Robert Slimbach

Cover photograph: A Tamil bride walking down the aisle toward the *manavarai* (wedding dais). Photograph courtesy of Eugine Vincent

23 22 21 20 19   5 4 3 2 1

All rights reserved. No part of this publication may be reproduced or transmitted in any form or by any means, electronic or mechanical, including photocopy, recording, or any information storage or retrieval system, without permission in writing from the publisher.

UNIVERSITY OF WASHINGTON PRESS
www.washington.edu/uwpress

LIBRARY OF CONGRESS CATALOGING-IN-PUBLICATION DATA
Names: Maunaguru, Sidharthan, author.
Title: Marrying for a future : transnational Sri Lankan Tamil marriages in the shadow of war / Sidharthan Maunaguru.
Description: Seattle : University of Washington Press, [2019] | Series: Global South Asia | Includes bibliographical references and index. |
Identifiers: LCCN 2018046904 (print) | LCCN 2018051514 (ebook) | ISBN 9780295745428 (ebook) | ISBN 9780295745435 (hardcover : alk. paper) | ISBN 9780295745411 (pbk. : alk. paper)
Subjects: LCSH: Marriage—Sri Lanka. | Tamil (Indic people)—Foreign countries. | Sri Lanka—Emigration and immigration—Social aspects. | Sri Lanka—History—Civil War, 1983–2009—Social aspects.
Classification:
LCC HQ666.8 (ebook) | LCC HQ666.8 .M38 2019 (print) | DDC 306.81095493—dc23
LC record available at https://lccn.loc.gov/2018046904

The paper used in this publication is acid free and meets the minimum requirements of American National Standard for Information Sciences—Permanence of Paper for Printed Library Materials, ANSI Z39.48–1984 .∞

To Sunila, Sanjay, and my parents, Maunaguru and Sitralega

Contents

Acknowledgments

This book would not have been possible without the tremendous support, generosity, guidance, and love of the many people who have journeyed with me during and after my graduate life. I wish to express my gratitude to all those individuals, families, friends, acquaintances, and informants, who so graciously opened their doors and hearts to me during my field research. Without their involvement, this work would not exist.

For the academic sinews of this work, I am indebted to Veena Das, Deborah Poole, Naveeda Khan, and Jonathan Spencer. Veena inspired me to delve into the field of Sri Lankan kinship. Her guidance, tireless engagement with my work, and unlimited support; her intellectual contributions; and her discerning balance of encouragement and criticism helped me to finish my project. Naveeda contributed immensely to this book with her sharp theoretical inputs, and the involvement and investment that she lavished on it. She helped me feel at home in Baltimore by providing a warm meal and hot intellectual arguments every Friday. Debby helped me to understand the many critical and theoretical concepts in anthropology. I am grateful to Jonathan for his thoughts, conversations, and critiques that have shaped this book in a significant way.

I am most thankful to the Wenner–Gren Foundation for the research grant and the National Science Foundation USA for the research grant (CA-DDRIG) that provided much-needed financial support to conduct my fieldwork. A book grant from the National University of Singapore helped me to cover the cost of preparing the manuscript. I also thank Orient Blackswan (Orient Longman) for allowing me to reuse material from "Transnational Marriages: Documents, Wedding Photos, Photographers, and Jaffna Tamil Marriages," which was originally published in *Marrying in South Asia*, edited by Rajni Palriwala and Ravinder Kaur (2004); and Routledge and Nicholas Van Der Hear for allowing me to reuse material from "Transnational Marriages in Conflict Settings: War, Dispersal, and Sri Lankan Tamil Marriages" (coauthored with Van Der Hear), which was originally published in *Transnational Marriage: New Perspectives from Europe and Beyond*, edited by Katherine Charsley (2012). I thank the two anonymous reviewers of the manuscript for the University of Washington Press who have given me insightful comments from which the book has developed and gained a lot. I thank the editors of the Global South Asia series for their interest in publishing my book, and finally I thank my editor at the University of Washington Press, Lorri Hagman, for her support and guidance in fine-tuning the manuscript. I also take this opportunity to thank Rochelle and Nick for their help in copyediting the various chapters.

The uniquely active intellectual community that is the Department of Anthropology at Johns Hopkins University has played an important role in the writing of this book. Many friends and colleagues from different parts of the world and institutions offered help in diverse ways at various points of my work, helping me build this book. I would like to express my appreciation and warm gratitude to Hopkins friends Aaron Goodfellow, Sameena Mulla, Richard Baxstrom, Sylvain Perdigon, Valeria Procupez, Bhrigupati Singh, Thomas Cousins, Andrew Bush, Amrita Ibrahim, Ross Parsons, and Hester Betlem, who spurred me along with their thought-provoking comments, encouragement, and constructive criticism at different stages of my writing. Many friends at different steps of the process helped me in various ways. I particularly thank Francis Cody and Bhavani Raman for their support and guidance in shaping this book. I thank Menaha and Sathiya for helping me to collect some data for the research.

I thank my dear friends Neena Mahadev, Citlalli Reyes-Kipp, Maya Ratnam, Christopher Kolb, Young-Gyung Paik, James Williams, Chitra Venkataramani, Andrew Brandel, Aditi Saraf, Abigail Baim-Lance, Sandra Eder, Fouad Halbouni, and Thaera Bardan for their friendship and support during my time at Hopkins. Special thanks to Anand Pandian for encouraging and advising me in the publication of my manuscript. It was their wonderful friendship that helped make Johns Hopkins a second home for me. Similarly, I deeply value the great friendship and insightful comments that Harini, Mihirini, Eshani, Jayanithi, Lisa, Lotte, Ruth, and Luke shared so freely with me, making me feel so much at home during my stay at Edinburgh that I count it a third home. I will always be thankful for the friendship of so many wonderful people at University of Edinburgh and in the city itself. During the writing time of this book, Janet, Julia, Paul, and Nayanika made Edinburgh a lovely welcoming place for me—my deepest thanks to them.

My friends and colleagues at the National University of Singapore have helped and supported me in various ways. I thank all of them, especially Noorman Abdullah, Kelvin Low, Prasenjit Duara, Rajesh Rai, Elaine Ho, the late Bernard Bate, and Rahul Mukherjee. Special thanks go to Vineeta Sinha and Arunima Datta, who have offered comments at various points of this process, and to Ranjana Ragunathan and Lavanya Balachandran for editing the book proposal.

Through the years, many others from around the world have not only contributed in important ways to this research but also have, through their love and care, invested much in me. My deepest thanks to Sabesan and Suba from London; Sathiya, Sudarshan, and Cheran mama from Canada; Cholan mama and Kalpana akka from the United States; Ponni, Mangai, Arasu, Sibi, Chithra, Meghana, and Param from India; and Jeyaruban, Nuhuman mama, Ratna, Sutharshan, Murali, Ananda, Sarala, Sithi mama, Usha, Kumi, Nimal, and Anoka from Sri Lanka.

I cannot imagine my life without the support of the late Sunila, sister Suba, my late brother Sanjay, Rajapopathi Mama, Mano Aunty, and Mama. Their encouragement and belief have given me that extra strength to rise during difficult times and keep journeying forward. My parents, in particular, have always supported, encouraged, and stood by me during the ups and downs of life, helping me to keep pushing toward the goal of finishing this book. I cannot express my love for them in words.

Finally, I want to thank Anojaa. She is the driving force behind this work. She has not only tolerated me, my anxiety, and my stress regarding the writing of this book, but also has tirelessly read and reread the chapters, provided critical comments, and patiently edited the book many times. Without her this book would have been just a dream.

Marrying for a Future

Introduction

IN MAY 2006 I LANDED AT HEATHROW AIRPORT ON MY WAY TO Sri Lanka, where I would be starting fieldwork to study Sri Lankan transnational marriages. My childhood friend Gnani, whom I had not seen for fifteen years, was waiting to receive me. We had grown up together in Jaffna, in northern Sri Lanka, during the civil war. We played, ran, and hid together behind the trees and in the bunkers during the shelling between the Liberation Tigers of Tamil Eelam (or LTTE, a Tamil militant movement) and the Sri Lankan forces. We went to school together and ran away from there when bombs exploded in its vicinity. We saw our friends disappear, be killed, and be arrested. We lived with an uncertain future, frightened for our lives and those of our parents. However, we also had dreams of doing well in school, entering university, falling in love. Amid the war, we played and joked about narrow escapes from crossfire. We took part in dramas and roamed around on bicycles. The rhythm of our everyday life continued, though entangled with the violence of war. In the 1990s, when the war intensified, my parents managed to get me out of Jaffna, which was by then under LTTE control. It took me three days, on a dangerous and difficult journey, to reach Colombo, the Sri Lankan capital. I could not say goodbye to Gnani; there was no time for that. I had to leave my childhood friend behind. Years later, in 2005, I learned that he had escaped to London as a refugee and was living there. After many attempts, I was able to contact him.

Gnani told me that he had to leave Sri Lanka in 1996 when the war intensified. Living in Vavuniya, south of Jaffna, had become difficult. His brothers, who were already in Germany and the UK, managed to get him to London by paying an agent to traffic him across international borders. Gnani made three attempts to enter the UK. In his first attempt, he was caught at the Hong Kong International Airport and had to spend a year in jail for holding a forged passport. In his second attempt, he spent time in Southeast Asia and Africa for more than a year, moving from one country to another along with fellow Tamil travelers who were helped by the same agent to reach the UK. But this attempt, too, failed. Finally, in his third attempt, he managed to enter the UK as a refugee. While listening to his story on a cold winter night over the phone, I asked him why he persisted in his efforts despite his repeated failures.

Gnani told me that he feared for his life in Sri Lanka and that he had fallen in love there with a woman, Sujatha. He knew their parents would not agree to their marriage, but he could envision a life with her if he could leave Sri Lanka and start anew in another place. While waiting to reach the UK, he wrote letters to his lover. Sometimes he would not receive a reply, or he would have moved to another country before the reply arrived. But writing such letters had become part of his routine as he traveled. Gnani did not expect the replies, but he wanted to write. He added that his experience in these places had changed his perspective on life. The Tamil maxim of life, "We will see when it comes" (*Varaikka parkalaam*), was his guiding principle. When he finally arrived in the UK, Sujatha's journey as a refugee took her to Australia. Because they could not meet or visit each other since both were refugees and did not have proper travel documents, they continued their relationship, across vastly separated national borders, over the phone. After some years of a long-distance relationship characterized by difficulties and uncertainties, they were married in Australia in a small function as soon as Gnani and Sujatha acquired their permanent resident documents—all this despite objections from their families. Sujatha moved to London, but they then realized that she needed a spousal visa to live permanently with Gnani in the UK. When she had to return to Australia to apply for a spousal visa, a new period of uncertainty began for the couple. Eventually, Sujatha obtained the visa after producing all the required documents to prove that their marriage was "genuine," paving the way for her return to the UK. Gnani joked at the end of our conversation that his love and marriage had produced both a certain and an uncertain life.

In 2006 I finally met my friend Gnani in London after many years. I met his wife, Sujatha, for the first time when I visited their home. That night we were discussing our lives during the war and even laughing and joking. Curious about her citizenship, I asked Sujatha, "Are you a British citizen now?" She answered in the negative. They had decided that it was better for Sujatha to keep her Australian citizenship, while Gnani remained a British citizen. They thought that if something happened to either of them or if their status got revoked in one of these countries, then they would have an alternative. Having lived a life filled with so much uncertainty, they still planned for unforeseen complications—long after the war had officially ended in Sri Lanka. A life that emerged from war and violence continues to shadow them in London even now.

The thirty years of war created constant movements and displacements of individuals within and outside of Sri Lanka, which became a "sociality" for the Tamil community (Thiranagama 2011) and created the conditions of possibility for an uncertain life.[1] The Tamil community learned to live with such uncertainty in a time characterized by war and dispersion.[2] Scholars have argued that the conditions of war and violence froze the lives of refugees and suspended the survivors of war in limbo (Ferme 2004; Agamben 1998). However, the story of Gnani and Sujatha reveals a different narrative. Their romance struggled on as they moved from war zones to become refugees, and finally made a home in a new, unknown land. The constant struggle of making and remaking relationships across borders, through the institution of marriage and kinship in times of uncertainty due to war and violence, has become an integral part of the everyday life of the Tamil Jaffna community of Sri Lanka. Gnani's act of writing letters from temporary locales during his journey to the UK—despite not receiving replies or even knowing whether those letters reached Sujatha—forged an important link between them. Gnani did not receive replies because he was constantly on the move, so Sujatha's letters back often reached only his "old" address. His journey was full of danger and marked by constant movement. But the letters contained aspirational moments, imagined futures, and memories of a joyful past for Gnani and Sujatha. The anxieties and desires, sorrows and joys of their relationship were written, rewritten, and left behind in these documents.

This ethnographic study suggests that the Tamil community, fragmented as a result of war, was rekindled by "in-between" processes such as transnational marriages. Those marriages are most commonly arranged by the families of the bride and groom, even though elements of romantic love are present as well. The actors and documents involved in this process— marriage brokers, wedding photographs, legal documents, and transit places—were connected through their facilitation of individuals marrying. Here, the "in-between" is neither a limbo space or liminal stage (Turner 1969; Ferme 2004), nor a hybrid space (Bhabha 1994), but a zone through which certain transfigurations of life take place. The marriage process (from arranging the marriage to the reunion of the spouses in their adoptive country) as in-between is not necessarily a well-mapped journey, comprising an in-built unknowability concerning the future relationship. It fore-shadows the desires and anxieties arising in the formation of relatedness, as well as the imagination and memories of futures and pasts. This book is about stories of individual lives disrupted and torn apart by war—but not permanently so. Gnani and Sujatha's marriage process, visa applications, and constant struggle to "prove" to immigration officers that their marriage is "genuine," so as to be able to reunite across borders, is hardly atypical. It is encountered in multiple lives with endless empirical variations in the Jaffna Tamil community. The Sri Lankan war- and marriage-related migration provided the context within which this ethnography unfolds.

CIVIL WAR, DISPLACEMENT, AND THE SRI LANKAN DIASPORA

Three decades of war in Sri Lanka ended officially in 2009, but the era's prolonged violence devastated the social and economic landscape of the Tamils, leading to the mass migration of individuals and families escaping the violence of the Sri Lankan state and of the Tamil militants alike. The brutal ethnic war resulted in the loss of between eighty thousand and one hundred thousand lives.[3] The Sri Lankan ethnic conflict has a long history, starting in colonial times. However, many scholars have marked the 1983 ethnic riots—a pogrom against the Tamils that took place in the capital—as the key event that ignited the violent ethnic conflict long simmering between the Tamils and the Sri Lankan government.[4] The ethnic composition of Sri Lanka includes the majority Sinhala community as well as minority communities of Tamils, Muslims, Burghers, and Vedas. Language and ethnicity distinguish the Tamil community as an ethnic group (Thiranagama 2011; Spencer et al. 2015).[5] Most of the Tamil community lives in the north and east of Sri Lanka along with the Muslim community. One can trace the ethnic conflict and political tensions between the Tamil and Sinhala communities at different registers from colonial period to the introduction of the Sinhala Only Act in 1956, or to the university standardization based on ethnic representation introduced in the 1970s. It can also be found at moments when Buddhism was made an official state religion, and it finally came to a head with the brutal 1983 ethnic riots against the Tamil community.[6]

Many Tamil militant movements along with LTTE emerged in the north and east in the mid to late 1970s. The LTTE in mid-1980s eliminated those other groups in an attempt to be Sri Lanka's sole Tamil militant movement (Thiranagama 2011; Spencer et al. 2015). During this period of violent inter-Tamil militant conflict, many Tamils fled to other countries. By 1986, the

LTTE had proven its supremacy and continued to fight for an independent state for Tamils. During the 1990s the war intensified, which resulted in large internal displacements, forced migrations, and even more refugees moving within and outside Sri Lanka.[7] During the three decades of war numerous peace talks took place, but each failed, leading to a further escalation of war and violence. The LTTE was finally defeated and its leadership killed after a bitter battle in May 2009. Many civilians who were caught up in the last days of war between the LTTE and Sri Lankan armed forces died or disappeared. A number of reports that have emerged since the end of war depict the brutality of these last days. The political solution to protecting the rights of ethnic minorities and managing the reconciliation process are still ongoing struggles in Sri Lanka even after the war has ended.

Against this background of conflict, which escalated in the early 1980s, Sri Lankan Tamils have resorted to a number of migration strategies to escape the violence: internal forced migration to safer parts of Sri Lanka; labor migration, usually to the Middle East; asylum seeking, initially in India and later in Europe and North America; marriage to Sri Lankan Tamils based in Europe and North America; and other forms of family reunion. In the 1980s, out-migration from the Jaffna peninsula increased due to the worsening conflict. Almost two-thirds of Jaffna Tamils lived elsewhere, and many who were living within the peninsula were internally displaced during the war. Overall, one in two Sri Lankan Tamils has been displaced and nearly one in four lives outside the country (Sriskandarajah 2002). The war has generated a substantial Tamil diaspora that includes both refugees and other kinds of migrants. By the 1990s, there were more than one hundred thousand Sri Lankan Tamil refugees in southern India, two hundred thousand in Europe, and more than a quarter of a million in North America, mainly Canada. Perhaps 25 percent of the Sri Lankan Tamil population of up to three million now lives outside Sri Lanka: not all of these are refugees, but the war has been a significant factor in driving most abroad.[8] At present, the Sri Lankan Tamil diaspora consists mainly of refugees and former refugees bringing families and friends to the adoptive land through chain migration, which is seen as re-creating a "homeland" in their host lands.[9] This continuous migration has been worked out also through marriage and the formation of communities in adoptive lands (Fuglerud 1999, 2004). The reach of this wider diaspora is substantial. Available statistics are not always consistent, but the most important destinations for Sri Lankan asylum seekers and refugees have been the UK, Canada, the US, Norway and other Scandinavian countries, France, Germany, Switzerland, and Australia. Major migration to the Western countries took place from Jaffna.

The first wave of migration happened way before the 1983 ethnic riots and consisted of privileged-caste Tamils immigrating mostly to UK or Australia for education or skilled work. The second wave of migration occurred after the political violence and ethnic riots. This group consisted of people from the middle class as well as the privileged and middle castes.[10] After the 1983 riots, many countries opened their borders to Tamil refugees. Therefore, many Tamils migrated beyond the English-speaking countries, such as UK, Australia, and Canada, to France, Germany, and other European countries (Daniel and Thangaraj 1995). In the 1990s, numerous Tamils from marginalized castes and the middle class managed to migrate as refugees to European countries, Australia, and Canada. These refugees received help from their friends or relatives already present in these countries, who sent them money and arranged for the necessary documents. Since 1990 the migration pattern of Tamil refugees has been a mix of middle-class, marginalized-class, and privileged- to marginalized-caste individuals with the means to sponsor their travel to these countries as refugees. The poorest of the poor and the lower class went to refugee camps in India as temporary migrants, since it cost less. Furthermore, India also became the place to which a number of Tamils migrated as a transit place before moving to another country, predominantly as refugees or through marriage. But many marginalized caste members and middle-class (privileged- and marginalized-caste) Tamils in government jobs continued to stay in Jaffna. Many others remained there for various reasons, ranging from looking after their property to having a son or daughter in the LTTE. However, overall, most migrants or refugees who ended up in Canada, the UK, or Australia were from the privileged to middle castes, and the upper to middle classes.

The constant movement combined with the challenges of being classified as a refugee constituted a form of life that the Tamil community has learned to live with (Thiranagama 2011). Anthropological literature on violence and war in Sri Lanka, especially the works of early writers on violence,[11] has argued that the collective violence affected individuals, dislocated families, and tore apart their everyday life, and the Sri Lankan war has been the context in which a series of transformations and redefinitions occurred: individual to collective and home to kinship ties alike (Thiranagama 2011). Yet the world of dispersed communities is being remade (Das 2007) amid movement and dispersion through the reproduction and transfiguration of classical institutions such as marriage.

JAFFNA TAMIL TRANSNATIONAL MARRIAGES
AND FIELD SITES

The Jaffna Tamils were exposed to the social life of migration not only through the introduction of war: this phenomenon was a constant, starting in the colonial era (Thiranagama 2011, 15–16). Most of the middle-class youth and government servants were employed in Colombo and moved constantly between the capital and Jaffna.[12] However, with the intensification of the ethnic conflict and violence in the 1980s, both migration and forced migration rose to unprecedented levels among the Jaffna Tamils. Furthermore, by the year 2000, refugees who migrated to Canada, the UK, France, Switzerland, Australia, India, and Germany became citizens and permanent residents of these countries. Transnational marriages and war-related marriage migration have to be situated within this larger historical context of war rather than in relation solely to labor and economic factors.[13] Most individuals from the Sri Lankan Tamil diaspora choose their partner from Jaffna, especially in the case of first-generation migrants. Cases exist where brides or grooms originated from other locations, such as the UK, continental Europe, and Australia, but this is not as common.

This study focuses on Tamil transnational marriages between Canadian and Sri Lankan Tamils before the war ended in 2009. The largest Sri Lankan Tamil refugee and migrant population lives in Canada, mostly originating from Jaffna. Due to this sizable Sri Lankan diaspora, a number of Hindu temples, restaurants, grocery stores, and Tamil radio and TV stations were established in Canada, along with the publication of a number of Tamil newspapers (Cheran 2001). Furthermore, many Tamils, migrants or refugees in Europe and the UK, later moved to Canada because the possibility of attaining citizenship there was perceived as easier than in any other country at that time. Because of these factors, a Jaffna atmosphere was recreated in Toronto and its suburbs, and now Scarborough (a suburb of Toronto) is known among the Tamils as "Little Jaffna." Canada is thus an ideal site for study because its large Sri Lankan Tamil diaspora has intensified the marriage migration among Sri Lankan Tamils, especially those from Jaffna. Marriage brokers confirm that more than 60 percent of the marriages they have arranged since 2000 were between a Canadian and someone from Jaffna. Moreover, the Canadian spousal visa enabled the recipients to obtain Canadian residential status immediately.[14] However, the process of granting this visa was made ever more difficult with the growing influx of migrants. During my fieldwork, I heard many stories about the difficulties of obtaining the Canadian spousal visa and the requirement to provide many documents, including photos of wedding rituals. Though visa procedures of other countries, such as the UK, France, Australia, and Switzerland, differ from those of Canada (e.g., in France, one need not provide marriage photos but is expected to declare beforehand at the French embassy where the potential spouse is living the will to marry and obtain a clearance), the cases related here necessarily focus on Canadian procedures since the stories I collected from my interlocutors concerned mainly the Canadian visa process.

Arranging a marriage for a daughter or son during the war and subsequent displacement (especially in the latter part of the conflict, in the 1990s) was no easy task. Because of the war's intensification from the late 1990s to mid-2000s, Tamils were constantly on the move both within and outside Sri Lanka. Moreover, the conflict between the LTTE and other Tamil militants, as well as within the LTTE itself, led to the LTTE capturing and killing many young Tamils and their family members. As a result, in order to escape from the LTTE, many ex-militants worked in collaboration with the Sri Lankan forces to target members of the LTTE and *their* families. This set the stage for "victims" and "perpetrators" coming from the same social space and kin groups.[15] Within this context, personal networks within families, which were already dispersed and divided, broke down.[16] Under these conditions of enforced dispersion and internal differentiation, "marriage" emerged as one of the most significant ways not only that people could move out of places of insecurity, but also be brought together, often through marriage brokers. Marriage brokers acted as "mediators" between Tamil families from two countries by "holding" detailed information on brides and grooms and their family members. They became important figures in understanding transnational Tamil marriage and its transformation in a time of war (see chapter 1).

After the transnational marriage was arranged, most wedding ceremonies within the Tamil diaspora took place in India. This was because either the bride or the groom had not been granted citizenship in their adoptive country, and as such was only allowed to travel to countries other than Sri Lanka. Another compelling reason was to avoid returning to a war-torn Sri Lanka. After the marriage ceremony in India, the spouse who had to migrate, in order to be reunited with their partner in the adoptive country, had to navigate a maze of embassies, immigration laws, and migration practices of the various states involved. Transnational marriages involved not only arranging and contracting a marriage between parties in the Tamil community, who were divided by geopolitical borders, but also conducting the proceedings in such a way that various state officials were satisfied that the marriage was genuine (i.e., not one of convenience). As one had to provide evidence of the marriage, visa officers from different countries scrutinized such marriage practices to validate the migration, according to their own immigration laws.

This book specifically examines Canadian state practices. As part of the process of assessing the validity of a marriage, the Canadian immigration officer, who looked into the wedding albums and other documentation of the marriage, sought evidence for whether certain rituals had been performed, and whether the photographs taken revealed the presence of a large number of family members (see chapters 3 and 5). An important question then arises: Why did Canadian immigration officers seek evidence of customary marriage ceremonies over and above the evidence of a civil marriage? Interestingly, the discussion within immigration courtrooms and embassies of Tamil customary marriage ceremonies and the debates surrounding the validity of "legal" Tamil marriages according to the Tamil tradition, had already taken place during the colonial era in Sri Lanka (see chapter 4). The transnational marriage migration of Tamils and the various state practices cannot be separated from both the experiences of war and violence these Tamil migrants faced and from their refugee status in their adoptive lands. Most studies on transnational marriages[17] look at the migrants' places of origin and where they decided to settle. But they rarely focus on the transit or temporary places the migrants or refugees sometimes passed through or where they celebrated their weddings. The Sri Lankan Tamil case necessitates looking not only at the home and host countries but also at the temporary places through which the Tamil migrants or refugees traveled. India was a key transit place where most arranged or love marriages between Sri Lankan Tamils actually took place; it became a location where the Sri Lankan Tamil community was made and remade during wedding season (see chapter 2).

THREE CITIES, MULTIPLE MOVEMENTS

This book is based on twenty-four months of fieldwork in three urban settings in different countries—Colombo (Sri Lanka), Chennai (India), and Toronto (Canada)—where I followed brides and grooms from the marriage arrangements to places where their actual marriage ceremonies took place to the adoptive countries where the spouses were reunited.[18] The circumstances have changed since the war ended, but its impact lingers and many issues resulting from the war remain unresolved in Sri Lanka and beyond. Since most Jaffna Tamil transnational marriages are arranged in Colombo, I worked primarily with marriage brokers and families there. Most of the brokers' files on brides and grooms include upper- or middle-class Tamils from the Jaffna diaspora. I started my work at the marriage brokers' offices, where I visited every day and helped them file information. I collected archival documents, files, and visual artifacts from the marriage broker. By being present during client visits at their office and witnessing the arrangement of marriages, I established relationships with those families and individuals. From there, I visited the families and took part in the marriage arrangements. I secured the data used in this book by obtaining narratives of family histories and interviewing informants. The majority of the actual marriage ceremonies (between a bride or groom from Sri Lanka and a prospective Sri Lankan Tamil spouse from Canada) took place in India. Therefore, I followed the families to India and participated in the wedding ceremonies themselves. I stayed with them in their guest houses during the time of the wedding ceremonies and recorded ceremonies, interviews, and interactions. Finally, I tracked two newly married individuals all the way to their adoptive country to find out how the imagined trajectories of relationships were being realized in the new setting. Furthermore, the connections I made in this network led me to trace and collect personal letters, refusal letters from visa officers, and transcripts of immigration court cases at these sites from the informants, courts, and archival offices. This also led me to work in the Sri Lankan archives to collect colonial court cases on customary marriage and the definition of marriage implemented by the colonial state.

My movements from Colombo to Chennai to Toronto did not follow a linear trajectory. I traveled back and forth between Colombo and Chennai within this two-year period, along with the families. In my ethnographic work, I do not consider Colombo, Chennai, and Toronto as three different sites, but rather as one "mobile social field" in which my interlocutors' journeys and experiences took place. My fieldwork does not unfold in a linear progression from marriage to migration, from home to adoptive countries. Unlike the place-centric approach of most conventional anthropological studies of kinship and marriage (as in village or urban settings), this one is person- and document-centric. In order to examine the role of documents as proof to convince visa officers of the genuineness of one's marriage to obtain a spousal visa in a transnational marriage, I compiled copies of a whole range of documents (marriage certificates, photographs, personal letters, and visa refusal letters) that had to be produced at the visa offices. I collected information on the immigration policies of Canada through the websites of the embassies and the immigration and refugees boards, and collected court cases from the Canadian Department of Justice. I compared current Canadian spousal immigration laws and the ways the Tamil customary marriage was framed and discussed by the colonial court in Sri Lanka. I conducted archival research on colonial court cases on customary marriage, Sri Lankan marriage laws, and Tamil customary marriage laws to trace marriage practices and colonial state interpretations of such marriages. By juxtaposing Sri Lankan colonial court cases and current Canadian spouse immigration court cases, I examine the main debates that framed (and continue to frame) the validity of marriages at different times and in different spaces.

I followed my interlocutors and their experience of the marriage process as they traveled across the globe. My interlocutors' experience of war-related marriage migration or displacement is interwoven with my own lived experience of conflict and migration. My friends, relatives, interlocutors, and I occupied the same social field of war and violence. We were displaced, full of fear about the war and thoughts of migration to foreign countries. But we learned to live in a dispersed life. My inquiry into how we assimilate to violence and war designed my research questions and framed my fieldwork. In other words, the choice of multiple places to gather data was not driven by an ideal conceptual consideration about "multisite" fieldwork, but rather by the politics of war, violence, and displacement, and by the milieu of the social field drawn by the experiences of my interlocutors. The scale and degree may differ from site to site, but my interlocutors' journey remains the same as a collective and singular experience.

MARRIAGE, KINSHIP: FUTURES AND UNCERTAINTIES

In the extensive literature on marriage and kinship relationships in South Asia, the focus has been on marriage as grounded in kinship rules and obligations as expressive of political, economic, and caste negotiations, ensuring social reproduction and continuity.[19] In recent times there have been changes to South Asian kinship and marriages owing to modernity, globalization, and urbanization. Therefore, migration processes have been revisited and re-conceptualized by recent kinship studies.[20] The main questions for scholars who study contemporary marriage and kinship are how the institution of marriage and its practices transform in response to the "newness" of the changing world. Feminist and Marxist scholars, however, have pointed out that marriage transactions embody social inequality, male domination, and power exerted over women's productive and reproductive labor.[21] Yet, most of these works tend to underestimate the importance of the individual's future linked with marriage. The process of marriage and its strategies incorporate strangers and affines into kinship (Carsten 2000, 2004; Bourdieu 1990a), allowing one to expect some certainty over the future.

While marriage in its traditional form has incorporated an orientation toward securing near and distant futures,[22] what is yet to be understood is how the institution of marriage has incorporated wartime insecurities and contingencies. How do we imagine the future during the marriage process as a way of reinhabiting the world and rebuilding a community that is now dispersed across many spaces? The idea of the uncertainty of the marriage process has been captured in the work of numerous scholars who have studied transnational marriage migrations or cross-border marriages in terms of instability in the marriages, divorces, and domestic violence after the marriages (Charsley 2012) within the context of the South Asian marriage system. Studies on marriage within modernity further highlight the uncertain nature of marriage practices. Work on right spouse and preferential marriage in Tamil Nadu has traced a breakdown of the "Dravidian kinship system" within the social transformation marked by modernity and urbanization (Clark-Decès 2014, 21). This captures the idea that social changes create uncertainty in preferential marriage, and result in desires and anxieties concerning such a loss. It also poses a question: How do actors within these historical changes inhabit and respond to changes through old and new forms of marriages? A study of Chhattisgarh demonstrates the need to differentiate primary marriages from secondary marriages (Parry 2001). Secondary marriages appear to be free of some of the rules set for primary marriages; for instance, such marriage unions increasingly breach caste endogamous marriage rules. These secondary marriages create a condition of possibility for multiple relationships and movements between partners, along with the resultant uncertainty. Only with the development of modern discourse and the emergence of a middle class does the idea of marriage stability enter this community (Parry 2001).

Both of these studies—on Tamil Nadu and Chhattisgarh—indirectly point to the notion of uncertainty in relation to marriage. In the former, the uncertainty of marriage institutions and practices is experienced vividly as a result of historical and social changes. In the latter, the idea of uncertainty of relationships and their constant renegotiation in second marriages lessens with the modern development of middle-class ideologies. While building on these insightful scholarly works, my study asks a slightly different question about marriage: Within the context of a prolonged war and the migration it caused, how does a community use the marriage process to reconnect, create relatedness, and work out uncertain futures? What is instructive about these studies is that the notion of uncertainty associated with marriage is *both* old and new. The uncertainty of the marriage process and of its aftermath call on us to rethink what kind of futures can be imagined, desired, practiced, and feared for during the marriage process.[23] If the marriage transforms two individuals into a couple and forges an alliance between families, then such a process works with certain ideas of imagined futures and current practices to bring some certainty to the uncertainty of marriage. Given the context of war and mass migration, transnational marriage processes have become moments in which another way of reinhabiting the world becomes possible for the Tamil community. In that sense, it is not just a strategy to escape the war, but also an effort to reinhabit the world, to make uncertainty into certainty, and to imagine a future for the Tamil community.

MARRIAGE PROCESS, WAR, AND THE IN-BETWEEN

As opposed to entering the issue of war-related marriage migration through the category of diaspora or refugees and/or migrants,[24] or through studies analyzing their marriage practices only as cross-border unions,[25] approaching it via the marriage process (Carsten 2000) connects and cuts across these given categories. Marriage is thus seen as a process rather than as an institution. The multiple moments of the marriage process, from arranging the marriage to the actual reunion of the couple, hold elements of uncertainty and possibilities for the future. Moving through the marriage process—from marriage brokers' offices, to wedding events, to immigration courtrooms— we encounter interlocutors, who were refugees or former refugees, marriage migrants, non-migrants or internally displaced, part of the Tamil diaspora or not. Migration patterns and trajectories are experienced in multiple ways by these different parties. The "marriage process" is a site in which these interlocutors from different current and former categories come together and where certain notions of futures, desires, and anxieties are made, imagined, and reinforced.

The core question I ask in this book is: How do marriage processes become spaces or zones through which dispersed communities affected by war mobilize to reunite with their fragmented members and reinhabit the world that may have been thought as lost for them?

Work on war and migration in Mozambique has shown that war conditions create a social life rather than suspend it (Lubkemann 2007). War as "social condition" transfigures the individual and subjectivities, and ethnographers need to understand the war condition as a point of departure to study new forms of social life that emerge while it's going on and afterward. On the other hand, war can be seen as a thick field, "not as along a continuum with other forms of social life, but as a powerful and distinct force, period, and subjectivity, a making on a site of unmaking" (Thiranagama 2011, 10). Through my interlocutors, I, too, could trace different journeys, as refugees, as marriage migrants, and as those who have been internally displaced. Some had experienced war and violence directly, while others had heard and lived vicariously through the experiences of their parents or friends. The details of war or violence, the dispersion of their life, and the impossibility of reuniting with family members are not openly discussed, but they emerge in conversations and expressions as a shadow that follows their stories. Family photos taken during wedding ceremonies evoke vividly memories of those who are absent: relatives and family members who could not join the couple or who died in the violence. Such photos remind all the family members of the impossibility of living together in one place, since different family members were settled in different countries because of the war and subsequent migration. In other instances, when parents arranged the marriage for their sons or daughters, they could not locate the right spouse, in terms of caste, village, or other traditional comparisons. Occasions of joy, happiness, gathering, and dining together come from temporary moments around special events in temporary places such as wedding events. Both the possibility of remaking the world and the remembrance of the scars left by the war appeared and disappeared within these temporary places, figures, events, and documents.

The violence of war appears here as a "fluid field" that follows the social life of the people caught up in the violence and war. My interlocutors' narratives of their marriage migration interweave their desires for social and economic mobility shared by any ordinary migrant, and their desires and anxieties to escape violence and war. These mingled narratives remind us of the paradox inherent in those marriage migrations: if the shadow of violence was kept alive in the aftermath of the war, the desires for a future and an ordinary life (Das 2007) were present as well in the migrants' everyday lives. Experiences of violence and losses, displacements and dispersion of family members, follow the Tamil community and emerge "here and there" in unexpected places: for instance, the couple confronted with the impossibility of gathering all family members use modern-day techniques to "insert" dead relatives in the wedding photos to create the ideal family. Therefore, to understand such complex narratives, the usual categories of refugee, diaspora, economic migration, or cross-border marriage migration are limited and insufficient. This study approaches marriage not through classical anthropological notions found in kinship studies, such as duty, rights, alliance, and honor,[26] but through a different lens that I call the "in-between." The marriage process as in-between is where the transformation of relatedness between individuals and families takes place, where certain desires and anxieties come together, and where futures are imagined and lived.

THE IN-BETWEEN

Here, the "in-between" is different from the one articulated by theorist Homi Bhabha as a space at the intersections of fixed categories. For him, the metaphor of the stairwell represents an in-between space: situated between the lower and higher levels, the stairwell allows temporary movement in which hybrid identities confront primordial ones. These "interstitial passages" (Bhabha 1994)—in-between categories where newness, differences, and possibilities are constantly produced—are crucial for understanding the possibilities of hybrid cultures. The marriage process and practices examined here are not hybrid practices that emerge between fixed categories and binaries. Crucial documents, figures, zones, and places associated with the marriage process are in-betweens that transform the uncertainty inherent in those transnational unions into certainty at given moments. Borrowing the idea from anthropologist Arnold van Gennep ([1909] 1960), Victor Turner's work on rituals introduces the idea of liminality in a broader sense. He suggests liminality as "between and betwixt": "Liminal entities are neither here nor there; they are betwixt and between the positions assigned and arrayed by law, custom, convention, and ceremonial" (1969, 95). This liminality is a process that an individual or a community goes through, from one state to another. It is anti-structural, and an unstable space, but also a space of transformation, one for all kinds of possibilities. I extend this idea to analyze the marriage process as a space for transfiguration, although it does not result from the ritual characteristics of marriage. How do we understand and study the marriage process as it happens and as it transfigures social life? How is the picture further complicated when, as in the Sri Lankan Tamil case, the marriage process is linked to migration and mobility? What are the crucial figures, documents, spaces, and places through which the transfiguration passes within marriage as a process?

The transfiguration suggested by Turner (1969), which is evident in the marriage process, needs to be understood as opening a set of possibilities. These figures, documents, spaces, and places in the marriage process appear as potential zones (Deleuze 1991, [1968] 1994, 2005) that allow the community to enter the rhythm of life in a time characterized by the uncertainty of war and marriage. The notion of potential can be linked to the idea of the virtual.[27] Regarding the virtual, the potential, and the actual, philosopher Gilles Deleuze points out that the virtual is real, but until it is actualized it could be "anything." The potential situated within the virtual and actual holds all possibilities, both actualized and not actualized. In other words, it is in the limitless potential that has yet to be actualized that forms of life can emerge. This ontology of potential has been further considered anthropologically by Elizabeth Povinelli (2011) in her work on the neoliberal world of surveillance and negligence, where alternative forms of life surface and endure. She makes a claim about taking the sociology of potential as an important point of departure and site of examination for understanding the forms of life that emerge in a neoliberal world:

> The life worth living is not necessarily found within these zones of maximal potential because the zones create such reduced conditions of life that the potential desire for them to spawn or foster alternative worlds can seem naive at best and sadistic at worst. But once we view potentiality as socially constitutive and materially distributed, then we found ourselves in a morally viscous realm of excess, exhaustion, and endurance, a realm that includes affective, physical, and social conditions that can depress the brain and immune system, rupture organs as well as bonds with families and friends, and orient violence inwards. *If we must persist in potentiality, we must endure it as a space, a materiality, and a temporality.* (Povinelli 2011, 128, emphasis added)

"In-between" moments (e.g., figures, documents, spaces, and places) of the marriage process are potential, where certain kinds of transfiguration of life and relatedness take place and all varieties of desires, futures, and anxieties become possible. The marriage as a process is not necessarily about social reproduction as assumed in classical approaches, but could be a number of things, which may include divorce, separation, and the like. The marriage process holds both certainty and uncertainty, but until it is actualized we cannot know what it will be. The potential endures even after such actualizations. The ideas of the virtual, the potential, and the actual cannot be located on a linear timeline, but should be perceived as entangled, at a point or a dot. Thus, the potential in-between and process as a zone endures not only in time but also in matter and space (Povinelli 2011). Studies of marriage in general or marriage related to migration should look closely at the process as it happens at the site of potential.

The in-between as *potential* is not only a zone, but can be traced in the steps of the marriage process. Documents such as wedding albums, for example, become important visual artifacts that capture the moment when individuals transform into married couples, or allow the possibility to create or imagine an "ideal family" in the absence of missing family members. These documents can also serve as visual proof in the application for a spousal visa to reunite with the other spouse in their adoptive country, and they have the ability to connect people across spaces. In the case of civil marriage and spousal immigration laws in relation to disputes over the validity of marriages for claiming property or for granting spousal visa, these cases, courtrooms, and laws function as in-between zones with the power to allow spouses to reunite or to transform two individuals into a married couple through debates about the intentionality of individuals at the time of marriage. Moreover, the in-between can be traced in the figures of the marriage brokers (as well as photographers or paralegals) as intermediaries who facilitate connections between individuals and families, across long distances. The marriage broker also holds fragments of familiarity that help the community to reconnect and rebuild its life during wartime. Finally, the notion of the in-between is incarnated in the transit or temporary places (e.g., India) where the actual marriages take place between Tamils from Sri Lanka and those from the diaspora, and where family members come together temporarily before, during, and after the ceremony. The concept of potential is not necessarily separated from the actual and virtual, but intermingles with them, as it both encompasses thinking about the future and holds multiple outcomes that contain both certainty and uncertainty. The visa officers' scrutiny of the marriage to grant or refuse the visa for the reunion of the couple, the marriage brokers' facilitation of matchmaking, and the wedding photographs' capture of the wedding and visual creation of an ideal family—all have the potential to unfold in different ways.

Rather than seeing the in-betweenness of the marriage process and its associated moments as momentary or temporary—that is, moments suspending each day—here, each day is perceived as becoming "eventful" (Das 2007) with a potential life and future. Such uncertainty and certainty, actualized and non-actualized relatedness, imagined future, and state practices within in-betweens, are worked out, lived through, imagined every day during the marriage process. It not only reconfigures subjectivity, kinships, and social order, but is an event that unfolds into everyday life (Das 2007). In-between spaces and the figures, documents, spaces, and places within such zones are important sites not only for the marriage process but also for an examination of how communities affected by violence strive to reinhabit the world. Reentering everyday life and remaking a world become possible through in-betweens that may be located not only at home or in adoptive countries, but also in temporary zones, whether they be figures, documents, spaces, or places.[28]

DOCUMENTS, CIRCULATIONS, AND FUTURES

Materials (e.g., documents, photographs, visa letters, court cases, marriage brokers' files on brides and grooms, astrological charts[29]) and human practices combine in the marriage process as an "in-between" space to transfigure the relationship and rebuild communities and families. The practices and materials come together as they circulate through the marriage process and actualize the union. As documents circulate in different spaces (from home to visa office to courtroom), they affect personal and collective relationships, and make or unmake communities. Documents can be seen to have a "life of their own" (Navaro-Yashin 2007; Hull 2012b) in their creation, circulation, and different readings in different spaces, by different actors (from photographers to immigration officers).

Documents interact with humans, and circulate within the human world through the representation and interpretation of social worlds, but they go beyond that.[30] Documents' mediation not only transforms the relations between humans and other humans, or between humans and documents, but also, in the process, changes the meaning the documents are supposed to carry (Latour 2005, 39; Hull 2012a). Wedding photos can mediate between visa officers and the married couples to validate a marriage as genuine, and thus allow spouses to reunite in Canada. Edited photos also may incorporate the faces of those unable to attend the wedding, as well as deceased relatives, thus re-creating kinship and mediating between the living and the dead.

Anthropological work analyzes documents and their associations with humans as documents create affect, relations, power, and capacity.[31] Further, in recent years the material and aesthetic aspects, as well as the social life of documents as artifacts, come to occupy a distinctive place in anthropological study.[32] Material documents can be seen to minimize the "emotional element" and take away the "person or an individual life story" (Fuglerud 2004, 36), but "documents themselves can provoke anxieties in bureaucrats who have to write on controversial matters" (Hull 2012a, 255), and in certain situations, "documents have the potentiality to discharge affective energies which are felt or experienced by persons" (Navaro-Yashin 2007, 81).

Among the Tamils, marriage migration's documents become part of "forms of sociality" not only as systems of control, deciding on the validity of marriages or re-creating ideal families, but also as vehicles for mobility and "imagination" (Hull 2012b, 260). In the case of Sri Lankan Tamils, state and bureaucratic practices mingle with the people through visa forms, court cases, or wedding photos as proof, but such moments of contact and circulation also produce the imagination of all kinds of possibility for the future—marriage, connections, leaving the site of violence, rebuilding a life—and come to occupy the space of the documents. The connection between things and humans can be seen as "assemblages as a collective" (Latour 2005). That is to say, both humans and materials come together as assemblages to produce sociality. Documents and the Tamil community, fragmented by the war and mass migration, assemble in in-between figures, documents, spaces, and places, where life gets transfigured and made possible for certain possibilities to be reimagined. Here, documents occupy both in-between zones (as a mediator between two individuals) and exist as associations within the in-between's temporal and social moments.

In this in-between temporal moment, the configuration of documents and humans generates affective energy, anxiety, fear, and happiness. The presence of the state and the immigration laws migrants must navigate or escape from becomes visible through tangible materiality. Futures are imagined and their possibilities felt more strongly through those tangible documents. The photographs, the immigration cases, or the court files at times recognize the marriage as genuine, which allow people to reconnect and imagine their life together. In the marriage brokers' offices, the documents containing the details of brides and grooms allow the fragmented Tamil community to trace their kinship and caste connections. These documents are not only archival elements to trace both the past and connections, but also important artifacts that have the capacity to turn the unknown subjects into known persons. Those persons are placed within the larger kinship and caste categories, and this movement creates a possibility of futures for rebuilding communities even within the uncertainty of life during a time of war.

The messiness and excessive potentiality of documents make them powerful (Navaro-Yashin 2007, 81), as their potential is uncertain at different temporal moments, even in instances of repeated associations between documents and humans. Professional wedding photographs may, in one circumstance, convince a visa officer to grant a visa to the spouse of a Canadian citizen to reunite with their partner in Canada; but, in another circumstance, other wedding photos taken by the same photographer might be considered unconvincing. The constant shifting, changing, and re-creating nature and affective mode of the documents when in contact with humans and other things produce all forms of possibilities and uncertainties. They bring out possibilities of relationships, actualized and non-actualized practices—a site of potential. Documents are part of the human life, and humans are part of the documents' life. Hull argues that documents' mediation enables construction of what people or things are (2012a, 259); looking at the documents' circulation allows us to see the artifacts not simply as information storage media but as shaping directly that information (2012b, 23). In the case of the Sri Lankan Tamil diaspora, documents not only mediate between the state and migrants or brides, grooms, and their families, but their circulation and assemblage in those temporal moments transfigures the relationships, allowing the participants to imagine a future. Circulation of the documents makes them come alive, acting and reacting with humans in everyday life, where life absorbs the potential life from the documents and documents absorb the potential life from humans. This absorption is also possible in temporary, short, limited times and spaces. The in-between temporal and temporary zone is a space where the rebuilding of life takes place for the Tamil community affected by war. The potential nature of documents holds not only imagination of the future but also past memories and their association and mediation with humans. Documents are thus in-between things, and their assemblage with humans in in-between zones produces the condition of possibility for transfiguring relationships of the Tamil community affected by war.

1   Brokering Marriages
in the Shadow of War

IN A TIME WHEN PERSONAL NETWORKS ARE BROKEN DOWN AND
mass displacement has taken place due to the war in Sri Lanka, the institution of marriage has emerged as a means to escape violence, and certain
traditional practices have acquired new forms to accommodate escape and to
rebuild relationships among widely dispersed kin. The marriage broker and
the documents they produce provide a lens through which we may understand the problems of social formations, political exigencies, and interstate
complexities that now relate to the union of couples across borders.

Of significance here is not the changing nature of Tamil marriage in the
time of war, tension between tradition and modernity, or social change
among the Tamils. Rather, it is how the marriage broker offers a community
torn apart by violence and multiple displacements the opportunity to step
back into the rhythm of everyday life by opening up conditions of possibility
for social continuity. Even though the marriage broker's services in Tamil
transnational marriages, as well as the newness of such offerings (i.e., the
bureaucratization and professionalization of marriage brokerage), have
created unfamiliar places for Tamils during the matchmaking process, the
marriage broker uses familiar modes (along with newly created documents
that contain detailed information on the bride and groom) that resemble
traditional matchmaking procedures. These familiar procedures help to
make the individuals and their families knowable in the time of war and
displacement. The prolonged violence and displacements evoked chaos,
uncertainty, "unknowability," instability, and mobility within Tamil communities in Sri Lanka. In the context of war and migration, marriage brokers
and the documents they provide are crucial in transfiguring unknown and
ambiguous persons into known ones through identifiable biography and
placement in the Tamil kinship universe.

The figure of the marriage broker reemerged as a product of forced
migration. Brokers are "pathways" in the matchmaking process, keeping
not only new detailed information on the spouses or expertise about

immigration regulations, but also making known or familiar traditions visible for the families to engage in marriage making (Maunaguru 2013). During the new process of transnational marriage, the familiar tradition of matchmaking was incorporated anew in documents and the reemerged figure of the marriage broker, which together help clients in the marriage process. They transfigure relationships and enable the Tamil community to imagine different futures. Although those fragmentary futures hold both certainty and uncertainty for the marriage, it is through such moments that the possibility of rebuilding life and imagining the future become possible as well.

THREE PHASES OF SRI LANKAN TRANSNATIONAL MIGRATION AND THE WAR

Sri Lankan transnational marriage practices date to three periods: (1) before the war; (2) during the war and refugee migration in the 1980s through the mid-1990s (when people claimed asylum in other countries but had not yet secured refugee status); and (3) from the late 1990s onward (when Tamils had acquired refugee status or citizenship in their adoptive countries) (Maunaguru and Van Hear 2012; Maunaguru 2013).

Tamil transnational marriages of the 1990s differ in many respects from those that took place prior to or in the early days of the conflict. In the first phase, only a small segment of privileged-caste or upper-class Tamils initiated migration (Daniel and Thangaraj 1995). Further, Sri Lankan Tamils (usually from the privileged caste) relocated to Malaysia or other colonial countries to take up clerical work during the colonial period and left their wives behind in Sri Lanka (Sathiyaselan 2004). One significant difference between the earlier and current migration in transnational marriages is that formerly, husbands either left their wives in their natal village in Jaffna and visited them frequently, or they migrated with their wife to a new country (Sathiyaselan 2004). Another difference is that, unlike now, stringent laws did not govern marriage-related migration. In the prewar era only a small segment of people migrated outside Sri Lanka, even though internal migration was common. The civil war in Sri Lanka brought about a drastic change, as nearly the entire Tamil community was either displaced within the country or moved out of the country legally or illegally. The protracted armed conflict made it impossible for individuals to return to their natal villages.

In stark contrast to the marriage migration of the prewar days, the current transnational marriage process takes an inordinate amount of time, from arranging the marriage until the couple's reunion in an adoptive land after marriage. The progression from the marriage proposal to the reunion of the couple after the marriage can take more than six months (and in some cases even several years). Interestingly, though, this inherent hurdle of the reunion does not always imperil the marriage; in fact, it seems to help foster intimacy among the newly married couple and their family members. Moreover, these transnational marriages have become the locus for the reunion of long-lost relatives, family members, and friends who have been scattered around the world in flight from war in Sri Lanka (Maunaguru and Van Hear 2012).

In the second phase, from late 1980s to early 1990s, Tamil refugees in the host countries did not have the required refugee or residency papers to enable them to travel to Sri Lanka or other neighboring countries to marry a Sri Lankan spouse. In most cases, as prospective grooms did not hold legal status in their adoptive countries, the brides would have to travel "illegally" to marry them. Most of these arrangements were made by Tamil agents who trafficked people for large sums of money and had extensive global networks (Maunaguru 2009). They, unlike marriage brokers, were not involved in arranging marriages or offering wedding-related services. In some cases the agent disappeared with clients' money without ensuring that the partner reached their destination. In the early 1990s, the prospective bride had to travel out of Sri Lanka to marry a Sri Lankan husband (Maunaguru 2013). Tales run rampant of how such prospective brides were abused by the agents, how the prospective husbands had relationships (and even fathered children) with other women in their host countries, and how the women migrating from Sri Lanka were subjected to domestic violence at the hands of their husbands. Despite these horrifying reports, the intensity of war and the urgent necessity of escaping from the violence and forced recruitment by the LTTE in Sri Lanka led many parents to send their daughters overseas (Maunaguru and Van Hear 2012; Maunaguru 2009). In some such marriages, Sri Lankan women became the vehicle for their entire family to move out of the site of violence through chain migration (Fuglerud 1999).

Since the early 2000s, in the third phase, a further change unfolded: many of the refugees who went to other countries in the late 1980s and early 1990s were now granted either permanent residence or citizenship in their host countries. As a result, grooms traveled to India, Malaysia, Singapore, or even Sri Lanka to marry Sri Lankan Tamil brides (my research indicates that brides' families preferred Tamil males who were citizens or permanent residents in a foreign country). After the wedding, the husband returned to his host country and the wife would return to Sri Lanka, where she would apply for spousal immigration to join her husband in the host country. In order to prove that the marriage was not one of convenience, the married couple had to submit multiple forms of proof, ranging from personal letters to wedding photographs. Despite the varied challenges of marrying a stranger, the traumatic spousal visa application procedures, and the hurdles of setting up a life in an unknown land, this practice prevailed among Sri Lankan Tamil females (Maunaguru and Van Hear 2012).

The situation was ripe for the emergence of a system to iron out the difficulties of transnational marriages, namely, compiling, classifying, and distributing to families in Sri Lanka information on prospective Sri Lankan spouses residing overseas. Both the men and women I interviewed in Sri Lanka told me that they did not believe in using matrimonial webpages to arrange marriages or to meet prospective partners. The primary reason for this was the lack of credibility of the information being presented, since there was no way of verifying either its accuracy or who generated it. These individuals seemed to prefer face-to-face communication when it came to arranging a marriage. This was further highlighted by several marriage brokers, who explained that they had set up websites especially for Sri Lankan Tamils, but that these pages did not generate much success. Thus, in the growing phenomenon of the transnational marriage, we see the old figure of the marriage broker reentering the scene, albeit in a new context. Unlike the agent, the marriage broker does not traffic young Tamil men and women as spouses to foreign countries. Rather, the marriage broker is involved in arranging a marriage between Tamil families across borders by providing them information about the prospective partner; furthermore, he participates in negotiating the marriage. However, like the agent, the marriage broker does not take responsibility regarding the reunification of spouses in the adoptive land after marriage (Maunaguru and Van Hear 2012).

THE MARRIAGE BROKER: A HISTORICAL BACKGROUND IN SRI LANKA, PAST AND PRESENT

The figure of the marriage broker is absent in the formulation of a love marriage and is marginal in an arranged marriage (Palriwala and Uberoi 2008a, 35). Lines cannot be easily drawn between marriage for social status and marriage for romance and its emotional satisfaction.[1] Though technically called "arranged marriage," the mechanisms through which it is contracted create a space for romance, intimacy, and love (Palriwala and Uberoi 2008a). The figure of the marriage broker is, in this context, associated with ambiguous behavior, untrustworthiness, profit-making motivation, money-oriented professionalism, and commercialization of marriage; unsurprisingly, all those connotations made the marriage broker an unpopular figure.[2] In earlier times, the role of the marriage broker was located within the domestic space or within kinship, relationship, or friendship circles. Their services were not offered to make a living. Sometimes such services were provided by estate or house brokers, and their work was limited to sharing information. This position gave the marriage broker a certain level of respectability, based on the trustworthy and respectable way they approached the matchmaking process. Also, the traditional professional marriage brokers, such as the Ghataks, were perceived as respectable because of their role in maintaining the genealogical and familial lineages of the wealthy Bengali families in Calcutta during the eighteenth century (Majumdar 2004).

Recent studies on marriage migration reveal the commercialization of marriage brokerage that has arisen, in terms of arranging tours, setting up offices, introducing prospective partners, conducting marriage ceremonies, and helping spouses to file visa applications.[3] With the increasing volume of labor and economic migration, matchmaking has emerged as a professionalized medium through which marriages are arranged and negotiated. However, a new type of marriage broker has emerged, owing to the required knowledge of legal matters in relation to navigating cross-border marriages according to the varied migration laws and requirements of different states. This modern marriage broker also appears to be incorporating the traditional methods of marriage brokerage to reduce the negative connotations surrounding the profession (Lu 2008).

The context in which the marriage broker emerges as a central figure in this study differs from the context of marriage migrations related to economic or labor reasons. Sri Lankan Tamil marriage brokers, operating within the context of war, carry a collective experience of violence, displacement, and their own personal histories of arranging their own children's marriages.

Although not a new occupation, the profile of the marriage broker has changed dramatically over the past few decades, marked by increasing professionalization and bureaucratization. As several interviewees pointed out, the marriage brokers of the 1950s and 1960s belonged mostly to the washerman (*vanar*) caste. The vanar is a service caste to the *vellalar* (a "high" landlord caste in Jaffna). The female members of the washerman caste, who washed privileged-caste women's clothing, had access to the internal spaces of their employers' houses. As a result, they knew personal information about each privileged-caste family and thus would know who had reached a marriageable age, and they would carry this information about prospective spouses from one vellalar house to another. A more formal type of matchmaker was the broker. While this figure was mostly involved in arranging marriages, they also engaged in house and land brokering. They would visit clients' homes and provide families with the necessary spousal information. The marriage broker generally carried information between privileged-caste households, making it a role looked down on in Tamil society. The marriage broker's low status is portrayed in Sri Lankan Tamil dramas. The Tamil melodramas of the 1960s through the 1980s represented the marriage broker as a dubious character, one who lied and got beaten up by the prospective spouse's family. Another common representation is that of a man who exaggerates information (e.g., about the wealth or status of the other family) for monetary gain and is always trying to make matches, since his survival depends on it.

Other types of matchmakers also intervened, such as family members, motivated not by material benefits but the desire to help their relatives find suitable partners for their sons and daughters. They performed this service by making suggestions about prospective spouses who would be suitable candidates to marry into their family circle. Another type of marriage broker was the village schoolteacher. This figure elicited much respect because of his status as an educated person and his role in negotiating local disputes. The teacher would pass the information about prospective marriage partners to the relevant families of his students. The one feature all these marriage brokers had in common was that they were known in the village (Maunaguru and Van Hear 2012).

Marriage brokerage was an old profession in the Tamil communities of Sri Lanka that acquired greater significance as a result of colonialism and the emergence of an elite middle-class among the Jaffna Tamils. Generally, the Tamil community promotes caste-endogenous marriage, resulting in unions among relatives (*sontham*) (Banks 1960). The rules of cross-cousin marriage,[4] as practiced in Jaffna Tamil society, made it possible for marriages to take place within the same sontham. Thus the role of the marriage broker was originally not so prominent in Jaffna society. However, with the emergence of a middle and educated class in Jaffna during the colonial period (Sivathamby 2000; Holmes 1982), families began seeking educated grooms for their daughters, in order to promote the upward social mobility of their family. This opened up the possibility of marrying outside the village or the sontham, to people who were considered strangers. This new phenomenon required a middleman to pass information regarding prospective spouses to interested families. The decision making and information gathering, however, were undertaken by the families themselves. Thus, while the emergence of a middle class in Jaffna made marriage brokers more prominent in Jaffna communities, they were still somewhat at the margins during marriage negotiations.

In the context of the war, however, more and more retired government officials and accounting staff from the private and public sectors have been gravitating toward the profession of marriage broker. The professionalization of marriage brokering started in the early 1990s. With the war and the resulting mass dispersion of families, the need arose for a figure to reconnect families across borders. The old figure of the marriage broker reemerged to facilitate transnational marriages. The fact that they come from the same community and social space, and that the families involved in marriage negotiations know them through personal networks, provides a certain accountability and authority to the marriage broker. Once the marriage is successfully arranged, the marriage broker charges each side (bride and groom) a fee of between 25,000 and 30,000 rupees (US$200). In addition, other types of fees are collected from clients for the communication of information about potential spouses, ranging from two to five US dollars. As the marriage broker is now marked by professionalism and brings with them the knowledge and experience of having worked in clerical and administrative contexts, the processes of collecting, codifying, cross-checking, and distributing spousal information gives them a niche in the community to facilitate matchmaking.

While in earlier times the marriage brokers were often nomads, now they have acquired more fixed locations. In addition to setting up offices, they also maintain databases on prospective clients, interact with clients through formal appointments, and solicit new clients via advertisements in the mass media. In short, the arrangement of marriages has moved out of the sphere of personal networks within bounded localities to the physical space of the marriage broker's office. Moreover, within this new professionalized space, the marriage broker operates on various, often contradictory, levels: as a priest determining an appropriate match, as an astrologer determining the appropriate matching of charts,[5] as a public authority providing both evidence and state-sanctioned authenticity to nuptials, and as a facilitator uniting partners across space and time. Even though the marriage broker appears as a local figure in Tamil transnational marriages, Canadian state documents recognize their part in arranging marriages. For example, the Spouse Migration Visa Forms questionnaire regarding basic background information on the relationship between the spouses, asks, "Was your marriage arranged?" At this point, the form defines that an arranged marriage is one "that was arranged by relatives, friends, or brokers (matchmakers)." However, despite such official recognition and professionalization of the trade, the marriage broker's origin in caste-bound services, combined with the obvious benefits that accrue from the misfortunes of others (i.e., arising from the earlier environment of political instability), have given the profession a somewhat dubious reputation, which begs the question: How does the marriage broker emerge as an indispensable figure between Tamil individuals who marry across borders?

THE MARRIAGE BROKERS: RAJAN, VIKRAM, AND NIMAL
RAJAN

In Colombo I met Rajan, who called himself a "marriage facilitator." Rajan started his marriage brokerage office in 1996 when he was displaced from Jaffna. He first worked as an account clerk in a firm in Colombo. During the 1983 ethnic riots in Colombo, he, his wife, and their two children were forced to leave and return to Jaffna. During this time he started a private academic institution, which he also developed into an organization that arranged Tamil literary conferences and facilitated meetings between local scholars. Rajan was a popular speaker at these public meetings and thus became well-known in Jaffna academic circles. Between 1987 and 1994 he was displaced several times and stayed in temporary shelters for months at a time. During that time, he offered a service of drafting letters for displaced people who needed to obtain government and NGO benefits. Later, in 1993, he arranged his son's marriage with the daughter of a highly influential businessperson in Jaffna. Through that marriage, Rajan developed contacts among Jaffna's wealthy population. After the Sri Lankan army captured the Jaffna peninsula, Rajan's wife, his daughter, and her family returned to Jaffna; Rajan, however, decided to go to Colombo to join his son and daughter-in-law.

Like many Tamils, Rajan's son has been living in the Colombo neighborhood of Wellawatte. Rajan's office is also located in this crowded borough, known as Kutty Yaalpaanam (Little Jaffna) because it is populated by Tamils who have come from Jaffna. Wellawatte was one of the areas affected most severely by the 1983 ethnic riots. Following the mass exodus from Jaffna in 1995, many Tamils set up shop in Wellawatte. Many high-rise apartment buildings have popped up in Wellawatte since then, targeting the new forced migrants from Jaffna. Thus, this place has become the Tamil hub in Colombo. Also, because of the constant fear of possible ethnic riots in the future, many Tamils felt safer staying close to their own community in Wellawatte (Maunaguru 2009).

Rajan told me that when he came to Colombo, he was keen to do something because he did not want to waste time. Some of his friends contacted him during that time to ask his help in finding prospective spouses for their children. This motivated him to start a marriage brokering institution, which had been in his mind for a long time. He had been considering the need for a professionalized brokerage to guide people in finding prospective partners. Success came after only a handful of years. He called his office a "marriage consultancy" (*thirumanam alosaniyaakam*) rather than a marriage brokering institute. The idea of establishing such a service was born out of his experience as a clerical worker and from running private institutions in Jaffna, his own marriage, his social networks established through his academic institution in Jaffna, the social service he had provided to the displaced communities in Jaffna, the extensive social and business networks he had made through his *sambandhi* (his son's father-in-law), and his own experience with displacement and war. In other words, his wide personal and professional networks, his experience in bureaucratic procedures and managing large institutions, and his charisma as a speaker and a well-known personality in the Jaffna Tamil community helped him quickly become a popular marriage broker.

Rajan runs his business out of one of the new high-rises, in the front room of his son's apartment. When I visited, we were first met by a signboard on the front door indicating whether he was in or out. When I walked into his office, I saw large rows of glass shelves, on which were colored files arranged in groups of blue, pink, yellow, and red. Next to the files, on the left side of the room, a television continuously aired Tamil programs. On top of the TV, Rajan had placed a black-and-white photo of his wedding. In the right-hand corner of the room, close to the entrance, was his desk and chair. Several chairs were arranged in line in front of his table, where clients could sit and go through the files. On both side walls of the room, enlarged pictures of Rajan with his books had been framed and hung. Rajan, dressed in a clean shirt and trousers, welcomed me to his office.

VIKRAM

I first met Vikram when he was visiting another marriage broker in Colombo to exchange client information. Vikram was living in Vavuniya, where he ran his marriage brokerage. Vavuniya is situated approximately 120 miles south of Jaffna, on the road to Colombo. A city highly populated by Tamils located between the predominantly Sinhala South and the pre-dominantly Tamil North, it served as a gateway for Tamils to move out of the war-affected northern region into the rest of Sri Lanka. Vavuniya hosted many displaced Tamils from Jaffna and Vanni (an LTTE-held area), and was also the location for many Tamil refugee camps during the civil war. During the hostilities, the region south of Vavuniya was under government control and the region north was held by the LTTE. Vavuniya was marked by many checkpoints and refugee camps, and the movement of people between the North and South was controlled and monitored—both by the army and the LTTE. In late 1990s, those who traveled from the North or from Vavuniya had to obtain a "pass" (i.e., clearance from the army)[6] to enter other parts of Sri Lanka.

Vikram worked in private firms as a stockkeeper and clerk in the south of Sri Lanka before he established his own business in Jaffna. Having become fluent in the Sinhala language through his work with the Sinhalese in the South, he established a bakery in Jaffna and did well until he and his family (a wife and four children) had to move from Jaffna to Vanni during the mass exodus in 1995. However, in 1997, after a few years in Vanni, he decided to move to Vavuniya to provide a proper education for his children and to safeguard them from forced recruitment by the LTTE. There he started a small business as a real estate broker. Moreover, since he could speak Sinhala, he became a mediator between the army and Tamil civilians who wanted to obtain passes to travel to other parts of Sri Lanka. Thus Vikram became a well-known person in Vavuniya. When the government abolished the pass system in 2005, Vikram moved on to set up a marriage brokerage. His established personal networks in Vavuniya, Jaffna, and Colombo; and his popularity, stemming from his services in obtaining passes and having run a business, enabled him to set up a successful marriage-brokering practice within a short period of time.

Vikram's service differs from Rajan's highly professionalized system. He visits the prospective spouses' families, relatives, and friends if he finds a matching astrological chart between his clients; he also negotiates over the phone if any of the partners' representatives live outside Sri Lanka. Vikram was planning to open his own office in Vavuniya in the near future, but at the time of writing he was operating from his house.

NIMAL

I met Nimal, a Sri Lankan Tamil refugee, in India. He lives in Chennai with his wife, and has two sons and two daughters. Nimal was running a business in the 1990s in Jaffna, where he and his family lived at the time. Because of the war, his sons were arrested and tortured by the army in 1990. Nimal managed to get them out of the Pusa prison in 1994 and send the elder son to Denmark as a refugee.[7] He never reached Denmark, but arrived instead in France, where he claimed refugee status in 1995. While he was waiting to be granted refugee status in France in 1997, a family approached Nimal to arrange a marriage between his elder son and their daughter. Nimal's family agreed to the marriage. As a result, Nimal's elder son moved to London to join his wife, a UK citizen. He lives there now as a citizen with his wife and two children. Since Nimal had to undergo medical treatment in India, he and his wife decided to move there with their other children, in 1999. They claimed refugee status in India and stayed on, even after his treatment was completed. Nimal's elder daughter's marriage was arranged by his elder son with a groom from Canada in 2000. Once the elder daughter moved to Canada, she took on the responsibility of looking after her father's family. According to Nimal, "Nowadays, daughters are the ones who are looking after the families who live in Sri Lanka or India and not the sons." Like Nimal, many marriage brokers I interviewed expressed the idea that married daughters are taking on the role of breadwinner for their natal families as well as arranging marriages for their siblings.

While Nimal's family was living in India, he managed to send his younger son to London with the help of his children overseas. The younger daughter continued to live with Nimal and his wife. They received a proposal for her from a family who had seen her at a friend's wedding. The prospective groom was living in London. According to Nimal, even though the rest of his family did not like the spouse, he went through with the marriage arrangements. The groom came from London, married Nimal's daughter in India, and returned to London fifteen days later. While Nimal was arranging for his daughter's travel to London, they found out that her husband was having an affair with another woman back in the UK. I asked him if he hadn't made inquiries about the groom before agreeing to the marriage. He responded that he had been fooled by the groom's family and their son's talk. He had asked some friends of his in London about the man, but they had not been able to give accurate information because the groom had kept moving from place to place. When they found out about the groom's affair, Nimal's elder daughter flew to London and found out first-hand information about the situation. Then, she tried to talk the groom out of it, but he said that conducting an affair was common in the UK and therefore was not willing to stop.

The elder daughter convinced her sister to file for a divorce, which was obtained in 2004. However, at a later date, Nimal found out that because the marriage had been contracted at the Sri Lankan embassy in India, the divorce papers they had obtained from the Indian court were not valid in Sri Lanka. Therefore, they filed for divorce in Sri Lanka and secured a divorce from the Sri Lankan courts. Nimal's younger daughter refused to attend any festivals or friends' and relatives' functions, and stayed at home most of the time. She also refused to speak to her father until, in 2006, a broker brought the chart of a possible marriage proposal. The groom was also a divorcee, living in Switzerland. Nimal matched the charts and was satisfied with the new groom, his family background, and other details, but he was scared to ask his daughter about it. Once again the elder daughter intervened; she talked to her sister and cross-checked the information on the groom. After a while, Nimal's younger daughter broke her years-long silence and asked him if he had matched the charts. The charts matched, the prospective spouses spoke with each other, and they agreed to marry. They now live in Switzerland and have a daughter.

When I met Nimal he was an established marriage broker in India. He mainly arranges marriages between Sri Lankan Tamils living in India and Tamils living in Western countries. He commenced his service in India in 2003. Nimal works from his home and does not have a specific office space set aside for his business. He limits his brokerage to people he knows personally. Nimal said that each time he arranges a marriage, he treats it as if he were arranging a marriage for one of his children. He also networks with other brokers, with whom he exchanges information about clients. If a marriage is arranged through such information sharing, the two brokers split the fee. Nimal also arranges marriages for those who are divorced as well as those who have been widowed. In such instances, he tries to connect divorcees or widows with partners in the same life situation. For Nimal, it is a way of giving both parties a second chance in life.

THE PROMISE OF THE MARRIAGE BROKER
SELF-SELECTION AND OFFICE SERVICES

Rajan claims that he has transformed the matchmaking process into a self-selection system—he provides all the detailed information via forms and sheets to the clients, who then can make their own choice. He went on to describe how a client comes to work with him. In order to obtain his services, an individual has to first sign up as a member, which requires an interview with Rajan, in which he notes down detailed information on the client and their family. They then must pay the annual membership fee of a thousand rupees (six US dollars). After all of that, they are given the forms and Rajan's set of rules and regulations. This includes statements such as "Though it is generally accepted that to find a suitable life partner is tedious, Rajan, with years of experience and careful study, has developed an easy system for self-selection." About making a successful selection, the handout states, "The success of a selection is a joint effort." It also details the matchmaking process: "(1) for a rich married life, the couple must like each other; (2) discrimination based on sex is unfair; (3) photographs help a lot to arrive at a quick and easy preliminary decision; (4) a single photo alone is insufficient to arrive at a correct decision; (5) annex current, color photos in different poses. One among these must be in passport size, and the other two must be in postcard size; (6) if the applicant is a female, one among the photos must be in a saree or in her traditional dress."

As noted above, the most noticeable feature in Rajan's office is the colorful files, which hold information about prospective spouses. The categories that interest him are place of residence, gender, and age. Each of his clients has a personalized file, coded with different colors for easy identification (Maunaguru 2009). Rajan explained to me how he arranged the color-coded files. Details of men under thirty years of age are coded in blue, and women in the same age category are coded in pink. Sri Lankan Tamil women over forty years of age are filed in A5-sized red folders. An analysis of this categorizing system reveals a particular type of gender stereotyping. It is interesting to see that he has filed the "difficult to find a suitable marriage partner" category—women over forty—in those differently sized red folders. This reflects the social reality of the Tamil community with regard to arranging marriages for women above a certain age. Further, each client is assigned a reference number they have to use in future dealings with Rajan. One day, he shared with me the rationale behind this. Each reference number is like a secret code, which only he can understand. It covers the gender, country of domicile, sponsorship ability, and first date of consultation of each client. At the top of each file is a form, which is divided into three parts.

The first part contains the basic details of the client, such as age, height, weight, complexion, appearance, job, country of domicile, and whether a person can serve as a sponsor, along with a passport-sized photo. The second part includes the astrological chart of the client, which contains minute details of that person's astrological data. It has been simplified to help an ordinary reader understand the basic astrological requirements for the best match. The third section contains details about the client's expectations regarding a marriage partner—such as from which country do they want to find a future partner, what kind of job or education level should the partner have, whether a dowry is expected, what civil status is acceptable (i.e., single, divorced, or widowed), and finally, the ideal height, weight, and complexion of the future partner.

Another form in the file contains the family details of the client, such as the names of the father and mother, their native villages, jobs, the number of siblings, their names and locations, and, if the siblings are married, details about their spouses. This form also covers details on the education levels and current employment status of the siblings and their spouses. The final part of this form lists detailed information on the client like the education level, the schools and universities attended, places of work, and jobs held in the past. This section also includes detailed information about their current living status (such as where they are living currently, how many years they have been living in the country, whether they are citizen or permanent resident of that country, and if so, whether they can sponsor a spouse, and whether that person can travel to Colombo for the wedding ceremony). The information also includes names and addresses of referees, who are generally friends from Colombo that know the client well. Even though there is a section to indicate preferences in terms of religion and/or caste (in cases of a mixed marriage), those details are often not filled in. However, the full details in the second form—on the parents' natal villages, to whom the spouses' siblings are married, and so forth—will, to some extent, indicate the potential spouse's caste background and social position. Locating the village of the spouse is an easy way to determine their caste order. The notion of caste appears to endure in transnational marriage through the work of the marriage broker.

During the time I spent in Rajan's office, I noticed that when a client was interested in a particular partner, they would ask Rajan about the caste details. In addition to the information in the files, Rajan has a private notebook in which he keeps the most personal details about his clients. When a client made such an inquiry, Rajan would take out this notebook. However, he would not directly articulate the caste name of the spouse. Instead, he would only say whether they were suitable. If suitable, he would say, "You can do it" (*Athu ningal seiyalaam*). When I asked Rajan why he does not include the caste details openly on the forms, he said that people do not like to make their caste background public knowledge. He thinks it is not a "civilized" (*nakariyam illai*) thing to discuss. This is in keeping with the Sri Lankan Tamil practice of not speaking openly about caste, even though it is an important consideration when it comes to marriage.

Rajan, like other marriage brokers, is familiar with the entire gamut of details pertaining to the caste order in Jaffna—which caste prefers to marry with which, and which belongs to which *ur* (village). Even though caste is not spoken about openly in his office, certain caste-related traditional marriage practices of Jaffna Tamils are processed through the figure of Rajan. On the other hand, by keeping this codified information, Rajan claims to provide scientific and rational information to his clients. When asked why he has been keeping such detailed information and copies of certificates, he explained that because of the war Tamils have been forced to move to different countries; as a result, all their networks have been destroyed and they have lost track of one another's whereabouts and family backgrounds. Thus, having access to copies of certificates and other relevant details gives interested parties a starting point from which to trace the background, status, friends, and relatives of a prospective partner; this, in turn, helps to develop a greater degree of trust and security about a prospective spouse.

The documents kept at Rajan's office are more than just a repository of information on potential partners—they are infused with history, connections of sociality, and traces of people's background, trust, and desire for a secure future. They are both "scientific" (classified and based on proof) and religious (astrological), both visual (photos) and written (documents). They contain elements of familiarity while reminding of the uncertainty about others and the newness of transnational marriages. Furthermore, the marriage broker's personal notebook holds hidden information on caste which is not explicitly listed in the main files. Therefore, these documents, put together, produce even more fragmented information on caste and the possibility of marriage. The traces of information contained in those different documents, and the anxieties, fear, and hope created when clients encounter them, further entangle with the figure of the marriage broker, who, as holder of information on Jaffna society, caste, and familiar marriage practices, is able to move between these documents and the clients. Marriage brokers enable the imagination of marriage and a future for their clients (both the potential spouses and their families) and thus insert a form of certainty into the uncertainty of the marriage process. The files, Rajan's personal notebook, and his personal knowledge together become in-betweens that not only connect people across borders, but also hold multiple potential futures. The marriage brokerage facilitates the imagined future of a new relationship in a new country through marriage, but also traces the people in the present and re-creates connections through the use of somewhat familiar traces of the past. Through these documents and the figure of the marriage broker, clients are able to imagine different futures every time they peruse the files.

PERSONAL SERVICE

Nimal's service is not as professionalized as Rajan's—he does not have an office, nor is the information on his clients codified and filed. Nonetheless, he does know the details of approximately two hundred to three hundred prospective spouses, all of which he stores in his briefcase. He stated that he generally arranges marriages among people personally known to him (e.g., friends and distant relatives). Nimal, unlike Rajan, resembles a traditional marriage broker in the sense that he carries information to the houses of the prospective partners living in India. Moreover, once he receives information and details about a spouse (such as photos and charts), he tries to match them with the astrological charts of those already in his possession. When two astrological charts match, he sends the materials of the prospective partners to their parents, siblings, or relatives. Thus, unlike Rajan, Nimal takes an active role in matching individuals. Even though Nimal's marriage brokerage services might seem traditional, he also has a vast knowledge of the various immigration rules of different states in relation to marriage migration, and offers or arranges marriage packages (see chapter 5) to couples who want to get married in India.

Moreover, even though his marriage services are motivated in some way by making money and are conducted using his business skills, his services are also shaped by his personal experience. The profession does not seem to be solely motivated by market forces, unlike others depicted in studies on the marriage broker in anthropology.[8] Nimal told me, "Ovoru kaliyanam seiyaka naan endra pilleikal mathiri yosithu thaan kaliyanam pannuranaan" (Whenever I arrange a marriage, I think of them as my own children and arrange the marriage for them). He further added, "We should help them in some way to have a better life. I have suffered and my family has suffered. I know what they go through." While the possibility exists that Nimal may have told me all this to impress me with the fact that he is performing a needed service rather than just doing all this to earn a living, his own experiences of the war and arranging marriages for his children, together with the impact of the failure of his younger daughter's first marriage, cannot be underplayed or ignored.

MOBILE SERVICES

Vikram's services differ from the other two in that he personally visits the prospective spouses' families, relatives, and friends; if he finds matching astrological charts among his clients, he commences negotiations over the phone. Vikram told me that he has information on both partners from Sri Lanka, the UK, Canada, Australia, Europe, and Australia. If the prospective spouse is located overseas, he then has dealings with their representatives (e.g., family members, parents, siblings, or friends) in Sri Lanka. In the present context, he tells me, the "foreign marriage is in high demand." Vikram differs from Rajan in the sense that he works with many other marriage brokers (exchanging clients' information). Vikram plays an important role in providing vital information (such as whom to contact, to whom the siblings are married, and where they were married) to the families of the prospective partners. Such information is needed by both sides to ascertain that the caste order or hierarchy is maintained through the proposed marriage.[9] His is a version of a mobile service. Unlike Rajan, he does not function from an office. Unlike Nimal, he does not get involved in arranging marriage packages, primarily because he operates in Sri Lanka, where the prospective partners can make the arrangements themselves.

PROMISES OF TRAVEL

Nimal, Rajan, and Vikram, like many marriage brokers, have amassed a comprehensive body of knowledge about the immigration processes, visa requirements, and the different citizenship statuses operative in different Western countries. They gained this expertise by talking to Sri Lankan Tamils living in Western countries, from their children, and from arranging Tamil transnational marriages. Vikram claimed that it was easier to go to the UK as a spouse than to Canada or France, as these two countries take a long time to process visas. He thinks that since the introduction of the Schengen visa system it has become more difficult to obtain a visa into European countries.[10] Vikram told me that if the spouse does not have a proper job in their adoptive country, then it is difficult for them to sponsor their partner from Sri Lanka. When I asked him who can sponsor from a foreign country, he replied, "Arasa angikaaram illaamal irupavarkal avangada pondatiyei kupudda elaathu" (People who stay in a host country without government recognition [legal status] cannot sponsor their wife from Sri Lanka). To illustrate this point, Vikram told me the story of Sritharan, one of his clients, who had been living in London for a long time but had not succeeded in getting his refugee status accepted by the UK government. Sritharan approached Vikram over the phone regarding a marriage. His main requirement was to find a woman with a permanent residence or citizenship in a foreign country. Vikram found the matching chart of a Sri Lankan Tamil woman who was a Canadian citizen and brokered the marriage. Both bride and groom and their families liked each other. Thus, the groom came back to Sri Lanka (because he could not marry in London since he did not have any legal status in that country), the bride came from Canada, and the marriage was performed. A few months after the wedding, Sritharan's wife sponsored him to Canada. While Vikram was narrating the story, I was surprised by his knowledge of the legal systems in different countries despite his lack of formal training in immigration law. Yet the knowledge Vikram has is sufficient to provide services to clients involved in transnational marriages who also need advice on immigration matters.

CASTE, *UR*, AND MARRIAGE BROKERS

These marriage brokers have gained fame as successful matchmakers among families seeking to contract transnational marriages not only because of their expertise on immigration procedures but also because of their knowledge of traditional caste hierarchies and other caste-related issues (such as which caste belongs to which *ur* or village in Jaffna, and which castes may intermarry). Such knowledge makes them important figures in connecting people through the traditional channels of matchmaking.

Inquiries about the ur of a prospective marriage partner are closely associated with questions of caste. Each village represents a composition of different castes or subcastes. The different caste members of a village are further segregated, and these divisions are marked by geographical boundaries. By asking a person to which side of the village they belong, one can identify their caste or subcaste. In the Sri Lankan case, earlier studies on marriage and kinship with regard to Jaffna Tamils before the war (Banks 1960; David 1973) indicate a high level of local endogamy: Jaffna Tamils appear to have married between different wards within and outside the village. The past preference of Jaffna people to marry on the basis of both territorial and kinship proximity (and social equality) is evidenced by the startling matrimonial statistics recorded by Kenneth David in the early 1970s in fishing villages along the Jaffna peninsula's northern coast. He claimed that the majority of the marriages take place within the same village but mostly outside wards (David 1973). Michael Banks (1960) introduces the concept of the *sondakara* caste to describe how in the village divided into wards (mostly among the privileged-caste vellalars), Jaffna Tamils would intermarry between wards from different villages. *Sondakara* literally means "people who are close" and includes marriageable relatives, consanguine relations, and those living in a specific ward (Tambiah 1973, 126). The category thus divides people along both caste and kinship lines. However, Jaffna vellalars appear to have idealized their sondakara as a closed grouping even it is not possible empirically, as this category is necessarily extended by definition (Banks 1960). The sondakara castes appear indeed to be "not mutually exclusive, but rather, overlapping entities" (Tambiah 1973, 126) in which a chain of marriages stretches out in many directions. Given the possibility of many directions taken by marriages with different wards, in actual fact the sondakara castes are not strictly endogamous, closed systems.[11] New marriages occur between previously unrelated wards but still within the Jaffna peninsula.

Tamil scholar Karthigesu Sivathamby (2000) points out a later mega caste formation among the Jaffna Tamils, in which the different subcastes of a particular privileged-caste merged and became a single caste, such as the vellalar caste of Jaffna Tamils. This led to marriages being contracted between subcastes of the vellalar caste. New members could be incorporated into bilateral kinship through marriage, to ensure political and economic gain, in a form of hypergamy (Tambiah 1973). Even though closed, ideal endogamy and hypergamy prevailed in Jaffna before the war, the possibility of making a larger kinship pool in which people could find their possible marriage partner was open due to the flexible boundaries of sondakara castes (Banks 1960; Tambiah 1973). The *sampathi* or *sampanthikarar*— that is, marriageable kinsmen who share bodily subsistence and are equal in levels of purity (David 1973)—are important, but a *prathiyar* (marriageable non-kinsman) also becomes a sampathi if they belong to the same caste with an equal level of purity (David 1973; Banks 1960). However, debates on Sri Lankan kinship and marriage mostly took place in the 1960s and 1970s, before the ethnic conflict.

With war-related marriage migration, the location where a marriage takes place has shifted from the village to other spaces. Most of the marriages of the Tamil diaspora occur in either Colombo or India. War, transnational marriages, and mass migrations have shifted from inter- or intraward marriages, within and between villages in Jaffna, to wider caste endogamy. However, caste endogamy still strongly prevailed even during the war: the flexibility of making the sondakara caste from many possible directions enabled the incorporation of new members into the sondakara pool, as long as they came from the same caste. The marriage brokers interviewed explained to me the caste statuses of the prospective spouses. They revealed that over 70 percent belong to the vellalar caste, followed by middle-caste members of Jaffna. Less than 10 percent of the field belonged to the "lower caste" of Jaffna. But all of them belonged to the middle class in the Sri Lankan sense: their occupations would range from doctors to accountants to teachers, or they would be living in a foreign country (in the Sri Lankan sense, having a job in a foreign country—or any job, really—would be considered as a middle-class qualification). The brides and grooms from Sri Lanka perceive marrying abroad as a form of status mobility. The Jaffna hypergamy has thus shifted to "global hypergamy" (Constable 2003).

Even though unknown people were incorporated into the sondakarar collective in Jaffna prior to the mass displacement, their caste background and other details could be traced through personal networks, as most of them lived in their natal villages within Jaffna (Tambiah 1973). Yet, with the onset of war and the resultant migrations, many Tamils were uprooted from their natal villages and spread across far-flung locales. Thus, tracing the background of such new and unknown figures, for the purposes of marriage, is no easy matter. To trace the caste backgrounds of potential spouses and incorporate them into the sondakara relationship at the time of war and migration, an intermediary who could gather such details and documents was required. We have seen how Rajan's documentation system provides information on the natal village of his clients' parents, as well as specifics about the urs from which the spouses' siblings' spouses hail. By recording such data, Rajan creates the possibility for his clients to trace the caste order and social hierarchy of the spouses' families within Jaffna society. The inquiry about the ur, even in a time of continuous displacement and breakdown of personal networks, points out that certain notions of caste and the social hierarchy associated with it persist in transnational Tamil marriages. In place of interward marriages, transnational Tamil marriages operate on the knowledge of ur and caste to determine marriage endogamy. Social hierarchy and hidden caste traced in the name of ur are kept in the spouses' files at the marriage broker's office. The files not only reveal the unknown people's backgrounds but also hold information in fragments and traces. Clients, files, and marriage brokers coming together to re-create the familiarity of marriages bring some certainty into the uncertainty of people's background, and thus make those people fit into known categories.

During my fieldwork, I did not hear anyone talk about caste differences in terms of "blood purity" or "pollution" (David 1973) and how it may adversely affect their family status or social order. However, many did mention the practical reasons for marrying within one's caste—for example, if one child marries outside the caste, it may be difficult to find partners for the other sons and daughters. However, several times I noted the impossibility of identifying a person's ancestral village or cross-checking the family's natal village. Thus, the minute details of the caste hierarchy are, generally, not observed. Other factors, such as education, foreign residence, wealth, civil war, and displacement, are important in making decisions and arrangements regarding marriage among Jaffna Tamils. Caste has been expanded to bring other subcastes within the vellalar caste as well as other middle castes close to it, and thus to transform those middle castes into a marriageable category. Rajan's filing and coding systems contain a certain continuity of the caste-endogamous rule in arranging marriages. What can be observed in his files reflects how marriage brokers and families try to maintain the traditional institution of marriage, and the classical structure of the marriage alliance between families on the basis of Jaffna society's caste hierarchy—even at a time of multiple displacements, dispersion of families, breakdown of personal networks, and political violence.

Although certain Tamil traditions of marriage arrangement have completely broken down due to the prolonged war and multiple displacements, fragments of such practices are still being passed down through marriage brokers and sustained through their documentation systems. Thus, on the surface, the war seems to have created a situation where cross-border Tamil marriages are contracted between two "strangers" for economic gain or to escape violence. Yet, through the matchmaking process's careful and complex systems, the strangers become sampanthikarar, thanks to the information provided on the kin's whereabouts. Marriage brokers and their files have the potential to connect families and individuals through multiple possibilities. Assemblages of different documents, personal notebook, files, astrological charts, and photos of prospective spouses, along with the figures of the marriage broker and their clients, re-create the social with fragments of familiarity and knowability at a time of war and societal dislocation. However, this situation does not necessarily imply that the social continuity or tradition of the Jaffna Tamil society remains unchanged. Rather, I would say that a fragmented social continuity and discontinuity of "traditions" passes through figures like Rajan, the marriage broker, housed in the files at his office.

PRACTICES, KNOWLEDGE, AND TECHNIQUES OF MARRIAGE BROKERS
RAJAN'S OFFICE

During the time I spent with Rajan in his office, I helped him compile files. Clients must make appointments to view the files of prospective brides or grooms. Rajan asks his clients which set of files they want. So, for example, if a client says that they are looking for women between the ages of twenty-five and thirty from Sri Lanka, Rajan would take out the first fifty files coded in pink and hand them over. For a copy of any prospective partner's astrological chart, the client must pay fifty rupees. The client then takes the chart to a known astrologer to find out whether their horoscopes match. Rajan also provides contact details for astrologers if needed. At the same time, he informs the other party that he has given out their chart, and encourages them to collect the chart of the requesting party. Once the charts are matched, the interested party contacts Rajan to inform him that they would like to talk to the other family. At this point they would also ask for more details about the prospective spouse, their family, character, caste background, as well as the names of other people they could ask about the bride or groom. Once this interest is expressed to Rajan, he informs the other party and sets up a meeting in his office between the two parties. These meetings usually take place after his regular office hours. Further inquiry and discussions take place outside Rajan's office. Once the negotiating parties reach an agreement to proceed, they inform the prospective bride and groom and ask them to talk to each other over the phone and exchange photos of themselves. After several such phone conversations, if they like each other, they inform their parents about how they want to proceed. In the case of a positive decision, the families will proceed with negotiating other factors, such as dowry, date, and venue of the marriage ceremony.

Among the middle-class and privileged-caste marriages of Jaffna, traditionally the dowry (*chidenam*) is given to the bride at the time of marriage.

An important part of vellalar caste marriage, chidenam includes land (sometimes a house), jewelry, and cash.[12] With transnational marriages involving a bride residing in Western countries, the groom does not expect cash or land because the possibility of migrating and becoming a citizen of that country becomes part of the dowry. However, if the groom resides in a Western country and the bride in Sri Lanka, her family is expected to provide cash and jewelry more than land (since most of the land during that time in Jaffna was not accessible because of military occupation). In some cases, apartments owned in Colombo substituted for the land as dowry during wartime. As a result, a number of apartments were bought by the Jaffna Tamils to give to their daughters as dowry, and those units were mostly occupied by the daughters' parents or relatives in Colombo. Thus, the scales and components of dowry change according to the locations of spouses and the ground situation of the war. Whenever deadlock would arise over negotiating the dowry or other matters, the client would come to Rajan and inform him of the problem. He would then advise them, often saying "that marriage is all about negotiating, that one has to give something to get something. It is a good family to have a marriage arrangement with, so it is OK to take or do a little bit extra to have this marriage."

One day Rajan asked me whether I would like to observe how a marriage is set up in his office. The meeting, which took place on a Wednesday evening, was between an uncle and aunt of the groom and the father and mother of the bride. Both sets of people were living in Colombo, but the groom and his family were living in Canada at that time. After Rajan made the initial introductions, they started inquiring about each other's native places and shared acquaintances from their natal villages. Rajan then left the office so that they could have a more intimate conversation. They tried to identify and get to know the family background of the other party in terms of natal village, schools, or mutual acquaintances. During the conversation, it came to light that both families had been displaced in the 1990s. Thus, they found it hard to identify many mutual contacts. Even when they did discover a common person known to each family, often neither party knew that person's whereabouts. After an hour of discussion, both parties decided to continue talks, so they fixed a date to meet again—at the bride's home. The bride's parents stayed behind to talk to Rajan about the groom's family. Rajan is well-versed in the art of persuasion. He mentioned many well-known people with whom the groom's family is associated. The name-dropping included famous doctors, lawyers, and teachers, which gave the groom's family status and credibility. His charming and charismatic behavior with clients goes a long way in influencing their decisions. He artfully moves back and forth between being an authoritative figure (one pushing the family to make a decision) and a facilitator (one merely offering information so that the family can make their own decisions), indicating his visibility and invisibility in the decision-making process of matchmaking.

Rajan would try his best to connect the person in the file with the client in front of him—through factors such as caste, background, village/town of origin, and social connections. He has a great amount of knowledge about each of his clients, and he constantly crosschecks the information provided by them with that of others who hail from the same village or school. Just like Rajan, during the marriage negotiations stage clients try to position the other family in terms of ur, caste, and acquaintances, so that the other family becomes somewhat "knowable" to them. Yet, as observed, this is not an easy task, given the multiple displacements and the related severing of social ties. Rajan's work of collecting comprehensive information on prospective spouses—from personal facts, to the marriage details of their siblings, to knowledge about family members and their marriage partners, to copies of certificates of education and employment—makes it possible to convert an unknown person into a somewhat known person.

When Jaffna Tamils arrange a marriage for a child, they make inquiries about the prospective partner through multiple channels (e.g., friends, neighbors, relatives, coworkers). The term in Tamil for such inquiry is *visarithal*, meaning "to acquire full knowledge of a person or inquire or find information about a person." The inquiry seeks to gather information on levels of education, caste background, character, wealth, and behavior. With the increasing tendency to look for prospective foreign grooms for Sri Lankan brides, gathering this kind of information through personal networks is no easy task, since it must include details about employment and the residency status of the groom and his family. Rajan pointed out that a Tamil marriage is not a marriage between a man and a woman, but rather a marriage between two families. Therefore, the clients who come to him require information not only about the prospective spouse, but also about their family. The marriage broker has become a figure of authority in matchmaking not only through their more professionalized approach to the marriage process (e.g., codifying and classifying information and conducting interviews with clients), but also by bringing back the known processes of inquiry (visarithal). The documents (such as copies of educational certificates) and the use of a filing system reflects not only the changing nature of marriage brokerage services, but also how the notion of inquiry has been transferred to reliance on documents at a time when face-to-face inquiry has become difficult. At the same time, we have seen how, in such spaces, documentary proof alone is not sufficient to get to know another person; a marriage broker's client also expects them to provide validation of this information on the prospective spouse and their family.

NIMAL'S SERVICES

Unlike Rajan, whose office-based services follow the self-selection method, Nimal uses astrological charts, his clients' personal requirements, and the information he already has to match the partners. Either he will visit clients in person to propose the matches or encourage them over the phone to look into the matches he has proposed. Nimal's service entails not only the arranging of a marriage between the spouses, but also that the organizing of a wedding package—such as arranging a guesthouse for both spouses traveling from another country and their families for the duration of the wedding period, hiring Sri Lankan photographers, finding priests, and booking wedding halls in India (chapter 5 will detail the Sri Lankan marriage ceremonies and how they take place in a transit place like India). The broker's role as a matchmaker does not stop with the marriage negotiation process, however, but continues until the marriage is contracted. The offer of marriage packages and facilitation of the marriage ceremony in India are unique features of Nimal's brokerage services, quite unlike his competitors in Sri Lanka. There are some similarities between Nimal's and Rajan's matchmaking services (e.g., exchanging information, matching astrological charts, facilitating negotiations between families, and finalizing the marriage); however, Nimal's involvement during the matchmaking process and marriage arrangement resembles that of a traditional marriage broker who operates within the domestic space where the marriage negotiations take place. Furthermore, Nimal generally arranges marriages between families who are personally known to him. Thus, he takes on a certain level of accountability and responsibility for the marriages he arranges.

Nimal told me the story of one of his clients, Malar, a woman living as a Sri Lankan refugee with her mother and sibling in India. Before she contacted Nimal, she had almost got married twice, but both attempts failed. In both cases, the groom's families had promised her that their son would come down from Canada and Germany, respectively, to marry her. However, after many months, the prospective spouse never turned up to marry her. In the last instance, she had even gone to live with her future husband's mother, in India, and was helping her soon-to-be mother-in-law around the house. However, after six months of this arrangement, the prospective in-laws did not want their son to go through with the marriage. Malar returned to her family, unmarried, without even seeing her prospective husband. Nimal was determined to arrange a successful union for her. For him, after what had happened to his own younger daughter, arranging a marriage for Malar became a personal challenge. Nimal found a groom from Canada for Malar. While arranging the marriage, Nimal made many inquiries about the potential partner and asked Malar's family to do the same. After matching their astrological charts and finalizing the dowry, the marriage was fixed and the groom and his family flew to India a few days before the ceremony. The *thali* (wedding amulet) had been made by the groom, the date was fixed, and the hall and marriage package were arranged. However, the day before the event, the groom called Nimal and said he wanted to cancel the marriage because he did not like the bride. Nimal tried to persuade him and his family to go ahead with the wedding, saying that it was too late since everything had been arranged. Yet the groom and his mother insisted they did not want to proceed and that they were leaving for Canada the next day.

Nimal, who was acquainted with a person working at the Human Rights Commission in Chennai, immediately complained to the Commission on the basis that the groom's family had agreed to the marriage and received in advance the dowry in cash. Nimal thought it was tantamount to cheating. He chose this course of action, first, because he thought the way the bride was deceived constituted a human rights violation; and, second, in case the groom's family left the country, so that the Commission could still take action back in Canada. When I inquired whether the Human Rights Commission was able to deal with such complaints, Nimal was not sure. But he explained that since money was involved (i.e., the cash dowry and the fact that the bride's family had spent money arranging the wedding ceremonies), his friends told him they could report the misconduct to the authorities. It is not clear whether the Human Rights Commission representative visited the groom's family only because he was Nimal's friend, to put pressure on them to recommit to the marriage. Nimal, his friends, and the Commission member all asked the groom for an explanation for canceling the marriage arrangements. Since he could not provide a satisfactory answer, the Commission representative told his family he was going to file a case against them if they refused to reconsider. This development forced the groom's party to agree to proceed with the marriage.

In this case, Nimal used his personal network and some sort of official power (through his friends) to make the marriage happen. He was not sure the Commission had any power in the matter, but by bringing an authority figure into the scene and keeping ambiguous the legality of one person's refusal to marry, Nimal managed to contract the union. The marriage took place the next day, as planned, and the groom left after a few weeks. Malar was still waiting for him to send the necessary documents so that she could apply for a Canadian visa. Thus, the uncertainty persists over her husband's acceptance of the marriage and her reunion with him across international borders. Even though the broker managed to bring certainty in arranging the marriage, the uncertainty of the marriage process endures after the wedding ceremony.

VIKRAM'S SERVICES

Vikram negotiates marriages between Sri Lankan Tamils he knows as well as those he doesn't. However, his service is not based on a self-selection method like Rajan's—once he receives the information about a prospective partner, he sets about finding a matching astrological chart. Once the horoscopes and the spouses' (and their families') desires and expectations are matched, he then approaches the families or the spouses' representatives, provides the information to each family, and asks them to consider the match. Vikram plays an active role in matchmaking and connecting the prospective spouses; he is also quite visible in the marriage negotiation process. Unlike Rajan's skilled, sophisticated, and subtle modes of influencing the match, Vikram is directly involved at every stage. His presence is quite visible, since he visits the houses of the spouses' families frequently during the process.

In order to gain personal knowledge to provide a better matchmaking service, marriage brokers have learned the art of matching certain astrological charts with others. Even though there are traditional astrologers who specialize in such services, marriage brokers nowadays consider astrological charts in their work. In Jaffna society, the matching of horoscopes is crucial in determining the marriage.[13] Vikram, who taught himself how to read and match horoscopes, told me that matching charts was not easy because there are many different methods of doing so in Sri Lanka (e.g., the *thrikantham* vs. the *vakiayam* systems). Thus, sometimes the astrological charts of a bride and groom that are matched under one system may not match under another. He is still puzzled as to why there are so many systems rather than a single common methodology. However, Vikram had decided to follow the thrikantham system to match his charts because he thinks this is the one used by most Tamils.

Once he gives the prospective charts to the two parties, they approach different astrologers to find out whether the charts do indeed match. Sometimes different astrologers give different interpretations. According to Vikram, it is difficult to get a consensus from different astrologers on one set of charts—not only because they may follow different systems of reading charts, but also because they keep inventing new forms within the existing systems. Vikram also pointed out that if it's a good match in terms of a highly educated or an overseas-based person, the parents are ready to overlook some details of the astrological match between their daughter and a prospective groom. Visiting different astrologers during marriage negotiations helps to overcome the uncertainty of marrying a stranger from an unknown land.

However, the astrologers and the documents they produce as part of the marriage process, as in-between figures and documents, contain many possibilities. The multiple astrologers consulted are not sought after to obtain the same result from the astrological charts, but rather for the possibility of slight differences between their reports. The slight gaps fostered by such differences enable the spouses' families to pick and choose among the astrologers' words to imagine a future and bring some certainty and stability in a time of uncertainty and dislocation. Astrological charts as documents play a crucial role in the marriage process, offering a pathway to read about the couple's potential future. These documents create both fear of the future and hope for a better life. But still those charts, so intricately weaving the past, present, and future life of their subjects, cannot be read by individuals themselves. Astrologers and marriage brokers are the needed figures who can read the documents and transmit the knowledge they contain regarding the right marriage, the possibilities of migration, and the couple's future life. The charts, astrologers, marriage brokers, and potential spouses all come together to produce their future sociality. But these potential spaces of the marriage process host the multiple possibilities of the future according to different associations. The rules of marriage and matchmaking are always reworked and reconfigured at the site of the marriage process, rather than following an established set of marriage and matchmaking rules. In other words, these moments, spaces, and the figures and documents within them hold both uncertainty and certainty, actualized and yet to be actualized moments, where uncertainty and differing perspectives create the possibility of certainty.

CHANGING DESIRES, MEETING DEMANDS,
AND ARRANGING MARRIAGES

One evening, after Rajan had finished his day's work, I asked him what his clients specifically look for from the other party. He answered that people still focus on the ur (i.e., whether they are from the same village, or which part of the village they are from) and the caste background (which is also traditionally linked with the ur). However, he also felt that nowadays people assigned more importance to education and employment. In terms of the more desirable locales, Sri Lankan women (or their parents and siblings) look for grooms in English-speaking countries, such as the UK, Canada, Australia, or the United States, because they feel it is easier to adapt in these countries since they are already familiar with English. Another important factor is the prospective spouse's ability to sponsor a partner for migration. Therefore, they look for whether such an individual has permanent residency or citizenship status in their adoptive country. Rajan told me, "Valaavetiya ipadi vevveru idathila iruka mudiyathu," meaning that a husband and wife cannot live in different places once they are married. Nimal also explained that while caste is important when arranging a marriage, there are times when families chose to ignore caste differences, such as when the groom is educated or well established in a Western country. However, this is not applicable to marriages between the marginalized and privileged castes, but rather only to those between the middle and privileged castes.

Commenting on the changing desires regarding marriage, Vikram shared Nimal's and Rajan's opinion. He explained that many Sri Lankans want to marry Tamils in foreign countries, especially English-speaking ones. The foreign grooms want to have Sri Lankan brides who have knowledge of English and are "fair" in complexion. When the women are dark complexioned, he works with the situation:

> You know, I ask these women's relatives or parents to take a good photo of the bride. You know you can make a woman look fair or lighter in the photo, with more lights on the face. So, I ask them to take a "good" photo of the bride. When the groom's parents like the bride's photo and the horoscopes are matched, I will make arrangements for the parents to see the bride directly in a *kovil* [temple]. When they see the woman face-to-face, her complexion will not be the same as the one they saw in the photo. They will then ask me or say the girl is bit "dark." I tell them that

I will arrange for them to get more dowry from the bride's side—like about one million rupees [US$7,000] or so. The parents are happy once they hear that they can get more dowry or money from the bride's family. So, they recommend the girl to their son.

When I asked how he would deal with the groom, he replied:

When the groom comes from Canada or from UK for the marriage, he will see the woman directly, and she will not be as fair as in the photos that he has seen. But, you know by that time, I would have arranged for him to talk to the bride over the phone for months. Then, of course, some love would have developed between them. Also, the marriage arrangements have already been made, and he has spent money to come here. Thus, it will be fine. He goes ahead with the marriage. . . . What they need is a good wife, not a fair woman. If they all want fair women, who will marry the dark girls?

The marriage broker is able to overcome the "skin color" issue by offering monetary incentives. The politics of skin color has a long history, going back to colonialism and remaining prominent in the new capitalist world of consumerism, which enables the sale of countless beauty products for lightening skin color. Edited photographs depict fair-skinned women, along with matching astrological charts, circulate in the groom's family circle and create an emotional feeling toward the future wife. Later, after the spouses meet in person, the politics of skin are overwritten by the increased dowry value of the bride for the groom's parents and by the romance and emotion created through photos and phone conversations. The photos have the power to create affection between the bride and groom, while other kinds of materiality in the marriage process (such as money and dowry items) reconfigure the desires and expectations concerning the bride and groom. Rather than a given set of kinship rules and obligations driving the process of matchmaking, it is the associations of different materiality and humans within the marriage negotiations that constantly reconfigure the desires for a certain future and the choice of a partner.

The marriage brokers have a vast store of knowledge regarding the changing desires of contemporary grooms and brides. Moreover, the new types of jobs and employment titles as well as academic qualifications of a Western Tamil spouse have to be translated into terms that can be understood by the families in Sri Lanka. The role of the marriage broker is

important not only in explaining or translating these titles or new categories of degrees, but also in providing details to the Sri Lankan spouse and
their families on the new places and lifestyles in the countries to which they
will be living. The marriage broker is the holder of this new information, a
channel where different desires meet, and a "translator" of new terms. On
many levels, therefore, the broker becomes an important figure, striking a
balance between fragments of traditions and the evolving desires of contemporary spouses.

It is not only the changing perspectives of Tamils about marriage that
affect traditions, but also the feeling shared by the brokers themselves that
they need to remove the stigma associated with their profession and gar-
ner recognition for their service in the community. I asked Rajan why he
chose for himself the term "marriage facilitator" rather than "marriage
broker." He replied that he created the term "marriage facilitator" because
"marriage broker" has too many negative connotations. In Tamil society,
marriage brokers have been looked down on and generally portrayed as
clowns. Therefore, he initially came up with the term "marriage consultant"
(*thirumana alosakar*). However, he was not satisfied with that, since he was
in the business of providing information to his clients, not advice. His next
option was "matchmaker" (*kalyana poruthunar*). However, this, too, did not
adequately capture the true nature of the service he was providing.

He settled on "marriage facilitator," which he translates as *thirumanam
attrupaduthunar*. In coining the Tamil term, Rajan drew *attrupaduthunar*
from the *Thirumurukatru Padai*, an ancient Tamil epic about the god
Murugan. Within that text, attrupaduthunar connotes "showing the path to
a person who got lost in the forest." He added that the term "facilitator" is
now commonly known among Tamils since the commencement of the
peace process (with the emergence of Norway in the role of facilitator in the
Sri Lankan conflict in 2002, the term began to be used often in the media
and in daily conversation). By introducing a new term to the sphere of marriage brokerage, Rajan is trying to induce a shift in the profession toward
the third-party role of "facilitator." Through this effort, Rajan is hoping not
only to eradicate the stigma associated with traditional marriage brokering
among Jaffna Tamils, but also to highlight the newness of his services. In
addition, the term "facilitator" brings in the notion of a third party, a person
who is there to smooth out difficulties and resolve conflicts that arise during
matchmaking and the arrangement of marriages. He told me that the new
label will help to eliminate the stigma of profit making associated with the
profession, making it seem more service oriented.

MARRIAGE BROKERS DEALING WITH
THE AMBIGUITY OF THE MARRIAGE PROCESS

Nimal, Rajan, and Vikram have each repeatedly mentioned that despite their best efforts to find suitable partners based on their clients' preferences, there have been times when such marriage negotiations have failed, or the spouse in Sri Lanka discovers that the other is having an affair or has lied about their situation overseas. They also indicated that there were cases where some of their clients could not join their spouses in their adoptive land because they could not get an immigration visa. Moreover, they admit that it is difficult to fully clarify and cross-check the information their clients provide, because those clients live in various locations around the world. The brokers themselves are familiar with the social reality of Tamil life as well as that of the communities concerned, which are constantly moving and dispersed across borders. Under such circumstances, it proves difficult to transform people from "unknown" to "known."

Nimal admits that he cannot trust anyone who lives in a "Western country" because there is no way of finding out their "real" situation, civil status, or lifestyle. When I asked him why it was difficult, he explained, "Because people are living in unknown lands and unknown places where sometime or most of the time inquiry about the grooms or brides is impossible." This is why he encourages the families involved in marriage negotiations to carry out a full inquiry about the prospective spouse before the marriage. He went on to say, "Sometimes no matter how much they inquire and organize the marriage it may not go the way they want it to go." Echoing the same sentiment, the three men told me that the war and displacement in Sri Lanka have "left us in a place where we do not know who is living where." Vikram said, "Naadu pireichaneila kalyanam ellam maripochu" (Marriage has changed due to the civil war). In reply to my question on exactly how it has changed, he replied, "You cannot trust anybody; and we do not know who is living where, what they are doing, and how they are behaving. There are many divorcees and widows nowadays. And, even if you arrange a marriage, sometimes fighting will start between the army and the LTTE, and roads will be closed, and we have to postpone the marriage for months." He made this comment at a time when the war was still ongoing and constant displacement was widespread. The reality has changed with the end of the war, but his words echo the social reality that lingers despite the peace. His words also clarify that what places a transnational marriage at stake is not only the inability of marriage brokers to verify clients' information, but also the uncertainty that surrounds such a union as well as the future uncertainty of the couple being reunited to make a life together in an adoptive land.

I asked Vikram whether any of his clients contacted him after the failure of a marriage he had brokered. He replied that he tells his clients that his responsibility is to arrange a marriage, not to ensure its longevity—after the wedding, that is their job, not his. He recalled one instance where he had brokered a marriage between a groom from Canada, Vel, and a bride, Rohini, from Vavuniya. After exchanging all the required information, matching the horoscopes, and arranging weeks of conversation between bride and groom, the wedding took place without incident. After a week, the groom contacted him and complained that his wife had only studied up to the Ordinary Level, whereas he had thought that she had gone up to the Advanced Level. He cited this as a reason that would make it difficult for him to take her to Canada, get her a job there, and build a life with her. Vikram told him, "I gave you all the information. Check your files: it says she has studied up to O/L not A/L. But look, you need a good wife in Canada. We all know that in Canada we do not work in high-flying jobs. You do not need higher education in Canada to find a job. She will be a good wife to you. Also, teach her English and computer while she waits for the visa, so that when she comes, she will be ready for Canada. Do not think it is a bad marriage."

The groom took his advice, brought his wife to Colombo, and arranged for English and computer classes while she was waiting for the Canadian visa. She left for Canada after eight months. At the time of our interview, Vikram did not know how they were faring. However much Nimal, Rajan, and Vikram hold the knowledge about the spouses and provide documents with detailed information, and however much they produce "scientific rationale" topped off with the religious and cosmic perfection of matchmaking, the marriage process resists certainty. The process of matchmaking—involving marriage brokers, documents, and clients—track an outcome that is constantly shifting and changing, entangled with uncertainty, as we have seen in the numerous cases narrated in this chapter. The potential of the marriage process, the figure of the marriage broker, and the documents they provide hold the promise of both certainty and uncertainty, possibilities of imagining the future paired with uncertainty about the future, failure and success. The practices of matchmaking, the process of the marriage, documents, marriage brokers, and future spouses involved, all are concerned not only with the present but also with imagination, anxiety, hope, and failure—the uncertainties of the future.

The future is both actualized and yet to be actualized during the marriage process, as illustrated by the story of Malar, still waiting for her husband to send the necessary papers to reunite with him in Canada, or the story of Vel and Rohini, trying to prepare for a future in their adoptive land. The uncertainty and ambiguity of marriage brokerage, the documents brokers use, and the repeated associations between documents and humans bring differences and surprises every time they assemble in the in-between space of the marriage process.

MARRIAGE BROKERS, FRAGMENTS, AND THE RHYTHM OF LIFE

War and violence in Sri Lanka have ripped apart entire communities and affected the stability of daily life. In the realm of marriage, certain traditional or customary practices have been destroyed or altered beyond recognition. With the disruption of community life has come the discontinuation of traditional channels of matchmaking (e.g., kinship and friendship networks). Figures like Vikram, Nimal, and Rajan emerged within settings of prolonged violence to re-create certain fragments of traditions, marriage rules, and customs, thus opening up the possibility for Tamil communities to rebuild, reconnect, and imagine futures through the familiar terrain of matchmaking. The services provided by these marriage brokers and the documents that circulate in this process give Tamil communities the opportunity to reenter the rhythm of life. Prolonged violence has given rise to a situation of uncertainty with regard to living with or marrying an "unknown" person (i.e., a person whose background and social circles are not easily traceable). In such a social landscape, marriage seems an obvious gateway to leave the site of violence—especially if one were to marry someone from outside the Tamil community, or a "stranger" who can offer one the opportunity of starting life anew in a different location and even the possibility of rebuilding a Tamil community there. Yet, the above stories of marriage brokerage show us that the transnational marriages of Sri Lankan Tamils do take place within the same Tamil community, to the extent of marrying a person sharing a similar social space and the same experience of war. The internal killings within Tamil militant movements made this space further complicated as the boundary between perpetrators and victims had been blurred (Thiranagama 2011).

Veena Das (2007) argues in her work on the partition in India that following violence people repair their relationships and reinhabit the world through everyday life. Here, the matchmaking provided by marriage brokers, and the traces and documents involved in such services, open up the possibility for the Tamil communities to return to fragmented but familiar practices, imagine multiple futures, and reconnect with members of their community. Vikram, Rajan, Nimal, and the documents they provide hold, and thus keep alive, certain traditionally known ways of arranging marriages among Tamils—such as "inquiring about the people," the notion of ur, caste, and astrological matches. The prospective spouse becomes known or trustworthy not because the clients or their families necessarily trust the marriage broker's word or the information in the documents (visual and written), but because the process used by the marriage broker and the circulation of these documents are in alignment with known and trusted notions of how a marriage should be arranged.

Even if all such avenues fail to provide the necessary connections, the marriage broker is able to provide a great deal of information and trustworthy documents (e.g., educational certificates, employment certificates, personal references) about a prospective spouse, making their family "knowable" to the other party. By providing a known and familiar space for matchmaking, the marriage broker facilitates the process of finding spouses for Sri Lankan Tamils within their own community. The marriage broker's work and the documents provided are one way these unknown categories are transformed into known categories through the familiar practice of matchmaking. This is perhaps one of the reasons why, as many marriage brokers pointed out to me, the matrimonial internet services have not been successful among the Jaffna Tamils. In addition to the documents certifying the details of potential spouses, Tamil communities seem to want a figure—made of flesh and blood, from the same social space, and part of the collective experience of war and displacement—to facilitate the matchmaking process.

It is not just the documents but the marriage brokers and the associations of the documents, brokers, spouses, and families in the in-between zone of the marriage process that turn the unknown into known. Every moment of these associations produces multiple possibilities for the future. The marriage brokers arrange unions not only through new forms of matchmaking—such as setting up offices, codifying and documenting information, and facilitating a self-selection process—but also through the familiar and known ways of the Tamil communities (e.g., by associations of caste and ur). The marriage process—fostering both uncertainty and certainty, emerging through the figures of the marriage brokers and the documents they produce on the spouses—has the potential of multiple outcomes. It connects present practices, past memories, as well as the imagination of futures in the form of leaving the site of violence, reconnecting with others from the community, and starting a new life amid the uncertainty of war. The transfiguring of relationships (old and new) within the context of violence happens not only through languages, voices, and bodies, but at the sites and moments of associations of documents and humans— in this case, the marriage brokers and their clients' information.

The marriage broker and the documents they provide in this instance are not only "holders" of information, but also a "channel" or "pathway" for a Tamil person to reconnect with the rhythm of everyday life (marriage, death, coming of age) through certain known categories while in an unsustainable place or condition—communities torn apart by war, made to live in social spaces where the categories of perpetrators and victims are blurred, where they have to resort to marrying off their children to unknown people in unknown lands, made to deal with unknown immigration rules, citizenship status, and the sponsorship ability of a prospective spouses. The traditional fragments (certain notions of traditional marriage, marriage practices, and marriage rules) are held by the marriage brokers and in the documents they provide. However, that does not mean that these rules and practices have remained static and unchanged. These fragmented yet known practices of the marriage process enable Tamil families to arrange marriages in an unknown space, in a context rife with uncertainty and instability and suspicion of others.

Veena Das, drawing on philosophers Ludwig Wittgenstein and Stanley Cavell, argues that putting together such fragments does not lead to imagining the whole or bringing it back: "The fragments mark the impossibility of such an imagination. Instead, fragments allude to a particular way of inhabiting the world" (Das 2007, 6). Here, the fragments in the marriage brokers' matchmaking process are the pieces of certain marriage rules and practices, sensitivity to caste, and traditional ways of arranging marriages. But assembling together each traditional fragment will not point to the whole because each fragment itself is something unique and singular. Each fragment not only represents a way of inhabiting the world but also holds the potential for the imagination of different futures. Through marriage brokers and their documents, certain traditions and familiarities of the marriage process travel in fragments and continue to play a crucial role in the life of Tamils. In a sense, people are hopping on the known stepping-stones of these fragments of tradition, rules, and practices to reach an imagined future. The stepping-stones are spaces and figures of familiarity that marriage brokers hold through their profession and documents. Associations of each fragment release different imaginations of futures, connections, and possibilities of reinhabiting a world torn apart by violence. These moments are important in-between zones within the marriage process in creating multiple fragments of familiarity. Such fragments of familiar practices in the process of arranging marriages open up the potential for certainty (that can be imagined and looked forward to) in a transnational marriage and in imagining and inhabiting multiple futures. It is also a site where new and old relationships transfigure through the marriage brokers and the documents they provide.

The shadow of war follows the rhythm of life. The uncertainty of future, constant displacements, and the uncertainty of migration after marriage, linger in the shadow of the marriage process. The presence of violence continues to remind marriage brokers of the impossibility of establishing certainty in the marriage process. The brokers also reflect the changing nature of marriage among Jaffna Tamils, the changing desires and new needs of their clients, the continuity and discontinuity of certain customs and traditions in the process of matchmaking, the effects of different countries' laws and customs on the lives of Tamils involved in the matchmaking process, and the ever-present shadow of violence cast on the life of Tamils.[14]

The figure of the marriage broker and the documents they provide are the sites within the marriage process where the uncertainty of future relatedness, and multiple imaginations and anxieties of futures for the prospective couples, are worked out, imagined, and lived. As seen in the cases of Nimal, Rajan, and Vikram, the uncertainty continues to hover over the rhythm of life—such as in marriage—and reminds people of war, violence, and displacement. The services of the marriage broker, and the different associations of documents, marriage brokers, and clients in the moments of the marriage process, also highlight the difficulties of making people known, the potential for failure in matchmaking, and the uncertainty of the marriage process itself. A constant tension remains in the process of matchmaking. Marriage brokerage services in the in-between zones and through in-between figures and documents not only hold the potential for imagining multiple futures, connecting past and present, tracing familiar practices to re-relate to others, transfiguring the relationships, creating new relations, and tracing old ones, but also hold the potential for uncertain futures, surprises, failures, and errors. This one site and moment of the marriage process is also where the Tamil communities imagine fragmented futures and inhabit a social landscape entangled with both certainty and uncertainty, marked by war, violence, and mass migration.

Once the marriage is arranged, the next step of the process unfolds through preparation for the wedding ceremony. India plays a crucial role as a transit place for the enactment of the wedding since most Sri Lankan diaspora Tamils cannot return home for the marriage. This is a site where the Sri Lankan Tamil community is made and remade.

2   Leaving behind the Trees

RAJA, A SRI LANKAN TAMIL, HAD MIGRATED TO THE UK AS A refugee during the war and had gained permanent residence there. Usha's marriage to Raja was arranged by her parents back home. Given the escalation of the war in 2007, Raja did not want to celebrate his wedding in Sri Lanka, preferring instead to hold the ceremony in India, where his mother was living as a refugee. Usha, accompanied by her parents, journeyed to India for the wedding ceremony. I had the opportunity to participate with Raja in *ponnuruku*, an important pre-wedding ritual in which the groom's party arranges to have a goldsmith melt a piece of gold on an auspicious day and make a *thali* out of it. A thali is a one-inch by half-inch rectangle, with two "horns" on the uppermost corners,[1] which allow it to be hooked onto a necklace and put around the bride's neck, constituting the most important ritual during the wedding ceremony. On a Friday morning, at the auspicious time, I went with Raja's family to see the ponnuruku rituals at Nathan's house. Nathan, a goldsmith, lives as a Sri Lankan refugee in India. Raja had signed up for a wedding package (costing US$3,000), so the logistics of the wedding ceremony and related needs of the bridal party would be handled. Sri Lankans who use India as the location for their wedding are in great need of these services offered by Sri Lankan refugees in India. Given the unfamiliarity of a new place and people, the wedding package helps to avoid the difficulties associated with organizing a marriage in a short time, yet it encompasses familiar elements of a Sri Lankan wedding.

Nathan had been living in India since 1996 and continued to practice his family business of making gold jewelry—especially the making of wedding thalis. Since he was fairly well-known in Jaffna for his ponnuruku services, many Sri Lankans who come to India for wedding ceremonies seek him out to have the thali made. Nathan told me that in India he has been meeting clients, conducting rituals, and making the thali in his home. Nathan explained that when he was in Jaffna he would visit the homes of privileged-caste grooms to perform the ritual. Those from other castes would have to come to his house to have the ritual performed. However, in India, he invites all his clients to his house for the ritual because he is unable to assess who is who.

While performing the ponnuruku ritual, Nathan also performed the *kannikal* ritual with Raja. Both rituals are linked. In response to my inquiries about the kannikal ritual, Nathan told me that according to the Jaffna Tamil tradition, after the marriage is fixed and during the ponnuruku ritual, the groom's party plants a *mulmuruku* (type of tree) in front of the groom's house. This serves as a sign announcing to the village that the date of the marriage is approaching. Once the tree is planted, the male relatives from the groom's side visit the bride's home to perform the same ritual. After the wedding, these two trees are transplanted in the garden of the newlywed couple's home. The growth of the trees also symbolizes the growth of the couple's family life. While he was offering me this explanation, I wondered what would happen to the trees he was planting for Usha and Raja, as each would be returning to Sri Lanka and the UK, respectively, after the wedding ceremony. When I asked Nathan what would happen to Raja's tree, he took me to his expansive backyard and showed me a sea of trees. He explained that the Sri Lankan spouses who come to India for their wedding ceremonies plant their trees in his garden. As they are unable to take the trees back with them, Nathan offers to keep the trees in his backyard. I was struck with wonder at seeing the trees, leading me to reflect on what it means to the newlyweds to leave behind a symbol of their togetherness in the transit site where their marriage was conducted.

After the marriage is arranged, most transnational wedding ceremonies between the Sri Lankan Tamil diaspora and the Sri Lankan Tamils take place in India or Singapore, usually because either the bride or groom has not been granted citizenship in their adoptive country and as such is only allowed to travel to countries other than Sri Lanka. Another reason is that given the war in Sri Lanka at that time, many Tamils in the diaspora preferred to have their weddings in other countries. In other words, transnational Sri Lankan Tamil wedding ceremonies took place neither in their "home country" nor in their "adoptive country," but in a third place. Tamil Nadu in India functions not only as a transit place for weddings, but also as a location in which large Sri Lankan Tamil communities live as refugees. The Sri Lankan Tamil community is made and remade here during the wedding season. Sri Lankan Tamils who live in Chennai often participate by providing the social texture (e.g., food, wedding services, and guesthouses), helping to create a "Sri Lankan Tamil village" atmosphere during weddings.

The Sri Lankan spouses who come from the UK, Canada, or Europe to marry partners from Sri Lanka seek the services of Sri Lankan agents in India.

The wedding package these agents offer will cost from between US$3,000 and US$5,000, depending on what is included. These wedding packages usually cover a Sri Lankan priest to perform the ceremony, a Sri Lankan photographer, Sri Lankan food for the reception, Sri Lankan musicians to play classical Tamil music, and, if required, even some Sri Lankan guests to attend the wedding. For an extra cost, these packages also offer fully furnished houses to accommodate wedding parties from overseas. Such a package is generally secured by friends or relatives living in India, who approach brokers, agents, or guesthouse keepers on behalf of the spouses' families. The other way these packages are accessed is through word of mouth—these service providers are recommended by friends or relatives living overseas, who have used their services for themselves or for a child's wedding. There are instances when the parents of the bride or groom are not able to attend the wedding in India: they may be unable to leave Jaffna due to the war, or are not granted an Indian visa, or do not have the necessary documents to travel overseas. In such situations, friends of the family in India or old couples arranged by the package provider are present to perform the rituals at the wedding ceremony on behalf of the spouses' parents. Wedding packages enable the spouses' families to perform the marriage in an unknown land. The families sometimes share the cost of the wedding packages, but the expense is usually borne by the spouse coming from the Tamil diaspora. In general, the spouses obtain loans to pay for these packages. Despite this burden, the spouses' families seek these arrangements to reunite their families and to re-create the familiarities and imagination of an authentic Jaffna wedding in a third place. Such packages enable the process of conducting a marriage in an unknown land to go smoothly and thus create a sense of certainty in the marriage process, thereby overwriting the uncertainty of a new and unknown place.

A transit or temporary place, in this context, is one where the spouses come to live for a few weeks before and after the wedding ceremony (their relatives, families, and friends coming for the wedding also stay for a few days afterward). During such marriages, the Sri Lankan Tamil refugees who live in and around Chennai participate. After the wedding, most of the couples never return to Chennai, as they have no reason to do so. However, during the wedding season, I observed that the Sri Lankan Tamil community in India was highly visible. At these times—temporary moments—dispersed Sri Lankan Tamil communities come together to create a traditional Sri

Lankan Tamil wedding in a temporary place. This temporary place in temporary moments of the process of the transnational marriage allows the Sri Lankan Tamil community to (re)imagine, (re)connect, and (re)create certain fragmented parts of its communal life and notions of Tamil traditions within a particular moment. This raises the question: How is the action of place making in a temporary site (even if for only a short period) crucial for a community to remake itself and imagine a future?

I was also particularly interested to find out why spouses and their families who come from different parts of the world prefer a Sri Lankan priest, photographer, and food for their wedding: Why were they not happy to have a Tamil Nadu priest or photographer instead, especially given that the wedding forms and rituals of both places respect the brahmanical rituals of Tamil marriage? How do Jaffna Tamils construct a notion of a Jaffna Tamil community by imagining wedding traditions and practices in a transit place like India, at a given moment? How does a transit and temporary location, as an in-between place in the marriage process, have the potential to hold moments of reconnection for families, re-creating fragments of familiarities of Jaffna Tamil wedding ceremonies through wedding packages and imagining futures of migration? How does it constitute, at the same time, a reminder of the ambiguity of the marriage process, the impossibility of togetherness in one place, and the uncertainty of marriage migration and futures? This chapter examines how this temporary site as in-between place in the marriage process plays a vital role in creating a notion of community, relatedness, and tradition through wedding-related events; and how place and a dispersed community, which are constantly shifting and moving, succeed in (re)making the sense of community and relatedness during these events in the marriage process.

SRI LANKA AND SOUTH INDIA: HISTORICAL CONNECTIONS

There is a long tradition of social, political, and economic connections between Tamil Nadu and Sri Lankan Tamils.[2] The relationship between the Jaffna Tamils and the Tamils of India predates the colonial period. The constant migrations between South India and Sri Lanka for trade, along with the South Indian Chola empire rule over parts of Sri Lanka during the ninth and tenth centuries, are well documented and point to the longtime connection (Daniel 1996; Meyer 2003). During the colonial period, many South Indian Tamils were taken as indentured laborers (coolies) to work in the tea plantation sector in the Sri Lankan Hill Country (Meyer 2003).

Moreover, South Indian Tamils who came to Sri Lanka for trade and business married Sri Lankan Tamils.

Links also existed between political parties in Sri Lanka and India. The emergence of the Dravidian movement in South India in the 1950s and 1960s had a powerful effect on Sri Lankan Tamil politics. The concept of Dravida Nadu (i.e., a country for Dravidians) was popular among Tamil politicians of the 1960s and 1970s (Muthulingam 1996). The idea of Dravida Nadu for the Tamils in India (i.e., a separate state to be ruled by Tamils) was promoted by the Dravida Munnettra Kazhagam (DMK), one of the strongest Tamil Nadu parties in South India in the 1950s and 1960s (Muthulingam 1996). Such an ideology about a separate state for Tamils influenced the Sri Lankan Tamil political parties of the time. The notion that Tamil culture, the Tamil nation, and the Tamil language are factors around which Tamils should come together as a community and create a state for themselves, as promoted by the Tamil Nadu political movements of the 1960s, trickled down to the Sri Lankan political parties (Muthulingam 1996). Many young Tamils were drawn to those ideas even before the militant movements emerged in Sri Lanka to advocate for a separate state for Tamils. In the 1970s, Selvanayagam, the Tamil leader of Tamilarasu Kachchi, was the first in Sri Lanka to demand a separate state for Tamils, basing his claim on the argument that the Tamils could not live under the Sinhala state or expect equal treatment. Tamil Nadu politicians supported his stance (Muthulingam 1996). He shared many links with Tamil Nadu politics and even met E. V. Periyar, a prominent figure of the Dravidian movement, in Tamil Nadu in the 1970s.

Eventually the Tamil Nadu political parties dropped their campaign for Dravida Nadu for Tamils in India. However, the ideological sentiment of creating a separate state for Tamils was transformed into the Sri Lankan ethnic conflict, where the cause of the LTTE closely identified with the notion of a separate state in Sri Lanka for Tamils, Tamil culture, and Tamil language. Thus, many Indian Tamils supported the separatist militant movements, imagining it possible to create an independent state for Tamils in Sri Lanka (Muthulingam 1996). Moreover, in Sri Lanka, the Sinhalese and the Sinhala politicians feared the forging of a strong link between the Tamils of Tamil Nadu and those of Sri Lanka, apprehensive that the Sri Lankan Tamils would be provided with financial and personnel support from Tamil Nadu to achieve their aims.

Moreover, since the 1980s, the Indian government was supportive of the Tamil militant movement that had emerged in Sri Lanka. Many Sri Lankan

Tamil militant groups used Tamil Nadu as a base from which they could carry out their activities against the Sri Lankan authorities. Many South Indian Tamil politicians supported the different Tamil movements' campaigns for either a separate state in Sri Lanka or the establishment of a federal system (Daniel 1996). The 1983 ethnic riots against the Tamils in Sri Lanka triggered a mass forced migration of Tamils to India (Daniel 1996; Suryanarayan and Sudarshan 2000). During these riots, many anti–Sri Lankan protests were held in Tamil Nadu, and functioning of the Tamil Nadu state came to a standstill as a result. Further, the Tamil Nadu government itself exerted strong pressure on India's central government to intervene in the affairs of Sri Lanka to stop the ethnic riots that had been launched by the Sinhala state against the Tamils. Since that time, many Sri Lankan Tamils have entered India as refugees.

Many civilians were killed when the Sri Lankan government launched a massive army operation to regain control of the Jaffna peninsula from the LTTE in 1987, which led, once again, to mass protests and campaigns by the Tamil Nadu state, urging the Indian government to intervene to stop the hostilities in Sri Lanka. Indian prime minister Rajiv Gandhi sent an Indian Peace-Keeping Force (IPKF) to Sri Lanka to stop the war and to facilitate a solution to end the ethnic conflict. These efforts resulted in the Sri Lanka–India Peace Accord between the Indian and Sri Lankan governments. However, the LTTE, which had become the largest and strongest Tamil military movement, opposed the agreement and declared war against the IPKF, a conflict that lasted until 1990, when the Sri Lankan army and the LTTE agreed to find a solution for the ethnic conflict. At the same time, in the South, Sinhala politicians wanted the Indian army removed; in 1990, at the request of the Sri Lankan state, India obliged. Yet, once again, the peace accord signed between the LTTE and the Sri Lankan government to end the war was nullified in 1991 when an LTTE suicide bomber killed Rajiv Gandhi on South Indian soil while he was campaigning for reelection as prime minister. Following this incident, the Indian state branded the LTTE a terrorist organization and banned it in India (Suryanarayan and Sudarshan 2000).

SRI LANKAN TAMIL REFUGEES IN INDIA

The Sri Lankan Tamil refugees felt that the assassination of Rajiv Gandhi served to drastically change the sentiments of Sri Lankan Tamils in Tamil Nadu for the LTTE. It also resulted in a change of attitude toward the Sri Lankan refugees in Tamil Nadu, which turned from one of sympathy to suspicion. Every Sri Lankan refugee was viewed as a possible LTTE member or supporter. Along with banning the LTTE in India, both the central and the Tamil Nadu governments took all necessary measures to capture LTTE suspects within their borders. This climate of suspicion only made more difficult the challenges of the Sri Lankan Tamils in India, regardless of whether they lived in the refugee camps. They had to register themselves with the police on an annual basis and carry on them at all times their refugee status documents. Despite these worsening conditions, many Sri Lankan Tamils continued to cross the Indian Ocean in small boats to claim refugee status in India, owing to the hostilities that continued between the Sri Lankan state and the LTTE from 1991 to 2009. Most often these boat journeys of six to seven hours were made at night, in an attempt to avoid being apprehended by the Indian and Sri Lankan coast guards and naval patrols out at sea. The risky refugee journey to India produced many tragedies, since many lost their children, parents, or other relatives while traveling in the small boats.

Since 1983, many Sri Lankan Tamils have come to India as refugees. Currently there are more than one hundred refugee camps, housing around one hundred thousand people (Zutshi Trakroo 2008; Suryanarayan and Sudarshan 2000). A large number of the Sri Lankan Tamil refugees have lived in these camps for over two decades, meaning that their children who migrated with them or were born there are now of marriageable age. There is also another category of refugees, known as "returnees," referring to those who had gone to India during the war, returned by boat to Sri Lanka during a lull in the hostilities, and then returned to India when the war recommenced. Thus, the numbers in the refugee camps had been fluctuating according to the intensity of the war in Sri Lanka. It was estimated that approximately fifty thousand Sri Lankan Tamils lived independently outside the camps before the war ended. Often such individuals have children or close relatives living overseas who support them financially. Others run their own businesses, offering guesthouses, vehicle rental services, wedding packages, or work as wedding photographers, marriage brokers, and priests. Some of them, albeit only a few, have bought property in Tamil Nadu. Most of those who live outside the camps attempt to send their children overseas (either illegally or through marriage) and wait for their children to sponsor them to their host countries.

Many of the people I spoke with said that they did not have a future in India—especially since India had not signed the 1951 UN Refugee Convention, nor did it have any special laws regarding the refugee population living there. Despite those hindrances, India has been hosting Tibetan refugees, Nepali refugees from Bhutan, Tamils from Sri Lanka, and refugees from Afghanistan.[3] In general, India has granted protection to Tibetans and Sri Lankan Tamils. Other refugees, such as those from Iran, Afghanistan, and Sudan, must be recognized by the United Nations High Commissioner for Refugees in Delhi to continue living in India (Zutshi Trakroo 2008). Moreover, as referenced above, India has not passed any specific legislation applicable across the board to all refugees in the country. For that reason the judicial system is constrained, when dealing with refugees, to invoke laws applicable to foreigners in general, such as the Foreigners Act of 1946 (Zutshi Trakroo 2008). This law, along with the 1948 Foreigners Order, have given the government the power to restrict refugees and asylum seekers to reside in a particular place in order to control their movements, and to prohibit them from working (Zutshi Trakroo 2008). However, through a gazette notification, the central government does have the power to declare as refugees a category of people who have entered the country during a mass displacement. Sri Lankan Tamil refugees are recognized as such in India; they can travel to India without proper travel documents and claim asylum. Although India did not grant refugees the right to work, it has been practicing a policy of tolerance toward Tibetan and Sri Lankan refugees engaged in informal employment (Zutshi Trakroo 2008). Sri Lankan refugees can hold jobs in areas neighboring their camps. They are free to live outside the camps in Tamil Nadu, if they so wish, but they must register themselves with the nearest police station.[4]

Even though Indian laws regarding refugees restrict their movement and fail to grant them any rights to engage in official employment or obtain permanent residence or citizenship, I have observed that in everyday practice the Indian government officials have adopted a flexible approach regarding Sri Lankan Tamil refugees. The Tamil Nadu government provides a monthly allowance of eight hundred rupees per person for refugees living in the camps. Further, it sells rice and other essential items at highly subsidized prices to the refugees in the camps. The Tamil Nadu government had set up a quota system that offered Sri Lankan Tamil refugees the opportunity to gain free entrance into Indian colleges to study medicine, engineering, the arts, and other disciplines. Such concessions had been instituted because of the sympathy Tamil Nadu politicians feel for the Tamils in Sri Lanka. Though the assassination of Rajiv Gandhi by the LTTE in South India caused some state government officials to sour on Sri Lankan Tamil refugees, in 2009, after the end of the war in Sri Lanka, the chief minister of Tamil Nadu requested that the central government provide citizenship status to the refugees, since they have been living there for a long time, but no further developments have taken place on the question of Sri Lankan refugees in India. Also, some of them have been returning to Sri Lanka since the end of war.

The greatest difficulty for these refugees is that they cannot obtain employment, as they do not have a legal status in India. Sri Lankan refugees cannot become citizens of India, and even the children born in India cannot claim Indian citizenship. Such conditions make India only a temporary/transit place for many Sri Lankan Tamil refugees. There is no mechanism through which refugees could obtain citizenship or permanent residence in India. As such, it was not possible for Tamil refugees to look for permanent employment, nor could they obtain loans to buy properties or start their own businesses. The status of a Sri Lankan Tamil refugee in India is temporary, placing them in a state of limbo. As a result, many Sri Lankan Tamils try to leave India for other countries. Since it was relatively easy and inexpensive to escape from Sri Lanka to India by boat (as compared to going to any other country as a refugee), many Tamils migrated to India and then attempted to cross over to another country from there. The poorer classes of Tamils, who cannot afford the large sums of money required to travel to other countries, remain in the Indian refugee camps. Those Sri Lankan Tamil refugees who live outside the camps and run various businesses target the wedding industry—and specifically a Sri Lankan Tamil clientele that comes from various parts of the world to get married in India.

On the one hand, because of their refugee status in India, Sri Lankan Tamils expect to eventually return to Sri Lanka or move on to another country. On the other hand, because of the long-standing political and social connections as well as language and cultural similarities between the Sri Lankan Tamil community and Tamil Nadu, Sri Lankan Tamil refugees tend to also consider Tamil Nadu as a place-making space (even though it is a new place). In other words, Sri Lankan Tamil refugees who have been de-territorialized from their place of origin become re-territorialized into the site of refuge—even though it may be just a refugee camp in India for a temporary period and may only hold the reality of a place of transit in a mobile life (Malkki 1992). For Sri Lankan Tamil refugees, or even for those Sri Lankan diaspora Tamils who visit for a brief period in order to contract a transnational marriage, India is a place-making space rather than a space of comings and goings in a given movement. The presence of a Sri Lankan Tamil refugee community in India has made possible for Tamils who come to India for the purpose of marriage to think of it as their own place, despite the temporary nature of their stay.

PLACE MAKING

The concept of place is an important study in the field of anthropology—especially in the work of those anthropologists who have focused on the community, identity, and local knowledge and culture of "native" people. Earlier studies articulated that local communities were located in spaces with neat and clear boundaries with a specific culture associated with each place (Basso 1996; Feld and Basso 1996b). Writing that assumes communities are located in one place and speak in one voice has rightly been criticized, and anthropologists have been challenged to capture the multiplicity of places, communities, and subjects (Appadurai 1986b). Indeed, while changing global economic and political conditions de-territorialize lived spaces and produce hybridized subjects, space appears to re-territorialize itself at the same time (Gupta and Ferguson 1992, 19–20). This re-territorialization needs a new understanding of place, one that encompasses space and could be defined by local knowledge, experiences, memories, and layouts of landscapes: "On the one hand, place is something like a formal universal in that it functions like a general feature, even a condition of possibility of all human experience—however expansive the term 'experience' is taken to be. On the other hand, place is also quite a distinctive feature of such experience. Place is not a purely formal operator, empty of content but is always contentful, always specifiable as this particular place or that one" (Casey 1996, 29). Place not only gathers experiences, histories, memories, languages, and thoughts, it also allows for certain things (e.g., people, ideas, etc.) to overlap and "sometimes even to occlude" (26). Space and time coexist in place as its "coordinates" (36). The temporary place in the marriage process allows re-territorialization in such a place, in a time of mobility.

For the Sri Lankan Tamil refugees or those who come to conduct wedding ceremonies in India, place making (even within a short time) becomes possible because of the long-standing social, political, and historical ties the Sri Lankan Tamils have with Tamil Nadu, in addition to the language and cultural similarities. A further possibility for place making emerges through certain fragments of traditions, rituals, and practices put in place at transnational wedding ceremonies through wedding packages. However, the reconnection of the fragments of community (where families come together and share lived experiences as well as memories of places and marriages) may not be as permanent as in adoptive lands like Canada (where Tamils may imagine a stable future in which they eventually gain citizenship). Yet India, as an in-between place (albeit a transit place), provides an anchor that enables the Sri Lankan Tamils (from both Sri Lanka and the Tamil diaspora) to imagine a certain future, togetherness, and stability for the Tamil community in another place or back in their homeland. The potential of this temporary place, in temporary moments, keeps alive the certainty and the uncertainty of futures for Sri Lankan Tamils.

RUBAN'S MARRIAGE

My friend and I went to India with Nilini's family to take part in her wedding. Nilini's marriage to Ruban had been arranged by her parents through a broker. Nilini was displaced from Jaffna in 1995 and relocated to Vavuniya with her father, mother, and older sister. There, Nilini's sister got married and then migrated to London. When the marriage broker proposed Ruban as a prospective groom for Nilini, her sister met Ruban in London. After the meeting and subsequent inquiries about his background, Nilini's sister was satisfied with the proposal. She told her parents to go ahead with the marriage. In the meantime, Nilini and Ruban talked over the phone and started getting to know and even like each other. Ruban's father had passed away, and when the war intensified in Sri Lanka in the 1990s he and his mother migrated as refugees to India. Subsequently Ruban relocated to London as a refugee; but his mother stayed on in India and lived with her relatives. As his uncle and his family lived in India, Ruban felt it was safe for his mother to live there until he could sponsor her to London once he gained citizenship. However, because a marriage was arranged for him before he could do so, he decided to celebrate the wedding in India so that his mother could attend.

When Nilini and her family arrived in India ten days before the marriage, Ruban and his mother met them at the airport. Nilini's family did not know anybody in India, so they stayed at Ruban's mother's house for the duration of their visit. Nilini's father was somewhat hesitant about staying with the groom's family before the marriage, as he felt it was not in keeping with Tamil tradition. However, because it was more convenient and would help cut down on unnecessary expenses, he decided to do so. Nilini's sister could not come for the wedding, as she was soon due to give birth to her second child. Her father was concerned that they did not have enough relatives or friends from their side to participate in the wedding. Therefore, he was happy that my friend, who was known to them, would be at the ceremony. He also considered me part of the bride's party. He kept telling me that if the wedding had been held in Vavuniya he would have had many relatives attending and would have seen to all the arrangements. However, as he did not know his way around India, he felt that he was forced to take a backseat and could only wait and see how it went.

Before the wedding, Ruban and Nilini went out shopping together, buying saris and other clothing for the ceremony. Ruban bought many clothes for Nilini. They also visited temples and went to the movies. They were holding hands, talking, and joking with each other. Ruban kept telling me how he had fallen in love with Nilini through their phone conversations. He said that she had succeeded in mesmerizing (*mayaki podal*) him over the phone. They symbolized to me the changing nature of the Sri Lankan Tamil marriage. Traditionally spouses were not allowed to spend time with each other in public before the marriage. I was also struck by the idea that it was possible for intimacy and romance to develop between a couple before an arranged marriage.

The nature of the Jaffna Tamil arranged marriage is changing. The previous chapter detailed how, after a prospective bride and groom are "matched," they are asked to talk over the phone to see whether they like each other. These conversations continue until they meet each other for the wedding, a period of a few months. Many couples have told me that during this time they begin to fall in love. In addition, like Ruban and Nilini, many couples spend a few days before the wedding visiting places and shopping together. Such moments of intimacy and physical proximity help to develop a bond between the prospective couple. In comparison, many have told me that in the case of arranged marriages among Jaffna Tamils in the 1980s or before, the spouses were not allowed to meet before the wedding. One of my interviewees, an eighty-year-old gentleman I met in India, told me that his father arranged his marriage and simply told him the date of the wedding— he saw his wife for the first time at the ceremony. While cross-cousin marriages were considered part of the category of arranged marriages by anthropologists in the 1960s and 1970s, those unions appear to have a romantic element built into them. In those instances, the future spouses knew each other from childhood and were aware that they were going to get married one day; for that reason, there is an element of friendship and camaraderie between them before the marriage. In this light, what I observed between Ruban and Nilini is not a new phenomenon that emerged with the modern arranged marriage; rather, the notion of arranged marriage should be rethought in the anthropological literature. The dual notions of love and arranged marriage may lead to the misconception that an arranged marriage is less invested with romance and personal choice than socioeconomic and political strategies (Dumont 1961, 1983; Yalman 1967). However, boundaries seem blurred between an arranged and a love marriage in the case of transnational arranged unions among Jaffna Tamils.

Ruban's mother booked a wedding package and paid for most of it through a Sri Lankan Tamil broker in India. The package included a Sri Lankan photographer, a Sri Lankan priest, Sri Lankan food to be served at the wedding, and a reception hall. She had invited her friends and relatives, most of whom were Sri Lankan refugees in India. About 150 people attended the wedding, most of them Sri Lankan refugees. Others were relatives of Ruban who had come over from Sri Lanka for the wedding. However, there was only the bride's father, her mother, my friend, and myself from the bride's side. Thus my friend was asked to be the *mapillai tholan* (groomsman). The Jaffna Tamil tradition is that the bride's brother or a close male relative plays a role similar to that of a groomsman. My friend performed all the duties required of the bride's brother in connection with the groom— such as going to the groom's house and helping him get dressed, washing his feet, bringing him to the wedding hall, and sitting next to him in the *manavarai*[5] until the bride arrives for the wedding rituals. In the Jaffna Tamil kinship system, where cross-cousin marriage is preferred, the relationship between the brothers-in-law is important for the endurance of the marriage alliance (Dumont 1961). This is because a brother has the right to claim his sister's son or daughter as a marriage partner for his son or daughter. Although in the case of Ruban and Nilini's marriage this traditional role of the bride's brother was not significant or important, Nilini's father was extremely happy that he had someone from his side, on such short notice, to perform the duties of a brother of the bride, rather than having an unknown person or someone from the groom's side stand in. Of particular significance to me was the dichotomy of the situation—by having a family friend stand in and carry out the responsibilities of the brother of the bride, certain Tamil traditions were being adhered to; yet the meaning of it, in a classical sense, was not being fulfilled.

On the day of the wedding, the Sri Lankan Hindu priest fell ill and sent a South Indian Hindu priest in his place to conduct the wedding. This created some uneasiness among the spouses' families. While the wedding rituals were being carried out, Nilini's father was constantly telling me that a priest from his village in Jaffna would have conducted the wedding differently (i.e., properly). I asked him what differences he saw between a Sri Lankan priest and an Indian priest. He replied, "We normally crack a coconut before each ritual. Cracking the coconut is for Pillaiyar [the elephant-headed god]—so he will be able to do the rituals without making any mistakes. But here the *iyar* [priest] is not doing that." He was concerned that the way the Indian priest conducted his daughter's wedding would negatively affect her married life. He kept saying that since they had gone through so much trouble in Sri Lanka his daughter should live happily in London. He told me that if this situation with the priest had happened in Sri Lanka he would have voiced his concerns, but that in this situation he felt helpless because he did not know anyone to even organize for a different iyar. When I questioned him further as to the specific differences that he could see between how a Sri Lankan priest and an Indian priest would conduct the wedding rituals, he could not give me specifics in terms of *manthiram* (mantra—the way in which the rituals were conducted, or the symbolism of the rituals); what he did say was that the Indian priest was either taking too little or too much time to perform each ritual.

The other person who got irritated with the Indian iyar was the Sri Lankan photographer, Vijai. He, too, was annoyed that the Indian priest was not performing the wedding rituals according to Sri Lankan traditions. Vijai told me that he had photographed many Sri Lankan Tamil weddings and claimed to know exactly how they should be conducted. He said that he always works with a Sri Lankan priest who knows how to officiate a Jaffna Tamil wedding, and that the Indian priest was hurrying and/or abbreviating the rituals. This made it difficult for him to capture the event and the rituals in an acceptable manner. The iyar became annoyed with Vijai, feeling that the photographer was trying to usurp his authority in conducting the wedding rituals. Vijai was concerned not only about his photos but also that, if the rituals were not conducted properly, Ruban and Nilini's marriage would suffer. He told me, "These are our people, and marriage comes just once in their life. With great difficulties they have arranged this marriage and come to India—to an unknown place—to conduct the marriage. So, marriage ceremonies should be done properly, so that they will have a better life in the future."

Vijai's genuine concern that the marriage rituals be conducted in a proper way for the sake of "his people" (i.e., fellow Jaffna Tamils) connects him and married couples in a collective experience of community. This clarifies why a Sri Lankan priest is preferred over an Indian one. At this wedding, Vijai and the Indian priest were not working hand in hand, and therefore kept fighting over who had the ultimate authority over the marriage rituals. What struck me most was that the concern of the photographer was not only about producing wedding photos but also about ensuring an "authentic Jaffna Tamil" experience. Vijai's worries suggest that Sri Lankan photographers, the bridal couple, and their families share the same hope for a secure future, sharing as they do the experience of displacement, suffering, and the difficulties of war.

Once the wedding ceremonies were over, I met with the Indian priest to find out how he conducts weddings. He was quite clear that he was not pleased with how the photographer kept questioning his authority. He told me that he had overseen many Indian weddings and had been in this field for more than a decade. He also told me that he had conducted many Sri Lankan weddings and nobody had challenged him before. He claimed that his previous clients had all understood his manthirams and rituals. He explained that it took him all his life to learn the manthirams, so, he asked me, how could anyone say that he had not conducted the wedding properly? This raises the question of what, then, is the authentic way of conducting a Jaffna Tamil wedding? Why did Jaffna Tamils want to celebrate their weddings according to the traditional marriage forms even in a transit place like India? I came to understand that the emphasis on traditional rituals is not only to prove to the immigration authorities (e.g., those in the UK or Canada; see chapter 5) the genuineness of their marriage, but also because they felt that to operate otherwise would harm their future married life. Marriage for the Sri Lankan Tamil community means more than just a union between two families or two people—it brings back the possibility of being reconnected with fragments of their communities, even in a temporary place, for a brief moment. I tried to find out about the authentic Jaffna Tamil marriage to which those at Ruban and Nilini's wedding kept alluding.

THE STORY OF RATNA

Ratna was living in London and had come to India for his wedding. On a Sunday evening I went to meet him at the guesthouse he had rented for a month for his family. We sat in his room and talked about his forthcoming marriage, experiences of displacement, and life as a refugee in London. Ratna had an older brother who had joined the LTTE and been killed during the hostilities with the Sri Lankan army in Jaffna. After that, Ratna's parents had sent him to Colombo to safeguard him from the war in Jaffna. One day, while he was working in a shop, the police arrested and detained him for two years on the suspicion that he was involved with the LTTE. Finally, after many efforts and a bribe of a significant sum to the police, Ratna's parents managed to secure his release. A few months later Ratna left for London by paying a fee to an agent who smuggled him into the UK. Once in London he sought asylum. While narrating his experiences, he turned around to show me the scars on his back from when the police tortured him in Sri Lanka.

Once Ratna got to the UK, he sent money regularly to his parents to help them with their expenses in Colombo. The previous year, his sister had gained admission to a university in London and joined him overseas. Ratna was working double shifts seven days a week in a shop in order to support his family in Sri Lanka as well as repay the money they had borrowed from a relative to pay the agent who had smuggled him into London. He told me that he had borrowed more than £10,000 from a friend for his wedding in India. He had to pay for his and his parents' airfare to India, the guesthouse rental, and the wedding package. After his return to the UK, he would have to earn even more money to pay back his friend. Despite this dire state of affairs, Ratna was immensely happy to see his family after seven years and therefore did not mind spending the money.

Ratna's marriage was arranged by his parents through a broker. After the astrological charts had been matched, his parents met with the parents of the prospective bride—Rohini, a graduate of the University of Jaffna. Ratna and Rohini were sent each other's photos and connected over the phone. They took a liking to each other and told their parents they were willing to proceed with the marriage. Since Ratna could not return to Sri Lanka, they decided to celebrate the wedding in India. Ratna's paternal uncle, who lives in Canada, knew a guesthouse owner, a Sri Lankan Tamil refugee in India, who rented it to Sri Lankan Tamils coming there for weddings. Through his brother, Ratna's father contacted the owner and rented it for the duration of their stay in India.

Ratna and his sister traveled from London, while his mother and father traveled from Sri Lanka. His paternal uncle's sons, as well as some distant relatives, also made the trip from Sri Lanka. His maternal aunt's daughter, who happened to be close to Ratna's family, decided to come to the wedding by herself, leaving behind her husband and children, as she could not afford airfare for the entire family. Ratna's paternal grandmother, who lived in Jaffna and was eighty years old, also came for the wedding. They all stayed in one guesthouse. I, too, stayed with them and took part in the wedding. The house, which had three rooms (each with air-conditioning), was fully furnished and situated on a large parcel of land. With the arrival of Ratna, the guesthouse was turned into a wedding house. His parents were overjoyed to see their son after seven years of separation. Ratna's mother kept cooking food for him—especially his favorite dishes, for which she had brought Jaffna curry powder. His father would encourage her to do so. Ratna's grandmother, too, was overjoyed to see her grandson. She kept telling me stories of how her wedding had taken place back in Jaffna. She recalled how the whole village had come to help her family prepare for the wedding, and how such activities would take place for a month before the ceremony. She said that if not for the war, she would have preferred that her grandson's wedding be held in Sri Lanka, in her village; instead, she had to go through various difficulties, including flying all the way from Jaffna to Colombo and then to Chennai, to see her grandson get married. However, since this was the first marriage in her son's family, and it was also the marriage of her eldest grandson, and she had thought to herself that she would die soon, she decided she wanted to be there for the ceremony.

Every day someone was going out somewhere to shop for clothes and other items for the wedding. While we were busy arranging the house, shopping, sightseeing, and going to the cinema, Ratna's mother was cooking. Ratna was happy to be reunited with his parents and kept asking his mother to cook various dishes for him. He asked the guesthouse owner if he could ask a few Sri Lankan families staying nearby to attend the wedding. The owner agreed, and Ratna gave him some wedding invitations to distribute. Ratna told me he did this because he wanted people to come and bless them at the wedding: "Sanam irunthaalthan kaliyanam" (If there are no people, there is no wedding). On the night before the wedding, when we sat down for dinner, Ratna's father turned to me and said, "We do not know when we will be together like this again. After Ratna's marriage each one will go back to their place. I do not know if I will see my son or daughter again. It is our fate." This statement reminded all sitting down to eat that it was only a temporary moment of family reunification. That moment of coming together as a family would disappear as soon as the wedding was over. Ratna would return to London, his parents to Colombo, and his grandmother to Jaffna. Rohini, Ratna's newlywed wife, would return to Sri Lanka to apply for a visa to join her husband in the UK. Rohini and Ratna were constantly on the phone with each other. He consulted with her on many matters before making decisions about the wedding, which created some conflict between Ratna and his mother, who kept complaining that his future wife was already challenging her authority over her son.

The family's conflicts, joys, fights, feasts, and jokes all took place within the few days Ratna's family spent in India, in a house that was not even their own. They all knew they would be parting company in a few days and may not see one another again. Despite all this, the atmosphere in that guesthouse was one of everyday family life and routines; even in that brief time in a transit place, the habits of daily life were established. The family knew how to pick up the fragments from where they had left off, through those daily routines. The thought that after the wedding they would once again be scattered was temporarily kept at bay, as the family reunited in that transit place to celebrate a wedding. However, the scars of the war and impossibility of staying together in Sri Lanka would resurface now and again—such as when, after a few rounds of drinks at night, Ratna would remove his shirt and show me the scars on his back, or when his father alluded on the eve of Ratna's wedding to the uncertainty of reuniting with his children.

RATNA'S WEDDING, THE SRI LANKAN PRIEST, AND MARRIAGE RITUALS

On the day of the wedding, we all got up early and helped Ratna prepare. The wedding package included a Sri Lankan iyar, himself the son of a famous Sri Lankan iyar, who had been conducting Sri Lankan marriages in India for the past eight years. This iyar had been displaced from Sri Lanka during the war in 2000. Most of the wedding rituals he had performed were for Sri Lankan Tamils holding their weddings in India. As I sat next to him during the ceremony, I took notes and questioned him about the meanings of the rituals that were being performed. He told me they could be done elaborately or in abbreviated forms. He said that in general he performs the shorter versions, but that their complexity varies according to the iyar performing it.

He also explained that there were significant differences between the Jaffna Tamil and Indian rituals. For example, in a Jaffna Tamil wedding there are fourteen *kumpam* (a bronze pot with a coconut on top), representing different gods and goddesses. Nine kumpam represent the nine planets (e.g., *sani*, *suriyan*, etc.), one represents the god Siva and goddess Parvathi together, one the god Indran, and the remaining three represent three protecting gods. The iyar told me that these fourteen kumpam are not seen in an Indian wedding. Another difference he cited between the two marriage systems was that in the Jaffna Tamil tradition, a coconut is cracked before each ritual in order to safeguard against any error in how it is performed. However, he claimed that there were no differences in terms of the manthi-rams used by the Indian and Jaffna Tamil iyars. Highlighting another dif-ference, he said that at Jaffna Tamil weddings, the groom's family is asked whether they are willing to accept the bride, and the bride's family is asked during the *kaniyathanam* ritual whether they are willing to accept the groom. The iyar explained that this practice had probably been picked up from church weddings in Jaffna. Whatever the origin, he said that Jaffna Tamils have been performing it for as far back as he could remember. He recommended that I read a book written by a Sri Lankan priest. It is that format and the order of the rituals that he follows when performing wed-ding rituals.

Sometime after this conversation I tracked down the book in Colombo and made an appointment with its author. I visited him in his home and asked him to explain the marriage rituals among the Jaffna Tamils. During our discussion he got up, went into another room, and came back with a book. He started reading aloud descriptions of Jaffna Tamil rituals. When I asked him why he had to refer to a book, he replied, "I may forget. I should tell you in a right way, so it is better to read it from my book." The authentic-ity that I was looking for in the Jaffna Tamil marriage rituals lay neither in the performance of the rituals nor in the knowledge of the priests perform-ing them, but rather in the shared imagination or memory of the Jaffna Tamil marriage tradition, which, in effect, is a collective sharing of com-munity knowledge. Thus, the issue is not whether there is an authentic form of Jaffna Tamil marriage rituals but how collective belief creates a sense of community around such traditions. The Sri Lankan wedding package in India holds certain fragments of Jaffna Tamil rituals and traditions that seem to promote a sense of (re)creation of community.

In cases like Ratna's—unlike that of Ruban—there is close cooperation between the wedding photographer (Ravi) and the Sri Lankan iyar, who had been working together for five years. The iyar at Ratna's wedding kept ask-ing the couple to pose for the photos, ensured that the photographer had enough time to take the photos he wanted, and even repeated certain rituals so that the photographer could get a satisfactory shot (see chapter 3). After the ceremonies were completed, the fifty people at the wedding came for-ward to congratulate Ratna and Rohini and give them gifts. The guest list comprised a few relatives of the spouses, the guesthouse owners, and some Sri Lankan refugees who had been invited by the owner. Ratna's mother wanted more people to participate in the wedding even in a place where they did not have any relatives or friends—not for the sake of proving to the visa officer that the marriage was genuine (see chapter 5) but, more important, to secure the blessings of many for the married couple and their future life. Moreover, if the wedding had been celebrated in Sri Lanka, in their village, many relatives, friends, and neighbors would have taken part. Thus, by ensuring that at least a hundred people attend the wedding in India—preferably Sri Lankan Tamils—the bridal parties attempt to create a "Sri Lankan" atmosphere, as if the wedding were taking place in a village back home. In this sense, a marriage package is more than a package, in terms of monetary value and grand celebration. It (re)creates fragmented Jaffna Tamil traditions, a sense of home, a possibility of reconnecting the dispersed Tamil communities for at least a temporary moment, in a transit place, facilitating the conditions to reconnect, transfiguring relationships, and imagining certain futures.

Just one week after their wedding, Rohini left for Sri Lanka and Ratna for London. When I went to meet Ratna's father before they returned to Sri Lanka, he was carefully packing the wedding photos, because that was all he had left to keep with him. The next day I accompanied them to the airport. They hugged and thanked me for my help with their son's wedding. Ratna's mother said that I was a part of their family now, and that I should visit them whenever I was in Colombo. She said she wanted to cook for me.

THE SRI LANKAN HIGH COMMISSION AND SRI LANKAN CIVIL MARRIAGES IN CHENNAI

Most of the Sri Lankan Tamils who come to India to get married conduct their civil marriages at the Sri Lankan High Commission, even though they can have a civil marriage conducted by an Indian marriage registrar. I was told that this was because it made the process of applying for a UK or Canadian visa much easier. If a civil marriage is conducted by an Indian registrar, other embassies (namely, those in the UK and Canada) request that it be further certified by the Indian Home Ministry. This validation is indicated by a red government seal being placed on the marriage certificate. Sri Lankan Tamils call this procedure "obtaining the red seal." According to a number of Sri Lankan Tamils I spoke with, the process takes a while. At times, they resort to bribing the officers to expedite matters. Thus, many Sri Lankan Tamils prefer to hold their wedding registration at the Sri Lankan High Commission in Chennai. Once the spouses come to Chennai, they must lodge an application with the Sri Lankan High Commission in India requesting a date for a civil marriage at the High Commission. This application must be accompanied by several other documents from both the bride and groom: birth certificates, travel documents, citizenship documents, as well as a statement that they are single and free to marry. A date for the marriage registration is given mostly after a period of fourteen days from the date of submission. Only four or five others are permitted to accompany the couple into the High Commission premises to witness the marriage. In addition to the parents or siblings of the couple, a photographer counts as one of this limited number, ensuring that there will be a photographic record of the civil marriage.

Nimal (the marriage broker discussed in chapter 1) introduced me to Anoja and Parthipan, who had come to Chennai for their marriage. Their marriage was arranged by their mothers, both of whom lived in Jaffna. Nimal was helping them with the wedding arrangements in Chennai. Parthipan, who had gone to London in the late 1990s as a refugee, had since become a British citizen. His father had passed away and his mother was living in Jaffna with her younger daughter. Anoja had also lost her father; and she was living in Jaffna with her mother, younger sister, and younger brother. When I met Anoja in Parthipan's guesthouse, she told me that she and her younger brother had come to India for the marriage. The two had traveled earlier to Colombo, and their mother and sister were to follow in a few days but then could not leave Jaffna because the war had intensified and caused flights between Jaffna and Colombo to be temporarily halted. Those same travel disruptions prevented Parthipan's mother, too, from attending. Despite this unexpected turn of events, both families decided to proceed with the wedding as planned. Parthipan's mother had asked her brother and his family who lived in London to represent her at the ceremony. Parthipan's maternal uncle and family had undertaken the entire responsibility of organizing the wedding in India. Through Nimal, they rented a guesthouse in India for the duration of their stay. Parthipan, Anoja, Anoja's brother, Parthipan's uncle and his family, as well as Parthipan's two other uncles from Germany, all stayed in the same house. The Sri Lankan High Commission gave them a date for the civil marriage earlier than the date set for the religious ceremony.

On a Wednesday morning Parthipan and Anoja, Parthipan's uncle and his wife, Nimal, Parthipan's friend from London, a Sri Lankan photographer, and I traveled in a hired van to the Sri Lankan High Commission in Chennai. When we arrived, I saw another twelve Tamil couples waiting outside with their relatives and friends. The road outside the High Commission was

teeming with brides and grooms in their wedding attire, bedecked in garlands, awaiting their turn. Each couple was given a token number and was
being taken in according to this order. The entire road in front of the High
Commission had taken on the appearance of a Sri Lankan Tamil wedding
house. A common sight was that of the bride's family or friends constantly
touching up her makeup, which was being affected by perspiration. Those
who wanted to witness the wedding of each couple were waiting with them
outside the High Commission, and some of those parties had more than the
allowed four or five people with them. I learned later that not all of those
individuals would have the opportunity to witness the wedding. However,
by simply waiting outside they would be captured in the photographs and
greet the newlywed couple soon after the civil ceremony. The vernacular
Jaffna Tamil language was being spoken by all those waiting. There was an
atmosphere of tension and anticipation. When Anoja and Parthipan's number was called we went inside the High Commission. We were asked to sit
in the waiting area, where two other couples were already queued up. Parthipan and Anoja were slightly tense. They did not talk to each other, nor did
they chat with the others. I sat down with the photographer and chatted with
him about his experiences photographing civil marriages for Sri Lankan
Tamils. His mother and he had been living in Chennai as Tamil refugees
for the past ten years, during which time he had worked many such events.

Although the atmosphere outside the High Commission reminded me
of wedding houses in Sri Lanka, inside there was far less conversation and
noise. It had an obvious office atmosphere, and there was a notice board in
the hallway indicating that people should keep silent. When the couple's
number was called, we all went into a small conference room with a round
table in the middle, at which sat the registrar and his assistant. The registrar
verified the documents, including their passports. The spouses were then
asked to sign the marriage register and to exchange flower garlands. Parthipan's uncle signed as a witness from Parthipan's side, and Parthipan's friend
signed as a witness from Anoja's side. The photographer made sure that
he captured the signing rituals. After all the paperwork was completed, he
asked Parthipan and Anoja to pose next to the registrar for a photo. Several
group photos, with the registrar prominently featured, were also taken. We
then left the High Commission.

Parthipan and Anoja relaxed and began chatting with each other. The
photographer asked them to stand next to the Sri Lankan High Commission
signboard at the exterior wall of the office building. When I asked the photographer why he needed to take that photo, he replied, "This is the proof

for the visa officer that the marriage has taken place at the High Commission." The war between Tamil militants and the Sri Lankan state caused the dispersion of Tamil families, as family members were forced to flee the site of violence. Yet it is the same Sri Lankan state that functions as the agent of reuniting Tamil families by creating the possibility for married couples to convene in an adoptive land, by authorizing their marriage at the site of the Sri Lankan embassy in a foreign land.

TEMPORARY PLACES, MARRIAGE PACKAGES, AND FRAGMENTS OF COMMUNITIES

During the wedding season, the Sri Lankan Tamil community in India becomes highly visible in certain locations—in and around Nathan the goldsmith's house (where thalis are made and trees planted), the guesthouses run by Sri Lankan Tamils, and reception halls. Further, sometimes elderly Sri Lankan Tamil refugee couples play a specialized role, such as in the kaniyathanam ritual, because the spouses' parents are often not able to attend the wedding for various reasons. In such instances, elderly couples stand in for the parents of the couple and perform the kaniyathanam and other rituals carried out by parents during the wedding ceremony. In some instances the wedding packages even include such services. When I interviewed a member of one such elderly couple about playing this role, they explained, "These are our children. They have to get married; and if their parents cannot make it to their children's wedding because of what is happening to our community, we must help them to get married properly."

They feel that the marriage should be celebrated "properly" or else there might be adverse effects on the marital life of the newlywed couple. The collective and shared experience of war, displacement, and dispersion of families has made others from the same community take on the responsibility of performing the duties of missing parents. Through such adaptations, India has become a transit place, one that holds, keeps, and gathers (Casey 1996, 20–27) fragments of Sri Lankan traditions through which Tamils can reconnect with their communities and imagine a future. In this sense, it has become more than a transit place, as it allows Tamils, through the marriage process, to anchor themselves through memories, fragments of traditions, family reunification, and the imagination of a collective future.

The wedding package is a profitable business enterprise, satisfying the new demands created by Sri Lankan transnational marriages, and at times functioning as proof to visa officers that a "genuine" Sri Lankan Tamil wedding has taken place. The wedding package serves as a container of familiar fragmented traditional Sri Lankan practices, rituals, and customs; through such a package, the dispersed Sri Lankan Tamils can attempt to re-create some semblance of community. Wedding packages are not produced in a vacuum, but become possible in a place like Tamil Nadu, which (a) has cultural, social, and language similarities with the Sri Lankan Tamil community; (b) is host to a large number of Sri Lankan Tamil refugees (who form part of some wedding packages, such as the elderly couples discussed above); and (c) is situated in close proximity to Sri Lanka (which makes it possible for many Tamils to make the journey to India for the wedding of a child or relative). This leads to the creation of a context where the concept of a collective community can be (re)imagined. Wedding packages, further, include specific known and familiar fragments of marriage practices and textures through which the Sri Lankan Tamils try to reconnect and imagine futures of reuniting, even within only a brief space of time. Thus the Sri Lankan wedding packages have become a means of place making in India.

Though India may be a place of transit for the Sri Lankan Tamil community, it is unlike other adoptive places, where forced migrants and diaspora communities try to re-create a notion of "home" (Daniel and Thangaraj 1995; Werbner 1990). In such places, where a sense of permanency prevails for the immigrants, the rework or reparation of relationships takes place in daily life within a community sharing the experience of past violence in a common locality (Das 2007). In India, however, as seen in the stories of Ratna and Ruban, families from different parts of the world come together for a brief period to participate in a wedding ceremony. The reunion of family members and friends lasts for only a few days, because once the ceremony is over each one returns to their respective countries and may never return to India. However, as in Anoja and Parthipan's case, even such a possibility of temporary reunion with parents may not be possible. The moments of family reunion, fragmented familiarities of marriage ceremonies through wedding packages, and the very atmosphere of a Sri Lankan Tamil wedding—in Chennai—enable a temporary place that functions to create the possibility of remaking Tamil communities currently dispersed across borders. The picking up of the fragments of their lives occurs for the Tamils not only in their own place (i.e., Sri Lanka) or in the new place (i.e., their adoptive country), but in transit places like India in the moments of reunion, marriage ceremonies, and togetherness. However, it is not simply about re-creating the community, as it were, but also about picking up fragments in transit places and beginning to rebuild their lives and imagining their futures in those fragments and moments, either in the place of devastation or in an adoptive place. In Anoja's case, when family members could not come for the wedding, someone else from within the Tamil community took on the parents' role during the wedding rituals. While the "real" element may not be available, there are segments that can be re-created so that those involved can go imagine futures in their dispersed social world. The possibility of doing so happens in an in-between place like India in the process of marriage, where a sense of being in one's own place is created.

A transit place, like India, functions like the in-between figure of the marriage broker, becoming a pathway or container that provides the space and means to perform certain familiar Sri Lankan Tamil marriage customs and practices. India functions as an intermediary space where the past and future of Tamils are reproduced and imagined through the ability to observe particular marriage practices and the availability of comprehensive wedding packages. In Ratna's story, where his mother brought specific food items from Sri Lanka in order to make her son's favorite food, we see a continuity of a family's past. On the other hand, when Ratna removed his shirt and showed me his scarred body, it was a reminder of his tortured past and the impossibility of returning to Sri Lanka. When Ratna's father encouraged his wife to cook for their son, saying that he did not know when he would see his son again, they were thrown into an unknown future. Yet it is these same temporary moments that bring together Ratna's family from different parts of the world. These transit sites of place making are where the Tamil community is made and remade during the wedding ceremonies. Even though the time span is greatly limited, it is an important point where the imagination of a future togetherness is made possible.

Similarly, the disputes around the correct ways of officiating a Sri Lankan Tamil wedding, and beyond that the alleged differences between Sri Lankan Tamil marriage ceremonies and Indian Tamil marriage ceremonies, reveal the motive of holding on to the sense of community. Sri Lankan Tamils claimed the existence of those difference even though they had not attended even a single Indian wedding. When I tried to find out what exactly constituted "authentic" practices in a Sri Lankan Tamil wedding, I discovered that the rituals performed varied from priest to priest. If that was the case, why were the photographer and Ruban's father-in-law dissatisfied with the way the Indian priest was conducting the wedding ceremony? The presence of the Indian priest and his way of conducting the wedding disturbed the rhythm of life that helps fragments come together for a semblance of reunion. In other words, the possibility of coming together as Sri Lankan

Tamils around a Sri Lankan wedding is disrupted when a new or unknown fragment enters the scene—as in the case of the Indian priest at Ruban and Nilini's wedding.

Sri Lankan Tamils who come for a wedding in Chennai are known to comment that "the marriage should have happened as it takes place in our *ur*." The ur is both person-centric (Daniel 1987) and place-centric (Thiranagama 2007, 2011). Sri Lankan Tamils who want to conduct their weddings in Chennai according to the customs of their ur do so by having a Sri Lankan priest, a Sri Lankan photographer, Sri Lankan food, and even Sri Lankans "guests." This does not mean that the people participating in the wedding, either as guests or substitutes for parents, necessarily belong to the same ur or caste as the bride or groom. Yet, those involved in the ceremony told me that they are satisfied when it is performed according to the traditions of an ur marriage. Ur thus becomes a notion that enables differentiation between Sri Lankan Tamils and Indian Tamils. Even though there are many ways of conducting a Tamil marriage ceremony, Sri Lankan Tamils insist that a Jaffna wedding is different from an Indian one. Ensuring that a marriage process that takes place in Chennai is carried out in the "Jaffna" style signifies more than contracting a marriage.

The marriage process creates moments for Sri Lankan Tamil communities to imagine togetherness—through isolated moments of coming together—and thus creates the possibility of a more stable and certain future. Thus, such a place is an in-between zone where certain futures and pasts can be cultivated and imagined, relationships transfigured in temporary moments. In the words of philosopher Edward Casey, "A place is something for which we continually have to discover or invent new forms of understanding, new concepts in the literal sense of ways of 'grasping together'" (1996, 28). This place making of the Tamil community during transnational marriage processes in India appears to enable the Tamil community to discover and invent new forms of understanding how to live and imagine futures, both in adoptive and "home" places. Transit places within the marriage process hold the potential for gathering familiar marriage practices, moments of togetherness, and imaginations of futures and new connections. It rebuilds communities through forms of certainty while holding uncertainty of reunions in the future, remembrance of permanent separation, reality of war and migration, and ambiguous futures.

3   Picturing Marriages

AFTER THE CELEBRATION OF THE TRANSNATIONAL MARRIAGE, the spouse who needs to migrate to be reunited with a partner has to navigate through embassies, immigration laws, and practices of the different states, for which they must produce a number of documents. An interesting phenomenon in transnational marriages is the importance—to couples and their extended families—of wedding photographs and albums. Wedding photos have become an item of crucial documentary evidence for Canadian state officials when granting visas to wives and husbands seeking reunion with their spouse. Immigration rules and procedures of the host countries, which are weighted toward restricting marriage migration (Gell 1994; Hall 2002), utilize the perceived "traditional" and "cultural" norms of the migrants' own community to validate a marriage as genuine (Palriwala and Uberoi 2008a).[1]

A vital feature of a transnational marriage is the necessity of proving to others that the marriage is legitimate. Toward this end, multiple documents—ranging from personal letters to wedding photos—must be provided. This raises an interesting anthropological question: How do such documents and the people who produce and scrutinize them come together to create a notion of what constitutes a "Tamil marriage," "Tamil marriage traditions," and "Tamil kinship relationships"?[2] Couples trying to prove to the state that their marriage is genuine are anxious to produce documentation that will be accepted as authentic, and in this process photographs take a special precedence. For the immigration officer, visual documents like photographs are assumed to prove that event took place.

Such photographs submitted as supporting documents in Canadian Immigration petitions are assessed by authorities to determine whether the marriage is "genuine"—specifically, whether the ceremony pictured in the photographs was carried out according to certain "Tamil traditions" and shows a certain intimacy between the couple. Did family members and relatives participate in and perform the ritual duties? How do the bride and groom look to be acting toward each other in the photographs? The wedding photos hold the potential to come "alive" as a witness in the immigration offices where they are reviewed. Such moments of association between the immigration officers and wedding photos reenact intimacies, traditional ceremonies, and relations between the couples and families during the marriage process. Relatives and friends who could not attend the wedding are sometimes inserted through photo editing to create an ideal family within the space of those documents.

The photographs as witness and as proof of genuine marriage hold the power for spouses to be reunited in Canada after the marriage process, and thus allow the spouses to imagine a certain future. At the same time, although certain family members are absent from the wedding ceremony, photos can create virtual families that hold memories of the past and imagine possible futures by capturing the wedding. How do photographs as in-between documents during the marriage process (along with other documents) circulate, produce, and come together with different actors at different moments to re-create a particular past and capture the transfiguration of relatedness between two individuals and their family members? How do they produce intimacy? At such moments, the photographs create hopes, anxieties, memories (Navaro-Yashin 2007), and uncertainties for the future.

STORY OF NITHI AND RAMANI

Ramani, a Sri Lankan Tamil woman, went to Canada in 2002 and obtained refugee status. In 2006 her marriage was fixed with Nithi, her cross-cousin (i.e., her father's sister's son). Nithi's parents had died in the war, and as a result he left for India in 1990 with his grandparents as a refugee. His brother and sister, both married, continued to live in Jaffna. Nithi's grandmother and Ramani's mother had arranged the match. Ramani and Nithi had not been in contact since 1990—due to the civil war, Ramani went to Canada along with her mother, two sisters, and brother; Nithi, on the other hand, left Sri Lanka for India, with his grandparents.

As they were unable to leave Sri Lanka, Nithi's brother and sister could not attend the wedding. Furthermore, Ramani's mother and two of her siblings could not attend the wedding either—her mother was obtaining her Canadian citizenship during that period, and the two siblings could not procure Indian visas in time. Therefore, Ramani arrived in India accompanied only by one of her sisters and a cousin. Ramani and Nithi wed in 2007. Their wedding was performed according to "Hindu customs" at a marriage hall in Chennai, followed by a civil marriage on the same day. They invited many people to the ceremony to ensure a large turnout and therefore prove to the Canadian embassy that their marriage was "real." Ramani returned to her host country, where she arranged for her husband to join her. In the meantime, Nithi applied for a spousal visa. At the embassy he had to produce clearance reports from the police, photographs of the marriage ceremonies, personal letters and gifts, and a marriage certificate. However, even after producing all the above documents, he was refused a visa.

The officer explained, in a letter to Nithi on December 11, 2007, the grounds on which the visa was refused: "The circumstances surrounding your marriage cause me to doubt that it is a genuine marriage." He pointed out that the marriage was arranged too hastily, that the couple did not meet prior to the wedding, and that important family members did not attend the ceremony.

> Parents play an important role in the marriage ceremonies according to the customs prevalent in your community. You did not provide any credible explanation for their absence at this important event. . . . Your wedding appeared staged. Photographs submitted in support of your marriage do not show you and your sponsor appearing natural and comfortable. The photographs suggest a lack of solemnity, spirit of celebration and festivity customarily seen in marriage in your community. Though you stated that your wedding was attended by 70–75 persons, the wedding photographs show a much smaller gathering. You and the sponsor did not go for the customary honeymoon or any exclusive outings. The outing photographs appear posed, taken only to support this application. You and your sponsor appear disjoint. The natural level of closeness and comfort as seen in newly married couple is not visible.

Ramani filed against the decision at the Immigration Appeal Division in Canada. While she was awaiting a hearing, Nithi was caught up between living in India and expecting to join his wife in Canada.

Many of the official visa refusal letters describe how a particular marriage is not genuine or how it was performed under questionable circumstances. The reasons given include the following: the marriage was not performed according to the Sri Lankan Tamil marriage customs; a lack of "sufficient" knowledge of one's partner; insufficient number of family members in the wedding photographs; and no immediate family members of the spouses at the marriage ceremony. Other reasons given for refusal include that the newly married couple do not look intimate and comfortable with each other in the photographs, or that the financial support indicated by the sponsoring person is inadequate.

These letters and the transcribed documents from the visa interviews often mention notions of Sri Lankan Tamil arranged marriages and/or Tamil customs and traditions. In one of its decisions the Canadian immigration authority stated that "the failure to use an elderly person to tie the thali at the marriage celebration was culturally inappropriate for Sri Lankan Tamils" (September 27, 2004, TA3-17873, Immigration and Refugees Board [Immigration Appeal Division]).

Another letter, sent by the Canadian authorities to another of my subjects on May 22, 2006, refers to a "definition" of a Sri Lankan Tamil marriage: "The circumstances of the marriage between you and your alleged sponsor are not consistent with Sri Lankan arranged marriages. Marriage is seen as celebration of union of two persons and always involves close members of families. In your case, your marriage was held with almost no one from either immediate family attending marriage ceremonies. No religious ceremony was held, which is highly unusual in Sri Lanka."

In the course of my fieldwork, I have compiled many such cases where visas were refused because of insufficient documentary evidence and inability to demonstrate to a visa officer the ongoing relationship and knowledge about each other. Interestingly, photographs often seemed to carry the greatest weight in providing documentary proof of a valid wedding or a legitimate marriage. This raises the question of why wedding photographs—a visual medium—have become a form of authentic evidence over a civil marriage document in the visa officer's process of determining whether a marriage is genuine.

PHOTOGRAPHS AS WITNESSES

Unlike other representational forms, the French literary theorist and philosopher Roland Barthes writes, photography holds a unique relation to the real—defined not through the discourse of artistic representation, but that of magic, alchemy, and indexicality: "I call the 'photographic referent' not the *optionally* [emphasis in original] real thing to which an image or sign refers but the *necessarily* [emphasis in original] real thing which has been placed before the lens, without which there would be no photograph . . . in photography I cannot deny that *things have been there* [emphasis added]" (1981, 76).

Therefore, the photograph is linked to a truth in the past that cannot be questioned:

> The photograph is literally an emanation of the referent. From a real body, which was there, proceed radiations which ultimately touch me, who am here. . . . The realists, of whom I am one, . . . do not take the photograph for a "copy" of reality, but for an emanation of the past reality; a magic not an art. . . . The important thing is that the photograph possesses an evidential force, and that its testimony bears not on the object but on time. From a phenomenological viewpoint, in the photograph, the power of authentication exceeds the power of representation. . . . In the image, the object yields itself wholly, and our vision of it is *certain*—contrary to the text or to other perception which gives me the object in a vague, arguable manner, and therefore incites me to suspicions as to what I think I am seeing. (Barthes 1981, 76–108, emphasis in original)

In the context of the visa office, wedding photographs are often referred to by the immigration officers as a witness to a wedding—somewhat like a human witness—as well as an "authentic piece of documentary" evidence (and they believe their "vision of it is certain") that captures and shows within its frame that the families, relatives, and friends of the spouses took part in the wedding ceremonies and witnessed the event. The dual role that photographs play here is (1) as a medium of witnessing the event itself (i.e., freezing the moment and capturing the event); and (2) capturing the presence and involvement of witnesses at the wedding (e.g., relatives, parents, and friends of the spouses).

Nithi's story highlights that the Canadian immigration officers are looking for specific clues in the wedding album along with a credible narrative in the application forms to establish beyond doubt that the marriage is genuine. The authorities seek evidence for whether (a) certain rituals had been performed and (b) a large number of family members attended the event (along with the proof of other factors). It appears that immigration officers do not accept a civil marriage as valid unless evidence of Tamil customary marriage practices—presented to the visa officer through the eye of the camera—is provided.

THE NOTION OF WITNESSING AMONG SRI LANKAN TAMILS

In Nithi's case, even after he had submitted the civil marriage certificate, his demand for a visa was rejected not because the document was forged or faulty but because the wedding photographs showed "insufficient" intimacy between the couple, and not enough close relatives attended the ceremony, especially Ramani's mother. Therefore, the visa officer concluded that the key family members had not witnessed the event. The notion of witnessing a marriage can be traced back to two sources in Jaffna Tamil culture: the early Tamil literature (which is always referred to whenever I ask people to describe Tamil marriages and ceremonies) and the court cases of the colonial period in Sri Lanka (especially those regarding property disputes, where the court had to validate marriages in order to determine the property rights of the parties concerned).

A wide range of marriage rituals and forms of marriage are referenced in early Tamil literature. A helpful illustration can be found in the Sangam poems, written sometime before the second century CE, according to which there are two kinds of marriages: the "arranged marriage" (where a man marries the woman with whom he falls in love, with the acceptance and in the presence of villagers, relatives, and/or parents) and the "love marriage." The "love marriage" is further divided into the *udan poku*, in which the woman runs away with the man with whom she falls in love; and the *mada-leruthal*, where the man who has fallen in love with a woman makes a wooden horse, which is then pulled by his friends around the village, and forces her to agree to their marriage (Sasivalli 1984). A point of particular importance is that in all these marriage forms, the idea of staging the marriage for the community or for the gods and goddesses was obviously demonstrated. Even in the *kalavu manam*, or love marriage, a friend of the bride witnesses the ceremony. Moreover, the Sangam poems describe how the love marriage, also called *kantharuva manam*, was witnessed by the five elements (*aim pothankals*) of nature (i.e., earth, moon, wind, sky, and sun). By their presence, these witnesses transform what could simply be a sexual relationship into a marriage, and give it the status of a public event. The notion of "public" includes the presence of (and witness by) gods and goddesses, relatives of the spouses, or even a single friend of the couple (Sasivalli 1984).

Further illustrations are seen in Tholkappiyam, another work of early Tamil literature. Here, two forms of marriage are described: *kalavu manam* and *karpu manam*. The literary translation of kalavu manam is "love marriage," where the male and the female are in a relationship (Sasivalli 1984), known to no one else except a female friend of the woman. Karpu manam refers to a situation in which, after a man and woman fall in love, they make a public announcement to the village and marry in public. Tholkappiyar, the author of the Tholkappiyam, notes that in the kalavu manam the woman's friend pressures the couple to disclose their love to the public and to start their life with a public marriage. This, then, converts the kalavu manam into karpu manam. While there are no descriptions of marriage rituals in this text, it states, "Poyium valuvum thonriya pinarr iyar yathanar karaman enpa" (The elders have made the rule that the marriage must take place in front of the people in public only, for if not, a person involved in kalavu manam will not take responsibility for the love marriage in cases where cheating or abandonment have taken place) (Shanmugampillai 2006, 97).

These works show that the witnessing of a marriage is important not only because the formation of a new kinship relationship is as much a public event as a private one, but also because witnesses to the union can be called on in cases of injustice against one of the parties to the marriage contract (e.g., in cases of infidelity or denial of marriage). This same notion regarding the witnessing of a marriage was expressed by those who spoke to me about Tamil marriages, and they often referred to Tamil literature to support their view. In other words, the role of the witness is to change the private affair into a socially accepted institution that can be recognized and validated.

This idea of witnessing is also seen in many Sri Lankan colonial court cases related to Jaffna customary marriages in the absence of civil marriage. For example, *Selvaratnam et al. v. Anandavelu* (42 NLR 486 [1941]) clearly demonstrates how, based on the criterion of social acceptance, colonial courts considered the customary marriage legal. The judge did not consider this marriage valid because there was no evidence that a thali had been tied at the marriage ceremony, and because figures like an *iyar* (priest), a *dhobi* (washerman), and an *ambatan* (barber) were absent. The ruling was based on the fact that (a) only a few relatives and family members attended and (b) no proper Hindu rituals took place (e.g., breaking of coconut or burning camphor). According to the vellalar wedding traditions, the washerman and barber must attend because they represent service castes and are responsible for decorating the house and the marriage site, and doing the bride and groom's makeup, respectively. Therefore, the judge held that "the account of the marriage reads more like a farce than a reality" and judged the union invalid.

The lack of relatives and service castes as witnesses to the marriage and participants in the customary ceremonies, as in the case cited above, highlights the importance of a union being accepted by the "public." Viewed through a different lens, it could be said that marriage ceremonies serve to provide a public image to the marriage. This institutionalization of customary marriages through the colonial legal framework can be perceived in the presumption that a proper or legal marriage required the acceptance of parents, friends, and relatives. Here, the "public" does not mean just random individuals but close friends and family.[3] The focus was on ensuring public acceptance of the union as a form of customary marriage, which was closely linked to the notion of the event being witnessed by the community. Even the move to register marriages by the state during the colonial period in Sri Lanka was an attempt to bring marriage into the public domain. But in the absence of civil marriage during colonial times, customary marriages were still brought into the public domain by the colonial state through the notion of societal acceptance (by the family or community) in order to validate a union. Some continuity in practices seems to exist in the validation of marriages by immigration officers and colonial courts (see chapters 4 and 5). In both cases, there is an air of suspicion that hangs over the marriage, especially regarding the authenticity of legal documents offered by the couple as proof. Ironically, it is the yardstick of customs—in particular those relating to certain iconic moments in the performance of rituals—as well as acceptance by the community, as a form of public witnessing, by which the legal status of a marriage as valid comes to be established.

This is a significant clue as to why Canadian visa officers[4] still call for proof of the observance of customary marriage forms, even when a civil marriage has been contracted, in order to validate a legal relationship. Here again, "public" is not constituted through the presence of random individuals or strangers who witness the event, but through the presence of parents, specific relatives, close kinsmen, and figures who take part in ritual performances. Thus the criterion used by immigration officers, and earlier by colonial judges, in assessing the validity of a marriage through the presence of witnesses brings back into the notions of blood ties and affinal relationships.

In the case of Nithi and Ramani, the visa officer was skeptical about the validity of the marriage because Ramani's mother was not present at the ceremony, which he could see in the photographs. It seems that wedding photographs are transferring the notion of "witnessing" from the human eye to the eye of the camera. Witnessing, in this context, is not only about capturing a particular past, and witnessing the event, but also about ensuring a certain future for the spouses by helping to reunite them in their adoptive country. Wedding photographs have become a zone where the proof of marriage rituals, intimacy of couples, and presence of kin are captured and witnessed. They stand as visual documents of the ritualistic and witnessing process of an in-between time and space where two individuals become a married couple. At the same time, the photographs witness the marriage process not only to capture and hold past events but also to prove, to some future immigration office, the marriage to be genuine. They carry both the past and the future of the marriage process and enact differently at different times in their circulation between different actors, such as from photographer to visa officer to the spouses' families. They thus create possibilities of hopes, anxieties, failures, loves, futures, and memories. The photographs are associated not only with immigration officers as a form of witness, but also with other documents to re-create the marriage process at the visa office.

The visa application form (narrated by the applicant) unfolds the narrative of the relationship's development, backed up with documentary proof. It covers the date of the marriage proposal, through the ceremony, to the current living status of the applicant and spouse. These narratives are read by visa officers along with, or against, the wedding photographs. Thus, because the medium of photography entails an act of witnessing, the question is, how are these wedding albums or photographs created by the photographers? The next section explores how the technique of capturing photos and the in-between figure of the photographer come together to produce wedding albums or photos, to determine how the notion of witnessing is transferred from the human eye to the eye of the camera.

WEDDING ALBUMS AND WEDDING PHOTOGRAPHERS

In October 2007, in Chennai, I met Ravi, a wedding photographer, who had come to India as a refugee from Sri Lanka. I met him while he was photographing a wedding. He and his three assistants were actively involved in producing photographs and videos of the ceremony. Ravi, like the director of a movie, was calling the shots and giving advice to his colleagues. He was telling them where to focus, from which angle to take the shots, when to take a close-up, and whether the shots should be long or short for a given part of the event. For example, before the groom was asked to tie the thali, Ravi told the groom that he needed to look directly into the camera while

FIGURE 1. The wedding photographer talking to the groom, while the iyar is preparing the next ritual

he did so (see figures 1 and 2). Moreover, Ravi and the priest who performed the ceremony were in constant communication, with the priest ensuring that Ravi captured all of the ceremony's important points. Also, after each important event, the iyar asked the couple to face the camera. At times Ravi asked the wedding couple to repeat certain moments in the ceremony when he was not satisfied with his shots. He took more than four or five photos of every single step of the ceremony; he told me that he would later select

FIGURE 2. The tying of the thali during a wedding. The photographer has assembled the photos, capturing the groom tying the thali around the bride's neck on the left side, and on the right side, the photo where the groom was asked to look straight into the camera.

the best one, meaning the one that looked the most "natural." He even challenged the authority of the priest at certain points, claiming he was not performing the rituals according to the "real" tradition, or complaining that the priest was hurrying through certain portions of the ceremony.

Once the ceremony was completed, Ravi asked the groom to put his arms around his bride's shoulder or around her hips, and he asked the bride to hug the groom and hold him tight. When the couple felt shy or uncomfortable, he would tell them, "Relax, be yourself, you are married now. Come closer and smile, do not be nervous, you are a hero today." He tried to put them at ease for these intimate but staged photographs (see figure 4). At times, when Ravi wanted to capture more affection through his photos, he would take the couple to a corner of the wedding hall and ask others to leave the area. He informed me that if the others were present, the spouses may feel shy and embarrassed about holding each other. "You know," he told me, "they should look natural in the photos."

Moreover, he said that these days he had to take an almost-180-degree shot to show the gathering of a large crowd on one side of the photo and the couple performing the ceremony on the other side. He had to do this, he explained, to dispel any doubt in the mind of the visa officer about the marriage. This is what I call the "double move" of the photographs, as they serve

FIGURE 3. The wedding photographer capturing details of the ceremony, while the couple and the iyar wait

FIGURE 4. Captioned wedding album photos

FIGURE 5. Facing pages in a wedding album, with an enlarged photo of the thali (right)

both to witness the event as well as to capture the act of witnessing by the audience. Ravi told me a marriage happened only once, whether it is for the people or for the visa officer, and therefore it must be done properly.

Ravi claimed that he knew the ceremonies well. While showing me his wedding albums, he explained that he tried to make them resemble storybooks. He normally took around four or five hundred shots of the event, from which he selected the best photos. His album looked like a moving picture. The way the photos were arranged told a story in a chronological way: from morning to evening, from the groom's family to the bride's family, from the minute details of the ceremonies to how two individuals at the end of the ceremony became intimate and close to each other. The album captures the transfiguration of relatedness between the couple and their families within the marriage process. It also documents important symbols or events, such as tying the thali or wearing the *metti* (a toe ring the groom places on the bride's toe during the wedding). Ravi enlarges these shots and places them next to the photos of particular rituals or ceremonies (see figure 7). He explained that he enlarges these photos because a non-Tamil person who looked at the album might not see the symbols or recognize their importance. By looking at enlarged photos, non-Tamils would see more clearly what the couple was doing during the wedding. Ravi was also

FIGURE 6. A couple performing a ritual during their wedding

aware that these photos were crucial evidence needed to obtain a visa after the marriage so that the spouses could reunite in a foreign country.

Ravi added that it was much more difficult to take wedding pictures now than it had been in the past. He explained that in the past, wedding photographers were worried primarily about the quality and outcome of the photos, "but nowadays, we need to think about the frame, who has to be there, who is going to see it, which rituals have to be captured, and where do we place

FIGURE 7. The *ammi mithithal* ritual, in which the bride puts her feet on a stone so that the groom can put a ring on her toe

relatives who did not come to the wedding in the wedding photos?" The new wedding photos are captured not just to remember the past event, but also to answer future needs. The future-oriented photos of the marriage process hold the potential of both actualized and yet to be actualized moments.

OLD PHOTOS AND NEW PHOTOS: ROMANCE, TRADITION, AND RITUALS

When I collected old photos of Sri Lankan Tamil weddings from the 1940s through the 1970s, I noticed that neither the bride nor the groom was look-ing at the camera; they were focused on the rituals, involved in the ceremo-nies, or looking down or away from the camera or from each other. The photos clearly show that when they were posing for the photos, the spouses were sitting or standing away from each other. The photographs captured their timidity being so close to each other. The couple is the focus here, rather than the events. Moreover, these photos did not capture the audience or even the close relatives present at the wedding. In Ravi's wedding photos, by contrast, we could see all the attendees, especially any close relatives and friends in attendance.

Furthermore, the old wedding photos do not focus on the minute details of rituals performed during the wedding. For instance, these photos show the thali-tying ritual as a part of the wedding without emphasizing the faces of the couple or providing close-up shots of the thali, unlike in the modern wedding albums. Moreover, the bride and groom do not portray a smiling, happy, and romantic couple; rather, the couple looks extremely tense and shy.

The wedding photographs from past decades do not include any written statements next to the photographs or imprinted within the photo frame. Ravi's wedding albums, on the other hand, include brief written statements such as "Lovely memories, made for each other," "Congratulations! Dreams never end," and "With pleasant memories," which explicitly express particular notions of romance, stable marriages, and enduring relationships. Printed alongside photos where the spouses are holding each other, hugging, or standing in close proximity, the short statements usually share such sentiments as "Made for each other" and "Love your wife, live your life," inviting the viewer to read into the photos normative understandings of love and marriage (see figure 4). The viewer's observations are manipulated and drawn to a particular story of the marriage process.

Furthermore, the same photographs show the couple as heroic figures, as if in a movie. Even though such photos seem like they are produced for the visa officer to highlight certain predetermined notions of romance, when analyzed by others in different contexts (Adrian 2003) they are interpreted in a completely different manner. For example, when viewed in the Taiwanese context, such glamorous wedding photos of the bride indicate an attempt to compensate for unfulfilled womanhood; in the global context of modernity, such photos show how moments of intimacy are translated in contemporary terms (Adrian 2003). Weddings' visuals could be read as expressions of class, social relationships, and identity formation (Bourdieu 1990b; Pinney 1997). Even within the Sri Lankan transnational marriage process, the wedding album has the potential to carry different affects at different moments during its circulation.

Many individual pictures of the couple before the marriage are inserted and placed at the start of the album. The couple poses for the camera in many positions, somewhat like a model or a film star on the red carpet. As mentioned above, it was Ravi who directed the spouses about how to position themselves and behave. Thus, a kind of "performance" is expected from the couple in front of the camera. Further, the individual photos are often edited to enhance their effect. For instance, a photo of a bride might show her walking over a body of water, sitting on the clouds, or standing in a temple. The background of the photo is manipulated or sometimes completely replaced in order to give the photos an exotic touch (Pinney 1997).

In his work on Indian wedding photos and images, anthropologist Christopher Pinney argues that the varying backgrounds, color schemes, and poses of contemporary wedding photos reflect certain imagined life desires of the Indian couple. For that effect, elements of fantasy are built into the photographs (e.g., being enveloped in a cloud). Moreover, such images are derived from or inspired by popular Indian films and have given rise to a specific genre of photography in India. Similarly, Ravi's wedding albums do not only serve the articulated need of providing the visa officer with authentic evidence of the marriage, they also cater to the changing needs and desires of the Sri Lankan Tamil community, which is seen in the unmistakable modeling on images from popular Indian Tamil films. Ravi's wedding albums are created in such a way as to evoke a certain kind of romantic love, which is accomplished through spectacular settings and the use of digitally manipulated backgrounds. Is it then, paradoxically, such staging that the visa officer is so keen to see in the photos, when these wedding albums are so carefully produced to present an imaginary world to the viewer? The power of the photographs to produce and re-create an event so that it presents what "really" took place is modified by this element of imagination. Thus, the power of the medium and its production show us that it can be "read" on multiple levels, from photographers to the couple to the visa officers, and that perception is located in the eye of the camera, the photographer, the viewer, and the eyes of the individuals in the photos when they associate at different moments within the marriage process.

When I flipped through Nithi's wedding album, I noticed that the thali ritual was given particular prominence. The thali itself is captured separately and placed in the album next to photos of the thali-tying ceremony. Thus, on one side of the album, one sees the thali-tying ritual and the people taking part in it, and on the other side, one sees the enlarged photo of the thali (see figure 5). I also noticed in Nithi's album that the word *mangaliyam* (another term for the thali) was written in English next to the photo of the thali. Similarly, enlarged photos of other rituals, such as the tying of the metti and the *ammi mithithal* (where the bride places her feet on a stone), are featured in most contemporary wedding albums, vividly bringing out the performance of the rituals and enabling the human eye to see the minute details of the ceremony. The camera eye's ability to capture such details and the photographer's role in enlarging and highlighting them in the wedding album bring a sense of staging and drama to the wedding-album production.

In other words, the modern wedding album brings out a more performance-oriented view of the marriage, and presents the rituals in more elaborate and dramatic forms. The modern wedding albums are characterized by certain dramatized and staged elements, as the photographer re-creates what they consider important traditions of a Tamil marriage, knowing full well that these photos are going to circulate among Tamils as well as non-Tamils. Moreover, in the modern wedding albums certain rituals are given more prominence; thus, certain fragments of tradition are not only captured and enlarged but also re-created, while other fragments are not. For instance, the thali-tying ritual is given more prominence than other rituals are. There is usually a color photo of the tying ritual on the right side of the page, and on the left side is a black-and-white version of the same frame with only the thali highlighted in gold. In this way, the viewer's eyes are immediately drawn to the thali. The thali ritual in Tamil weddings only emerged in Tamil literature as an important part of the wedding ceremony beginning around the thirteenth century. Even among the Jaffna Tamils, the thali ritual is not observed in the same way across every caste. Ravi's albums have not only helped re-create the actual event through photography, but have also created certain notions of tradition and romance.

PHOTOGRAPHS AS EVIDENCE

Ravi asks the couple to relax and look "normal" or "natural" for the camera. He produces a certain kind of intimacy between them through the medium of photography, anticipating the visa officer's reading of such moments of romance. By asking the couple to look at the camera when they perform important rituals during their wedding, Ravi provides visual evidence of the faces to the visa officer, indicating that the people who are applying for the visa are the same people "truly" marrying each other. By facing the camera, the spouses appear to be looking directly at the visa officer through the photographic lens. Through these photos, the photographer, the camera, and the subjects come together to create a face-to-face relationship with the visa officer in their faraway office (thus contracting the distance between them). This telescoping of time and space, by means of photographs, enables the visa officer to witness the event. The photographs make present the absent spouse when the visa officer poses questions about the wedding photos. The photographs come alive, staging a type of intimacy between the couple as they perform certain traditions, while also standing as the witness of the marriage process. They create a "reciprocal" relation whereby viewers, the photographer, and the photographed interact: "As photography immobilizes the flow of family life into a series of snapshots; it perpetuates familial myths while seeming merely to record actual moments in family history.... The still picture is captured by a single camera eye whose point of view, that of the photographer, determines the viewer's position ... but the structure of looking is reciprocal ... : between the viewer and the recorded object, the viewer encounters, and/or projects, a screen made up of dominant mythologies and preconceptions that shapes the representation" (Hirsh 1997, 7).

Even though photographers have the power to immobilize past events through the production of snapshots, a specific future is being projected in the wedding photos I encountered. The photograph should not end with the captured event; rather, it should have the power to come alive and re-create the intended effect (i.e., emphasizing traditions and intimacy) for the visa officer to convince them that this particular wedding is "genuine." This association between the visa officer and the wedding photographs also creates anxiety and doubt (Navaro-Yashin 2007; Hull 2012b), which certainly affects this government official's decision-making process. The photographs should show an actual intimacy between the couple, and also that the wedding was witnessed by relatives who accepted the union. Thus, we have seen that the wedding photos require a certain element of performance and staging. However, because a photograph functions not only as a "witness" to the wedding but also as a medium to capture the presence of witnesses at the wedding, the "stagey" element is mitigated. This, in turn, enables the visa officer to view the photo as an authentic record of an actual moment in time. The photographs have the potential of both being the witness and capturing the witnesses of the wedding. They hold the past and the future together as a medium of both actualized and yet to be actualized memories and imaginations.

Thus, in wedding photography—contrary to Roland Barthes's suggestion that photography is an evidential force, communicates the real past, and therefore cannot be penetrated—the visa officer's eyes seem to penetrate the images, searching for clues that certain traditions and customs have been followed. The state official looks for evidence of certain affects and particular activities of "witnessing" to prove the marriage's validity. However, I also learned from Ravi that no matter how carefully he takes these photos, with the same priest performing the same ceremony, there were instances where the visas were rejected on suspicion of being "staged." Similar photos from the same photographer appear to become indifferently legible or illegible in the office of different visa officers.

Photography is able to manipulate reality and pass it off as truth. "Countless observers have documented the myriad ways that photographs can lie, cheat, and steal," writes Bonnie Adrian. "The camera de-contextualizes; it fragments space, freezes time, manipulates light, and settings in which they were photographed and in the way photographs are displaced, captioned, sequenced, and viewed" (2003, 6). She continues, "A photograph's tendency to serve as an invisible medium makes it doubly powerful" (205).

In this context, the medium of wedding photographs carries a double burden, both as an "evidence force" and an "invisible medium." It can be read and unread at the same time. The photographs in the visa officer's offices come alive, breaking away from both the frozen time and the past (the assumption is that the event in the picture is dead now)—they become a penetrable evidence. The production of the photographs, the perception of the viewer, the photographer, the eye of the camera, and the performance of the subjects lead a photograph to be read in many ways. It has the potential of holding both certainty and uncertainty of its effect. Despite the photographer's intentions, the photographs do not always produce their intended effects on visa officers. The temporality surrounding the production of these photos and their circulation within the marriage process (from arranging the marriage to the reunion of spouses across borders) open the possibility that the images can be considered both genuine and not genuine, simultaneously, at every moment of their associations in the immigration office. It is possible that the question for us is not about how the photographs show that "*this thing has been there*" (Barthes 1981, 76, emphasis added), but about why and how this thing was made to be there to be read in the future. The photographs operate in the realm of potential.

WITNESSING FROM HERE AND BEYOND

Modern states come to be experienced by people through documents, as states are built through their writing practices.[5] However, these written forms also evoke the possibility of forgery, so the documents constantly come under suspicion, making some of them illegible even to state officials (Das and Poole 2004a, 15). The illegibility of written legal documents requires the state to call for "visual documents" and incorporate them into a legal regime. Photographs are perceived as evidential proof that cannot be penetrated, as they bring out the real past and, ultimately, the truth (Barthes 1981). Perhaps that explains why some see the visual documents as providing more authentic proof of a genuine marriage. Visuality contracts the distance between the viewer and the subjects engaging in a past event, through the ability of the eye of the camera to witness both an event and its witnesses, and its ability to empower photos to produce minute details of the event in a realistic visual form. However, photos can be read in multiple ways in different times and different places, through their association at different moments in the marriage process. Thus, the production and circulation of wedding photos and the interplay between camera, photographers, traditions, and visa officers show that the images submitted to embassies simultaneously carry the legibility and illegibility of the state's practices.

Visual documents are required to help create the notion of a "Tamil marriage," to capture the ceremony, and to show the key participants at the event and the active roles they played according to the customs of Tamils in Sri Lanka. The production of all these visual documents is designed to convince the visa officer that a specific marriage is genuine and not merely one of convenience. Further, the notion of witnessing the wedding (through both the camera eye and the human eye) revives the importance of not only blood ties and familial relationships in the marriage rituals but also witnessing as a form of social acceptance of the marriage by friends, relatives, and close family. Affection, love, intimacy, loss, and happiness—imprinted in the photos at one moment of the marriage process (i.e., the wedding ceremony)—then circulate to the immigration offices to create different effects of social acceptance, authority, and validity when presented to the visa officers. Through the constant future moments of association between photos and humans, the image carries its potential to be ambiguous, authentic, staged, certain, and uncertain, holding all these together in its body.

These wedding photographs also become important documents that help dispersed Tamils to reconnect. The images circulate among the couple's relatives who live in various far-flung locations. Moreover, through the medium of photography, photographers, priests, and the spouses' relatives attempt to (re)create a sense of a fragmented "Jaffna Tamil marriage." While working with Ravi, I learned that attempts were made to paste into the images pictures of relatives who were dead, disappeared, or could not attend the wedding. In Tamil culture, the dead are respected but kept at a distance during the wedding ceremony out of consideration for what is auspicious for the couple's future. But in these moments of inclusion, the wedding photos literally become a record of the living relatives as well as the spectral presence of the dead.

These visual documents, where the living and dead relatives become part of one living family, open up conditions of possibility for making the dead relatives part of the important events of a living person's life. In the in-between space and time of the marriage process, such photos are able to create space for the missing, the dead, and living members of families to inhabit the same visual space. They make possible the re-creation of kinship and the imagination of futures with the living presence of the past. The wedding photos in this sense not only capture the transfiguration of related-ness between bride and groom during the marriage process, but also rei-magine and transfigure the relatedness between dead and living persons. Thus, they keep open the possibility for the dead, absent, and missing to reinhabit a space in a way that would otherwise be impossible. Such visual moments make the photographs "living" documents, as they turn the dead into living participants in the marriage process. Photos act as a space where learning to live with death and the past becomes possible while at the same time learning to live with the uncertainty of marriage migration and its futures. The wedding photographer, as an in-between figure of the marriage process, not unlike the marriage broker, helps to gather fragments of a dis-persed community while opening up the possibility of various futures.

In one moment a photo is taken as proof and witness; at another moment it promotes the imagination of romance between the bride and groom; at yet another moment, it re-creates unions between the dead and the living and encourages the envisioning of different futures. In one context, it becomes authentic proof of the event, and in another it fails to stand as an authentic witness for the visa officer. The potential of photos to hold both certainty and uncertainty resides in their moments of association. The photos encompass differences in the reading of the same affects or repeti-tions of practices. They bring surprises, shifts, changes, and different futures in their circulation within the marriage process. Affects such as hope, failure, anxiety, and romance reside in the photos, which also hold the potential to reconnect the dead and the living in a world marked by war and migration. When I asked Nithi why he wanted to insert his relatives into his wedding photos, he said, "These people would have lived with us and participated in this marriage, except for this war."

4 Framing Tamil Marriages in Colonial Courtrooms

THE TRANSNATIONAL MILIEU WITHIN WHICH IMMIGRANTS SEEK to create families makes it important that a marriage is validated at the levels of both community and formal legal regimes. Certain similarities can be found between the adjudication of laws regarding the validity of specific marriages in the colonial courts and in the eyes of the contemporary visa officers. There are, of course, important differences in the process. In colonial courts, Tamil disputants brought cases to contest matters of property and inheritance; the validation of a marriage was a necessary precondition. Colonial courts were primarily concerned with settling such issues in order to create secure rights over land and other sources of property. In the case of immigration officials, the focus is more on issues of family reunification than on the relevance of marriage for the devolution of property. However, ethnic customary marriage practices play an important role in a Canadian immigration officer deciding whether a marriage is genuine, just as in the colonial courts.

The main difference between these two sets of practices lies in the underlying motives. The colonial regime's aim was to implement laws to govern its Sri Lankan subjects. The complexity of implementing new laws and challenging the practicality of their subjects' everyday lives made the alien state flexible about the implementation of certain marriage laws. The Canadian state, on the other hand, receives the married spouses of its citizens as potential future citizens, and therefore tries to implement more rigid forms of immigration laws on spouse migration to protect its borders. Even though motives behind the formation and implementation of laws differ for these two regimes, the process by which they sought/seek to validate a marriage as "legal" or "genuine" reveals similar questions and modi operandi.

The couple's intention becomes the focal point on which both courts (colonial and Canadian) and legal processes focus to measure the marriage's validity. However, the degrees and scales of the intention and its measurement have shifted since colonial times, due to the variation in motivations. In its anthropological study, the notion of intention has been explored as it links to the inner self located at the individual level and expressed through others (Strathern 1995). Intention is entangled with power, moral, and legal understandings. It varies depending on the cultural context (Rosen 1995; Duranti 2015). These studies also bring out the difficulty in studying intention and extracting meaning from the action. Intention is usually associated with the inner self, but it could be located at the same time within social and cultural relations; therefore, it carries certain elements of uncertainty (Rosen 1995). Intention appears as an intersubjective idea that is always perceived and performed, but would be in constant tension with others when interpreted by the community or other individuals (Duranti 2015).

The intention of the human action, when expressed, does not necessarily include all the intentions that were associated with it. In other words, the intention when acted on includes both actualized and not actualized intentions. "Intention" is obviously present in the arrangement of marriage through astrological matching of the couple, the dowry, and gift-giving practices during and after the marriage (Dumont 1964, 1983). The intention of the couple to marry can be observed in the performance of rituals during the marriage as well, or in public inquiries about potential spouses during marriage negotiations, as we have seen in the previous chapters. However, this chapter and the next one trace how the notion of the marrying couple's intention was determined within the courtrooms of the colonial period and continues in the immigration regimes of the present day. The discussion will illustrate how courtrooms as in-between spaces have the power to rearrange and transfigure relationships. I look at the process of measuring intention in customary marriages and the ways in which it folds, merges, and is adapted into legal languages through the colonial courtrooms, by conserving, changing, and re-creating the notions of Jaffna Tamil cultures, traditions, and customs. The process of legalizing and measuring the intention of the marrying couples through legal languages within the colonial courtrooms led to the crystallization of certain traditions and practices. Traditions and local practices appear to be produced, changed, or adapted through the legal recapture of "intention."

The laws and practices introduced by colonialism greatly affected the lives of the colonial subjects and led to major structural changes in colonized countries (Dirks 1992, 2003; Uberoi 1996a). Indeed, "culture" appeared to have been "invented in relationship to a variety of internal colonialisms" (Dirks 1992, 4). However, these new practices and laws appear to have been contested not only at the legislative level but also at the level of adjudication, showcasing the resistance shown by colonial subjects.[1] The encounter between the colonial authorities and colonial subjects refashioned new legal languages, traditions, and subjects (Sarkar 1993).[2]

Although the introduction of colonial marriage laws has affected property rights and the practices of sale, transfer, and inheritance in Sri Lanka, of concern here is how the marriage laws and debates in the colonial courtrooms—through the legal framing of the intention to marry as a way of validating the customary marriage—not only produced certain ideas of customs and practices in legal language, but also enabled revisiting the marriage process itself. The assemblages of new colonial laws, the legal language of intention, local practices, and individuals, in the absence of legal civil marriage documents, opened up the possibility of making and breaking relationships. By revisiting the marriage process in courtrooms, its uncertainty and certainty were made visible again.

Within the colonial court spaces, authorities invented and reinforced the local people's traditions and marriage practices, and local subjects challenged, reinterpreted, and explored the possibilities of their own marriage practices. Within the contested space of colonial courtrooms, the assemblages of these elements revisited the customary marriage process, its intention, and its legal validity. Thus, they brought out the potential of transfiguring relationships, uncovering the actualized and not actualized intentions of married couples, and producing "tradition and customs." The courtrooms as in-between spaces of making and breaking relationship, based on the validity of the marriage between two individuals, not only revisited the past but opened the future for those individuals. The court cases became documents, and as such, the verdicts become the carriers of notions of customs, traditions, and cultures for future court cases.

A study of disputed Sri Lankan Tamil marriage court cases between 1810 and 1948 forms the basis on which I consider the question of which type of Tamil customary marriages were considered "legal," as well as how the different caste-based marriage practices and customs were crystallized through the legalization of those practices. These court cases will be helpful in mapping out how colonial laws and the customary practices of Sri Lanka came together to create a legal language, which in turn affected how the Sri Lankan subjects thought about "tradition" during the colonial period.

REGISTRATION AND LEGALIZATION OF MARRIAGES
BY THE BRITISH COLONIAL REGIME

Marriage and kinship rules in the southern part of Sri Lanka, before the colonial marriage legislation was introduced, appear to have been flexible and fluid; the British regime brought a uniform policy of land sale and transfer, however, which affected marriage patterns (Risseeuw 1988). The legalization of marriage and the introduction of new marriage laws in colonial Sri Lanka and India were closely linked with property ownership, the sale and transfer of property, and inheritance practices.[3] They aimed to establish marriage as a legitimized public event and promote the use of a legal language associated not only with the governance of property and ownership, but also with the control and manipulation of women's sexuality. The existence of multiple marriage forms in Sri Lanka meant that the British found it difficult to determine who were the "legitimate" children and what was a "legitimate" marriage.[4] Thus, the colonial state needed to regulate marriage through law to ensure that "legitimate" children had the legal right to claim the property of their parents (Risseeuw 1988). In response, the British colonial rulers introduced registration as a form of validating marriages.

The Marriage Ordinance of 1907 was introduced to regulate all marriages except for those of Kandyans and Muslims. The transformation of marriage laws had started, however, prior to the arrival of the British, who simply made further changes to the systems set up by previous colonizers. During the time of Dutch and Portuguese rule, a comprehensive process of collecting, codifying, and re-creating "customs" of the "natives" had commenced with the help of the privileged-caste elites from different regions (Goonesekere 1984; Tambiah 2004). However, British colonizers, unlike their predecessors, institutionalized and normalized monogamous marriage throughout the island (Goonesekere 1984). Furthermore, they changed the age of consent for marriage and regulations regarding parental consent, and introduced rigid divorce laws (Goonesekere 1984; Tambiah 2004, Risseeuw 1988). Through such formalization, the colonial state established itself in Sri Lanka and institutionalized marriage, which affected the daily lives of Sri Lankans (Goonesekere 1984, 31). However, this does not necessarily mean the laws were having their intended impact—a close study of the practices at the adjudication level makes it abundantly clear that the colonial subjects were not adhering to the new laws (this will be demonstrated in subsequent cases). As a result, the colonial authorities, who faced problems implementing the legislation, changed the laws to suit the contexts of their colonial subjects. Further, at the adjudicatory level, it was discovered that a more flexible way of implementing the colonial marriage laws was to promote practices that incorporated colonial subjects' social realities. It is against this backdrop that the importance of registering a marriage to establish its validity will be analyzed.

The British 1847 ordinance introduced to Sri Lanka registration of marriages. Several similar ordinances were adopted during this period in an attempt "to remove uncertainties attached to the law of marriage through the island" (Hayley 1923, 188) and provide legal legitimacy to the union. The many ordinances and amendments issued by the British authorities (in 1867, 1859, 1895) confirmed the need for marriage registration and brought into effect strict regulations regarding marriage, namely (a) the institutionalization of monogamous marriage as the legal marriage form and (b) the abolishment of polygamous marriage forms (Goonesekere 1984).[5] This meant that a marriage not sanctioned *publicly* by the state was considered invalid.

These measures were hotly debated not by nationalist or reform movements, as in the Indian context (Sarkar 1993; Dirks 2003), but by the colonial authorities themselves, because many Sri Lankans did not register their marriages, even after the legislation was passed.[6] The colonial authorities were compelled to find a solution since most marriages would be deemed illegal and their offspring illegitimate if the registration was maintained as an absolute requirement (Risseeuw 1988).[7] The legislative debates on the topic, the failure to implement the registration of marriages, and the concerns voiced by various colonial authorities and judges regarding the rigidity of the new laws eventually brought about an amendment of the marriage laws in the late twentieth century.

Now, a marriage did not need to be registered to be legally valid; in such a case, the validity of a marriage was based on other evidence (Goonesekere 1984). The colonial authorities accepted the observance of customary marriage ceremonies as a way of solemnizing a legally valid union. Even though the state did away with the mandatory registration of a marriage, it brought back a different form of validation: proof that either (a) the marriage had taken place according to customs or (b) there had been long-term cohabitation (Goonesekere 1984, 1987). This move led to a new legal debate within the courts about customs of a "native" marriage through which the language of customs entered the discourse.

The colonial regime attempted to legalize customary marriages as a form of valid legal marriage in the absence of registration. The reintroduction of certain marriage ceremonies and the presence of witnesses (e.g., close family members, relatives, and friends) as proof of a valid marriage demonstrates the colonial state's key objective of bringing marriage into the public domain as a way of reading the couples' intention to marry. In the process of legalizing customary marriage practices, the alien laws incorporated the social realities of caste hierarchy and the heterogeneity of the subjects' marriage practices. Prior to addressing issues of the colonial courts' discussion on the validity of customary Tamil marriage, it is important to understand the workings of Sri Lankan customary laws, which provide insight into the nature of marriage among the Jaffna Tamils.

THE THESAWALAMAI CODE AND JAFFNA TAMIL CUSTOMARY MARRIAGES

The Dutch, the area's second colonial rulers, first compiled the so-called customary laws of Jaffna (Tambiah 1954). The Jaffna Tamils' customary laws, or the Thesawalamai code, were codified by Class Isaacs, a Dutch officer, with the help of twelve *muthaliyara* (privileged caste) in 1707 (Tambiah 1954, 20; 2004). Nowadays the Thesawalamai code is related to the transfer and sale of property as well as inheritance that can be used by the Jaffna Tamils only (Tambiah 2004, 46–73). This chapter will cover only the relevance of the Thesawalamai code with regard to Hindu marriage and in light of the Sri Lankan marriage ordinances, as its purpose is to understand how the validity of a marriage is defined both in customary and colonial laws through established court cases. While discussions abound on the origin of the Thesawalamai, a detailed discussion of this aspect is outside the scope of the present volume (see Tambiah 1954, 2004). In general, customary laws in different colonies are found to have been codified, classified, and produced by the colonial authorities (Dirks 1992; Comaroff and Comaroff 2004). The governance of colonial states and their direct and indirect rules over the colonized populations occurred through the "customary law that different colonial regimes over time codified if not invented" (Hansen and Stepputat 2005a, 25).

"Thesawalamai, originally, was a collection of Dravidian usages" (Tambiah 2004, 4). Many other customary laws, from within the region and from Asia, influenced and shaped it, such as the Mukkuvar laws of Batticaloa, Hindu law of India, Mohammedan law, and the Marumakattayam laws of South India (Tambiah 1954, 30; 2004). The Dutch, the Portuguese, and the British changed and transformed the Thesawalamai code when they

FRAMING TAMIL MARRIAGES   115

governed Jaffna (Tambiah 1958, 2004). After the Thesawalamai was codified
by the Dutch, it was later translated by the British chief justice of Ceylon,
Sir Alexander Johnston.[8] The multiple translations of the Thesawalamai
code—from Dutch to English to Tamil—further complicated their reading
and understanding.

According to the Thesawalamai code, in order for a marriage to be considered valid the following requirements had to be satisfied: "(1) the consent
of the parents, or if the parents are dead, of the guardians; (2) the attainment
of the age of maturity; (3) the requirement that the bride and bridegroom
must be of the same caste; (4) the necessary ceremonies" (Tambiah 2004, 112).
While the British introduced a marriage ordinance to govern the marriage
of Tamils of Sri Lanka that ignored a great number of these requirements, it
still recognized the weight of Hindu customary rituals for the validation of
customary marriage in the absence of civil marriage (Tambiah 2004, 112–13).
Moreover, even though the Thesawalamai code states that necessary ceremonies must be performed in order for a marriage to be considered proper,
it does not explain what the specific ceremonies are. Section 1.18, however, is
one of the rare instances where it deals openly with ceremonial symbols of
marriage. The Thesawalamai code states, "Pagans consider as their lawful
wife or wives those around whose neck they bound the Taly with the usual
pagan ceremonies; and should they have more women, they considered them
as concubines. If the wives, although they should be three or four in number,
should all and each of them have a child or children, such children inherit,
share and share alike, the father's property; but the child or children by concubines do not inherit anything" (Tambiah 2004, appendix).

The laws highlight the thali, investing it with importance as a ceremonial
symbol of a legitimate marriage. The lack of a thali on the neck of a woman
negated her status of wife—instead, she would be considered a concubine.
Thus, the observance of the thali ceremony at a wedding was of great importance according to the Thesawalamai. Interestingly, however, later on we
see that the thali ritual came to be considered a privileged-caste practice,
and court cases did not consider the thali-tying ritual as being of any legal
importance in marriage ceremonies of the marginalized castes, certain
segments of the privileged castes, and even those belonging to the privileged
caste if they hailed from other regions of Sri Lanka. Privileged-caste men had
concubines from the marginalized castes, who were not accorded the legal
status of wife in the language of the law (Tambiah 2004).

The Thesawalamai code also served to protect certain interests of the Saiva
vellalar privileged-caste group of Jaffna Tamils. Polygamy was recognized

by the Thesawalamai code, and children of such a union were recognized as legitimate. The code also recognized the practice of concubinage but did not consider it a marriage union, and the children from such union did not have any claim over the property of their fathers (Tambiah 2004). In other words, legitimacy was conferred on children of a polygamous union only if they were born from parents of the same caste; if the child was born out of an intra-caste union or the mother was a concubine from a marginalized caste, the child was considered illegitimate. The caste and legitimacy rules were reinforced, articulated, and practiced among the Jaffna Tamils through the Thesawalamai code. Despite this, the British abolished the practice of polygamy, and instituted monogamy as the only valid marriage practice among Tamils in Jaffna. However, within colonial courtrooms on questions of the validation of a marriage, the observance of Tamil marriage ceremonies, in the absence of a civil marriage, was discussed and debated, and traditions criticized, reinforced, and in some instances re-created. The courtroom confrontation between colonial laws and local marriage practices led to the emergence of a new legal language pertaining to Tamil marriage ceremonies and Tamil traditions.

TAMIL CUSTOMARY MARRIAGES, INTENTION TO MARRY, AND VALIDITY OF MARRIAGE WITHIN THE COLONIAL COURTROOM

In the case of a Sri Lankan Hindu, in the absence of a civil marriage the union's validity is determined on the basis of customary marriage practices of the Hindu religion in Sri Lanka. For a marriage among Tamils, the main rituals (even though varied) consist of the tying of the thali (necklace) by the groom around the bride's neck, the bride receiving a cloth (*kurai*)[9] from the groom, and the performance of those rituals in front of relatives (Tambiah 2004, 113). However, these customary rituals that validate a marriage tend to differ from caste to caste and region to region. The colonial court ruled on the validity of a customary marriage on the twin bases of whether the rituals had been performed and what the *intention* of the contracting parties appeared to have been. The colonial court's interpretation was that the performance of the customary rituals was a public expression of the intention of the parties to contract a marriage. The ambiguity around what the customary rituals of Hindu marriage were (in keeping with caste and regional differences) made it difficult for the colonial judges to determine a union's validity. As a result, it seems the colonial judges focused on the question of intention as a legal means through which to link up the practices of customary marriage rituals for the purposes of validation. Intention, associated with the inner self, is treated by the courts as that which can be read and interpreted from actions performed. Further, the customary rituals were performed with and in front of people and thus provided a public face to marriage.

In the context of criminal laws, the expression of intention is entangled with the questions of motivation, desire, and prior knowledge (Crawford and Quinn 1983). Those questions complicate the reading of intention. However, common law minimizes these complexities, as the choices of verdict are set between culpability and innocence. It consistently encompasses the "common sense assumption that legal requirements and findings can be set down with certainty in simple declarative sentences" (Crawford and Quinn 1983, 278). It is about what is knowable and certain in the action of an individual that provides the ground for the verdict's reasoning.

In the context of customary marriage, the individual intention of marrying another person was established by the new colonial courts through the performance of certain ceremonies, which were linked to public display and social acceptance of marriage by the public as they took part in and witnessed the event. Thus, through such a public display of intention as well as the social acceptance of the marriage, the union could be recognized as legitimate. The public display and social acceptance of various ceremonies seems to provide certainty to the couple's intention, though it's not definitive, and so uncertainty lies within these actions as well. The aim of the court was to seek certainty over the ambiguity of varying marriage ceremonies practiced by colonial subjects according to caste and region. The couple's legal intention to marry in the customary ceremony was placed within the cultural expression of marriage through which the colonial authorities had interpreted, governed, and read their subjects.

The following cases show that many different marriage customs were prevalent among the Tamil Hindus in Sri Lanka, which proved to be a unique challenge to the colonial court in its attempt to validate, institutionalize, and legalize customary marriage practices. It also shows how the customary marriage rituals were linked with the question of intention and through which particular caste hierarchy and customary practices were institutionalized.

The case of *Ponnammah v. Rajakulasingham* (50 NLR 135 [1948]) shows that while the thali-tying ritual is important among the Tamils of Jaffna, it is not equally important to Tamils of Batticaloa (eastern Sri Lanka). This case came to the Batticaloa civil court before Benayake, the magistrate of

Batticaloa. The applicant filed for a maintenance allowance on the grounds that the respondent (her husband) did not provide her with one. The applicant was the second wife of the respondent. The judge noted that several witnesses present at the wedding (such as the headman of the village and the dhobi who performed certain rituals at the ceremony) had testified that the marriage between the applicant and the respondent had been celebrated, that the customary rites had been performed, but not the thali ceremony. Justice Benayake declared that this fact alone could not rebut the presumption of a valid marriage.

> In the instant case there is no expert evidence either way, nor is there
> any evidence that according to the custom of the community of Hindus
> to which the appellant and the respondent belong the thali ceremony is a
> sine qua non of a valid marriage. . . . It appears from Mutukrishna's The-
> sawalamai that, even in Jaffna, the tying of the thali is not a custom com-
> mon to all Hindu communities and that there are certain communities
> at whose marriage ceremonies the thali is not tied. . . . *It is evident from*
> *the parties going through the form of marriage that they intended to be*
> *married*; and if they were not married according to the strict custom,
> it was not in consequence of their wish that it should be so. (50 NLR135
> [1948], emphasis added)

In this case the marriage was considered valid not only because all the important ceremonies had been observed but also because certain ceremonies had been performed in public. This was sufficient to demonstrate an *intention* to marry, which led the court to presume that the marriage had complied with all the essential customs of the community to which the contracting couple belonged. The colonial court did not follow the strict rules of customary practices in Tamil marriages. For the court, the different customary marriage practices served to ascertain the intention of the parties to contract a marriage. By stating that even if the couple "were not married according to the strict custom," it does not change the fact that "they intended to be married." The colonial judge, thus, argued that the court did not require *all* the customary marriage ceremonies to have been carried out in order for a marriage to be considered legally valid; rather, the performance of *some* marriage customs was sufficient evidence of the intention to marry.

That some ceremonies were enough to determine the couple's intention to marry was also mentioned in the *King v. Perumal* (14 NLR 496 [1911]) case, which maintained that performing certain ceremonies gave a public face and cultural meaning to the intention of two individuals to marry. However, the colonial courts took into consideration that the customary marriage rituals differed along caste and regional lines. This case makes clear that for the court, intention was associated with the performance of marriage rituals in which the community took part. It is given validity through social acceptance and social participation in the marriage ceremonies in public spaces. Therefore, the customary marriage rituals provided a language for the courts to interpret the intention behind a marriage in legal terms. In other words, the colonial state was able to overcome the ambiguity of customary marriage rituals by redirecting the question of marriage validity from "proper customary rituals" to the legal language of intention. Thus, it was accepted that intention could be demonstrated through varied forms of performing the customary rituals, which were not necessarily based on specific compulsory ritual rights.

As long as the ritual rights showed a degree of public performance and public presence, it was sufficient for the colonial judge to deem the marriage valid. But the contestation of intention within its legal framework at the site of colonial courtrooms also brought all kinds of possibilities for creating, legalizing, and crystalizing certain marriage customs on the one hand, and all kinds of possibilities for reinterpreting and playing with local marriage practices for the local people on the other. In its rulings on tradition and culture, the court became the site of contention, creation, playfulness, governance, and invention.

In 1947, Ratnamma filed a case against Rasiah in Jaffna at the magistrate's court before Judge Dias. The applicant was claiming a maintenance allowance from her husband. The respondent argued that their marriage had not taken place according to Hindu customs, as he had merely tied a piece of turmeric in place of the gold thali. In this instance, the question before the court was whether the tying of the thali was an essential feature of a Hindu customary marriage, and therefore whether the tying of a piece of turmeric in place of a thali (which could not be used in this instance for astrological reasons) could constitute a valid customary marriage. In his ruling Dias argued that the marriage took place in public, before guests in a temple. And the priest performed all the required rituals except that of the tying of a gold thali because of the belief that the gold thali would harm the groom (the turmeric thali was used symbolically in its place). On the issue of tying a symbolic thali the judge wrote, "I think, a symbolic thali— provided it was intended to be used as such and in fact was so used—may serve as a thali. *It is the spirit and the intention behind the act which matter. It is clear that after this ceremony the parties believed they were lawfully married and lived together as man and wife and were received by their relatives and friends as husband and wife"* (*Ratnamma v. Rasiah*, 48 NLR 487 [1947], emphasis added).

The judge's conclusion was that the marriage was valid because of the intention behind the ritual. The parties to the marriage contract must perform at least some of the required ceremonies in the presence of witnesses (i.e., relatives, friends, and headmen) to show their true intention. Therefore, the intention to marry cannot simply be articulated between the two parties—it must be publicly displayed through the observance of marriage customs. However, the public display of marriage ceremonies as a tool for reading the couple's intention also opens up the space for colonial subjects to contest the marriage process because of the omission of certain customary practices. For them the issue was not only that those omissions were important to show their intention regarding the marriage; such cases provided a site for them to show that their intentions could be multiple and that marriage ceremony practices were not homogenous. In other words, the courts served as a space to articulate their identities, differences, and heterogeneity, thereby revealing the difficulties of locating intention in fixed homogenous assumption of cultural idioms and practices.

THE HETEROGENEITY AND VALIDITY OF TAMIL CUSTOMARY MARRIAGES BETWEEN DIFFERENT CASTES

The study of Jaffna Tamil kinship and marriage systems has shown cross-cousin marriage patterns, but rituals have not been examined along the various caste lines.[10] Several court cases from the nineteenth and twentieth centuries illustrate the various ways marriage rituals were performed among the Tamils of Jaffna, and elucidate how customary marriage practices vary both from caste to caste and even within a single caste.

The case of *Cadergamer Welayden v. Maylie et al.* (1820, no. 1,118) (Mutukisna, Atherton, and Isaakzoon 1862, 188–90) illustrates how different marriage customs were practiced within a single caste. Cadergamer Welayden, the plaintiff, brought the case before the magistrate's court of Jaffna concerning the validity of his second marriage. He married the first defendant, Maylie, the sister of his first wife after her death, and demanded that she return to him and pay him damages. He claimed his wife, Maylie, had been asked by family members to chase him from their house, which he had received as dowry. Therefore, the validity of the marriage was under question, and subsequently the plaintiff's rights over the dowry property. Maylie claimed she was not married to Cadergamer but to another defendant since no marriage rituals had been performed, such as the thali ritual. Cadergamer countered her argument by claiming, "We are *Vellalars*, we are five hundred families who never tie *thalis*, or get Brahmins to attend."

Thus, he claimed, the marriage was valid, even though the thali was not tied. The court confirmed the marriage as valid, but the appeals court reversed the decision. In this case, the judge called the village chief to submit a report regarding the marriage customs of the vellalars of that district. The report of the headman of this district showed that there were three types of marriage ceremonies for those of the vellalar caste.

> First—the priest is called upon who performs the ceremony by kindling a fire commonly called Omesendy, as also another ceremony Pullear Paegah, in the midst of that ceremony, a necklace called Salu [thali] is tied to the neck of the bride and a piece of cloth is given to her, and the fire so kindled serves as a token of testimony, and these ceremonies are performed in the presence of the relations and barber and washerman, which constitutes a legal marriage. Second—the priest is called upon to perform the ceremony, called Pollayar Paegah, the Salu is tied to the neck of the bride and a piece of cloth is given to her, the relations together with the washerman and barber attend. Third—without the attendance of the priest the relations the washerman and barber attend and cloth is given to the bride.

This report was signed by two mudhaliars, a title which indicates that they belonged to the district's privileged caste.

In this case the colonial courts could not even pin down the exact characteristics of a vellalar-caste marriage ceremony. The magistrate's court held that this was a valid marriage according to the local customs, while the appeals court decided against it. The judge's move to call for information from local experts revealed that there were three equally valid ways a marriage could be solemnized in the community. The colonial regime recognized this fluidity and flexibility in the solemnization of Tamil marriages. Thus, the process of institutionalizing and legalizing this heterogeneity opened up debates in the courts on customary practices. The ambiguity surrounding the different customary marriages among Tamils made it difficult for the British colonial rulers to crystallize and institutionalize Tamil practices.

Even though the process of institutionalizing customary marriage practices had been put in place by the colonial state, in practice the colonial state exercised flexibility in order to accommodate the complex processes and practices of customs along various caste and regional lines.

The case of *Menachy Sidambie v. Perial Parmen* (1820, no. 1,1164) (Mutukisna, Atherton, and Isaakzoon 1862, 187) deals with the nallavar caste's marriage ceremonies. Perial Parmen, the defendant, denied being married to the plaintiff, Menachy Sidambie, and wished to enter another marriage. The judge had to examine whether the customary marriage rituals specific to this slave caste[11] had been performed to decide on the union's validity. To this end, the judge asked for witnesses to be produced to testify regarding the customary rituals. Arresenayaga Modliar and Tamoderan Cheety, acting as witnesses, stated, "I know the parties are husband and wife. There are three round huts in the plaintiff's father's house, in one of which they live together. Slaves do not marry in other fashions, only the owner of the female slave calls the male, who presents a piece of cloth to the female, they then cook together and live as man and wife."

Another witness, Tellanayaga Aromogam Chetty, affirmed, "About two or three years ago, the defendant wanted me to accompany him as he wanted to marry the plaintiff. . . . I accompanied the defendant and his brother-in-law to the house where the plaintiff lived. . . . On reaching the house, the defendant presented her with a piece of cloth which she accepted, they then boiled rice and ate together and the defendant took the plaintiff home to his father's house, accompanied by his brother-in-law." The court held that the marriage was valid and therefore the defendant could not enter into a new marriage.

This case shows that different customary marriage practices were observed among different Jaffna Tamil castes, and that colonial judges determined the validity of marriages according to the customs of each caste. Furthermore, this case reveals that the witnesses to the marriage, accepted by the court, were members of the privileged caste, even though the marriage was between two marginalized-caste individuals. Through their intervention in the courts, members of the privileged-caste Jaffna Tamil communities sought to maintain the differences in the marriage ceremonies as practiced by the different castes (Tambiah 2004). Thus, by trying to institutionalize customary marriages, the colonial courts joined hands with the privileged caste of Jaffna Tamils to maintain, re-create, and reinforce hierarchical authority along the caste lines among the Jaffna Tamils.

The proceedings of the case *Nagy v. Casy* (1820, no. 1,103) (Mutukisna, Atherton, and Isaakzoon 1862, 191–93) provide a view of the marriage ceremony of a service caste to the vellalars, the koviyars. Nagy, the plaintiff, filed a case against her husband, Silmemby Casy, to recover her dowry property. Two questions were considered: (1) the validity of the marriage according to the koviyar-caste rituals, and (2) the provision of a dowry during the wedding ceremony. The barber and the washerman were called to testify on the observance of koviyar marriage practices, which they acknowledged. The judge, referring to their testimonies, wrote, that the bridegroom, "dressed in gold earrings," was accompanied by his relations and friends to the bride's place "where the *dowary ola* [dowry deed] was executed" and rice was served by the bride to the bridegroom. He further noted that a ceremony was performed in front of a pillaiyar made out of cow dung.

The court held that it was a valid marriage, as the customary practices of the koviyar caste had been observed.[12] In this case, although the thali-tying ritual and the brahmanical rituals were not considered part of the marriage customs of the koviyar caste, the presentation of or exchange of *olai* (dowry deed) was deemed a vital part of the ceremony. In many cases, the exchange of dowry played an important role in the legal recognition of the marriage's validity. Even among the vellalar caste, the exchange of the olai was considered a key feature in the solemnization of a union (cf. *Canneger v. Mooder Mootan* [1822, no. 2,129)] [Mutukisna, Atherton, and Isaak-zoon 1862, 194]; *Sinnatangam v. Wettywalen* (1860, no. 173) [Mutukisna, Atherton, and Isaakzoon 1862, 185]). Here the materiality and monetary value in the form of dowry documents and their exchange between the marrying couple are seen as a tangible expression of intention to marry, and the whole act of presenting the dowry olai before the public brings back the notion of the marriage being conducted in a public place.

Customs such as tying a thali, giving the kurai, handing over the dowry olai, the presence of a barber and washerman and their involvement in the marriage ceremony, and even the presence of Brahmin priests, were all considered specific to the privileged-caste rituals. Even within the privileged caste, however, ceremonies would vary, which led to different forms being contested in court. Marginalized-caste marriage ceremonies were associated with cooking and serving rice by the bride, a *pillaiyar pooja* (worshipping the god Pillaiyar), the giving of a piece of cloth by the groom to the bride, and the presence of relatives (Tambiah 2004). This hierarchical social structure prevalent in the Jaffna Tamil society was revealed through the questions that arose in the colonial courts with regard to marriage ceremonies. The deliberations that followed paved the way for the legal institutionalization of different marriage ceremonies for different castes.

A particular difficulty in validating marriages was the wide range of regional difference, in addition to the heterogeneity of marriage ceremonies along the different caste lines or within the same caste (as explored above). This complex situation meant that, while at the legislative level attempts were made to standardize what constituted a marriage, at the level of adjudication great effort had to be made to balance the differences that arose based on region and caste. Thus, the colonial rulers were faced with the conundrum of how to rely on the specificity of caste and region to determine what was essential for a marriage to be considered valid. It is also interesting to observe how the privileged-caste men (who were called on to give accounts of the different types of customary marriage ceremonies) had a stake in maintaining the heterogeneity of the Tamil marriage ceremonies as a sign of their own hierarchical superiority in the community. Courtrooms became a space for the privileged caste to reinforce the social hierarchy through legal institutions. While many of the colonial authorities would have worked to standardize their practices for the sake of simplicity, the process of adjudication shows an interesting rift between those who established the laws and those responsible for implementing them in context.

SOCIAL ACCEPTANCE, MARRIAGE, AND COLONIAL COURTS

The cases discussed above show that, for a marriage to be recognized as valid, it required public presence, performance, and witnessing of customs as forms of measuring the intention to marry. The courts also interpreted the intention to marry in the performance of certain customary practices in which parents, relatives, and the wider community took part and acted as witnesses. This section analyzes two cases that illustrate how the colonial state linked the idea of social acceptance of a marriage, symbolized by the involvement of the family or community in the customary practices of the Tamils, as the measurement of the intention to marry which formed the basis for a marriage's legality.

In the case of *Carderan Comeran v. Mayly* (1820, no. 1,118) (Mutukisna, Atherton, and Isaakzoon 1862, 188–90),[13] Judge Moyaart made an important judgment about the validity of the contested marriage: "As there appears to be no rules established by law, to render marriage legal, and

different methods are pursued in solemnizing marriages ... the solemnization thereof, by certain rites, is proved, the Plaintiff's residence in the
Defendant's house, the report in the village, and the Plaintiff's cultivation of
his wife's Dowry Lands, are collateral evidences that the parties were legally
married." This constituted a landmark judgment, as the colonial judge
accorded greater weight to the verbal promises exchanged between the
couple, their cohabitation, the villagers' acceptance of them as married, and
the husband's cultivating of the dowry land, in determining the validity of
the marriage, than to any ceremonies performed. In other words, in legal
terms, the validity of a marriage was recognized based on material and visible evidence of intention.

Social acceptance of a marriage was established in the colonial court
cases in two ways: (1) through the marriage ceremonies, where relatives and
friends took part and accepted the union, and (2) through the provision of
a dowry as a material gift of land, house, or money (mostly for the privileged
caste). The giving of a dowry and/or the husband's cultivation of the dowry
land is another form of social acceptance made possible through material
items—that is, the transfer of the dowry property witnessed by those who
participated in the marriage ceremonies. They did not only witness the
transaction but also recognized the transfer as a part of a customary marriage. The husband lived in his dowry house with his wife, and the community recognized that. Thus, the colonial court interpreted the dowry
transaction and the husband living in the dowry house as evidence that the
marriage was recognized and accepted by the community to which the
couple belonged.

The key issue for the colonial courts in deciding on the validity of a
customary marriage, as mentioned above, was not whether all the customary marriage rituals had been performed, but whether the rituals that had
been performed were sufficient to demonstrate the intention to marry. The
colonial court believed that the public observance of some of the customary marriage practices, with the family and other individuals from the
community participating, was a sign that the marriage was accepted and
recognized by the group. Social acceptance is grounded in the act of the
community and family accepting a marriage by taking part in the customary rituals. Here, the public includes the relatives, family members (who
take part in the marriage rituals), and members of the wider community
who accept the marriage and thereby create a public authority over matri-
mony. The act of social acceptance by the family or community of a marriage is appropriated and articulated by the colonial state through the legal

medium of intention. In other words, the colonial state, drawing its authority from the family and community, reframed its laws (Das and Poole 2004b) to govern its colonial subjects in the absence of civil marriage or state documents. The colonial state thus emerged in colonial places by governing via "the formation of public authority through the language and performance of 'the law' and the creation of public domains" (Hansen and Stepputat 2005a, 20). Reading the customary marriage as public performance, and social acceptance of the marriage through the language of law and practices of colonial courtrooms, was a way for the colonial state to establish itself in Sri Lanka.

The case of *Selvaratnam et al. v. Anandavelu* (42 NLR 486 [1941]) clearly demonstrates how the colonial courts considered a marriage legal based on the criterion of social acceptance. The applicant (Selvaratnam) opposed the marriage between the first respondent (Anandavelu) and the third respondent (Rasaratnam), alleging that Anandavelu had already married her according to Hindu rites and ceremonies. The first respondent argued in the court that that customary marriage was not legal because the number of marriage ceremonies performed was not sufficient to form a valid marriage. He argued, "There was no kurukal [priest] present, no dhobi, no tying of thali; marriage is a social event, *requires a certain degree of publicity*, especially in the case of customary marriage. . . . The father of the bridegroom was not present. *The presence of a close relative is essential in a customary marriage of even the poorest*" (emphasis added).

It was also challenged on the basis that the father of the groom, Ramasamy, had not consented to his son's marriage. The son was only nineteen and therefore a minor at the time of ceremony. Since the father had not given his consent to the marriage, it was not a binding contract between the parties. Judge De Kretser, in his verdict, stated that there was no evidence that a thali was tied at the marriage ceremony. Moreover, a priest had not been present, nor had a washerman or barber taken part in the rituals: "Under the Hindu system, the marriage was arranged by the parents . . . *one of the inevitable concomitants of the ceremonial being the presence of the relatives and friends of the two contracting parties.* They took the vital interest in the marriage and, as article 12 of the *Thesawalamai* indicates, they took the place of deceased parents in seeing that the marriage was a suitable one, that suitable provision was made and that the ceremonies were properly carried out" (emphasis added).

To assess the validity of a customary marriage, the judge evoked the rules of Hindu traditional marriages and pointed out that among Tamils the marriage is arranged by the parents and the ceremonies are performed in the presence of relatives and friends. In other words, when the judge decided that "the ceremonies were not properly carried out," it means that the relatives had not taken part in the ceremonies and performed their specific roles. Second, on the question of the consent of the father to the marriage, the judge had a view that, according to the ordinance, as the defendant was under the age of twenty-one, consent from the father had to be obtained. Given the provisions of Roman–Dutch law, English law, and those of the general marriage ordinance, the judge took the view that in such customary marriages, if the prior consent of the father was not obtained, the marriage was null and void. The court, however, held that the marriage was not legal on the basis that most of the Hindu marriage ceremonies were not performed, rather than because of the missing parental consent (Tambiah 2004). It seems that because the community could not authorize the marriage, the judge then could not draw his legal authority from the community or family to assign legal validity to the marriage itself.

When the colonial courts could not rely on their practices of state regulation of a civil marriage (i.e., a marriage in a public setting, conducted by a state official, producing state documents), the colonial courts relied on the authority of the community. The legal reading of the intention to marry by the colonial courts was measured through the community's authority to accept or reject the marriage process. As discussed in prior chapter, the marriage process always holds both certainty and uncertainty, but the colonial courts and judges, by focusing on the couple's intention to marry in disputed cases, tried to capture the certainty of marriage and legally transfigure the relatedness. The complexity of measuring the certainty of intention within a process that holds both uncertainty and certainty seems to rely on others' participation in the intention of the individuals, its expression through local practices, human actions, and intra-subjective performance (Duranti 2015) read and sanctioned by the community, family, and colonial courts together. Colonial courtrooms became in-between spaces for couples to validate their marriage and transform the inherent uncertainty of human intention into certainty. In these in-between spaces, during the revisiting of the marriage process, a number of assemblages between judges, parties, lawyers, witnesses, documents, and court files come together to enable the legal transfiguration of relatedness. During colonial times, the marriage process ended after the marriage took place (unlike the transnational marriage) and opened again only over disputes within courtroom spaces, bringing out its potential of being both certain and uncertain.

By introducing the registration of marriage and marriage laws, the colonial state attempted to regulate and homogenize unions among the colonial subjects of Sri Lanka. However, failure to implement registration of marriages during the colonial period led the colonial state to incorporate customary practices as a way of validating marriage in the absence of registration. Thus, in its absence, the courts had to recognize customary marriage ceremonies as an alternate way of legalizing a union. However, in the process of legalizing customary marriages, the colonial state had to deal with the ambiguity surrounding customs and the tensions that arose between the legal interpretation of marriage and customary marriage rituals. In dealing with several customary marriage practices, the colonial state showed flexibility, within the space of the courtrooms, with the heterogeneity of marriage customs, and incorporated the social hierarchy of Tamils.

The tension between colonial law and local practices of validating a union paved the way to finding or redefining a new legal language of marriage validation based on the idea of intention, which was then legally measured and read through the notion of witness, public performance of ceremonies, and social acceptance. The legal lens of intention introduced by the colonial court to simplify and homogenize customary ceremonies was complicated by the potentiality of intentions that had both actualized and not actualized. Courtrooms became a space where each case had the potential of different outcomes based on different practices of customary marriage and different legal readings of intention. Even though the colonial courts tried to capture, define, and pinpoint customary marriage practices and the certainty of the couple's intention, this always eluded them. The potentiality of the couple's intention can be read in many ways, so that the marriage process holds both actualized and not actualized intentions and outcomes.

Intention remains a field for legal battle within the courtrooms around which the local marriage practices, legal languages, people, and court files come to associate over customary marriages. The complexity of measuring intention in the marriage process not only brings different associations between the authorities of communities and courts to determine this with certainty, but also in the process led to legalizing and institutionalizing customary marriages and social hierarchy among the Tamils in Jaffna. The different assemblages of practices, witnesses, colonial judges, and lawyers brought out, captured, and re-created different practices of the customary marriages and associations of different authorities (from communities to colonial laws) and resulted in various outcomes. However, these cases became the carriers of customs, traditions, and practices for future cases covering similar issues. They may or may not produce the same result, as the re-association of these court files, authorities, and people in another context will bring a different set of outcomes based on new knowledge, practices, and assemblages.

In cases where evidence of marriage is required by the visa officers, ideas similar to those of the colonial state surface with regard to the role played by marriage ceremonies in immigration law. The public acceptance of a marriage, as marked by the observance of specific marriage ceremonies, and the intention to marry surface as the evidence required for a genuine marriage in both the colonial laws of Sri Lanka and the immigration laws of Canada.

5 Reviewing "Genuine" Marriages in Spousal Migration

THE TRANSNATIONAL MARRIAGE PROCESS DOES NOT END AFTER the ceremony has taken place; rather, it continues until the married couple reunites in their adoptive country (in the case of this study, Canada). Refusal of a spousal visa leads to a legal battle in the immigration court to prove the marriage genuine and request that the couple be reunited in the West. Immigration officers look for evidence to gauge whether a marriage is simply one of convenience. Clues in this regard are the observance of customary marriage practices, civil marriage documents, evidence of an ongoing relationship between the couple after marriage, and other monetary and documentary evidence. The importance given to customary marriage practices in ascertaining the genuineness of a marriage involves criteria similar to that seen in the colonial courtrooms of Sri Lanka. However, in the case of the Canadian immigration laws and regulations, it is only one part of a wide array of evidence.

The couple's intention to stay together permanently after marriage is, in Canada, a key factor in assessing the union's genuineness. This intention is cross-checked against the level of intimacy shown between the couple, their knowledge of each other, and evidence of continuous communication between them before and after marriage (through documents such as personal letters, telephone bills, greeting cards, and wedding photos). In other words, the notion of *genuineness* seems to be placed between the authority of the couple's community or family and the decision of the two individuals who are the parties to the marriage contract. Unlike in the colonial court, where the validity of the marriage is placed within the notion of the ambiguity of customs, here the marriage's genuineness is placed within the specifics of the relationship. Yet, in order to grant or withhold a spousal visa, the Canadian immigration officers and judges pose questions that are similar to and in the idiom of the legal language of intention used in the colonial court in Sri Lanka to test the genuineness of a marriage.

Despite the background of a modern state, the key issue is not whether the marriage had been performed in accordance with civil marriage regulations, but whether a customary marriage had also been performed and what the nature of the relationship was between the couple before and after the ceremony. Why is it that, for the modern Canadian state, factors such as customary marriage practices and the couple's intention to stay together play such a crucial role in deciding the genuineness of a union even after the civil marriage contract has been produced? And what other documents and practices, along with customary marriage ceremonies, are used within the courts to prove the marriage is genuine?

The modern era of globalization and capital flow leads to forms of "flexible citizenship" (Ong 1999), resulting in greater mobility and skilled labor migration. However, border protection and restriction on migration by immigration regimes have become more rigid in the current Western world (Hansen and Stepputat 2005a). In his study of the processing of Sri Lankan asylum applications and migration cases by Norwegian immigration officers, Øivind Fuglerud argues convincingly that "one needs to see how state officials perceive themselves to understand the state practices and immigration regimes." Immigration officers in this globalization process perceive themselves as protectors of their state sovereignty and, thus, "look upon the law as an instrument in trying to recover a basis for government that is about to be lost" (2005, 299). Furthermore, they see themselves as officers who trace irregularities and decide based on their personal knowledge of the "people's background, their migration patterns, their characteristic manner of fraud and deception, and so on" (307) rather than based on legal knowledge and criteria.

In the Canadian immigration case, as we have seen in the chapter 3 discussion of wedding photos, to validate a marriage as genuine, the visa officers look at other forms of knowledge, such as interviews, photographs, and other personal documents, rather than the civil marriage contract. Indirectly, the visa officers try to pinpoint the intention of the married couple, namely, whether the marriage was contracted for the sole purpose of entering Canada or to be together and establish a family in Canada. The intention is read in terms of whether the couple is lying about the marriage arrangements or their plans, their effort to conduct ceremonies, and if they are serious in getting to know and support each other. To protect their state borders and to reduce the possible future burden on the welfare state from incoming migrants from other countries, Canadian officers in marriage immigration cases use multiple forms of knowledge regarding applicants and their communities to assess the real intention of married couples.

The bureaucratic and administrative practices of the immigration officers and the state (both the current state for the citizen and the future state for the marriage migration applicant) come to be experienced in everyday life (Ferguson and Gupta 2002; Gupta 2012). The state manages and controls its own population through technologies of power,[1] and people experience the state in their daily lives through its documenting practices.[2] However, those experiences are constituted not only through the legibility of the state's writing and documentary practices but also through the illegibility of those same practices (Das and Poole 2004a). In the case of the migration practices, the presence of the state is experienced differently by the "foreign insider" and the "foreign outsider" (i.e., the naturalized citizen and permanent resident versus applicant for migration): while the insider is subject to "ordinary mechanisms of the modern state structure" and disciplined by that state, the migrant applicant is treated as "nonperson caught in transit between different spheres of jurisdiction, he is subject to the old merum imperium, the ruler's absolute power over life and death" (Fuglerud 2005, 310–11). Thus, the investigation of asylum cases and the granting of visas is not just "a judicial but a political process" of the state (311). In the Canadian case, the visa officers' assessment of the spousal migration applicant cases based on the couples' "real" intentions can be seen as a political process through which the Canadian state enters into the life of both spouses.

But the measuring and reading of intention, the difficulty of pinning down with certainty a human action legally, the circulation of documents (Hull 2012b) and their associations with other documents and humans in the immigration offices, along with the illegibility of state documents and practices, create the possibility for applicants and their spouses in Canada to dispute their rejection in federal court. Through the different associations of documents, judicial processes, and knowledge around the measuring of intention through legal language, the genuineness of a marriage in court has the potential to be actualized differently. The state experienced through administrative practices, official documents, and immigration officers may be quite different from the one encountered through courtrooms, judges, and court files. The process of immigration applications, their travel through different state spaces, and their association in these spaces (from immigration offices to courtrooms) constantly open up spaces for applicants and their spouses in Canada to prove, challenge, and contest the immigration officers' decisions.

The process of reuniting with the spouse as part of the marriage process goes through different state spaces and produces varying results, and thus carries both certainty and uncertainty. The process of reuniting through different legal bodies of the state constantly transfigures and re-transfigures relatedness in legal terms. The state here is not perceived as a monotheistic entity, but as one with different arms, ranging from immigration offices to courtrooms. Given the state's illegibility in its own documents, along with varying practices of its various arms and the constant shifting in law making, immigrant applicants are able to find moments of possibility to contest, navigate, and resist the state controlling their destinies. However, regardless of whether the court finally allows the couple to reunite, the process itself holds both certainty and uncertainty for the future, anxieties and hopes for the applicants and their spouses in Canada. The refusal of the spousal visa protracts the marriage process for years after the ceremony. The following court cases on appeal may yield mostly favorable decisions to the couples, but the process and the time it took always carried the uncertainty of the marriage and their future relationship. During the process of the court cases, the couples constantly struggle to make their intention recognized by the state while imagining a certain future together after their wedding.

VISA APPLICATIONS, APPEALS AFTER VISA REJECTION, AND PROCEDURES

The foreign spouse of a Canadian citizen or permanent resident in Canada must apply for an immigration visa to reunite with their spouse at the Canadian embassy in their home country or country of residence. The application is processed by the immigration officer at the embassy of that particular country. If the spousal visa application is rejected, the sponsor has an option to execute his right for appeal against the immigration officer's decision within thirty days. The appeal is made at the Immigration Appeal Division (IAD) of the Immigration and Refugee Board of Canada (IRB).[3]

The IAD has been set up by the Canadian government to enable Canadian citizens or permanent residents to file appeals against immigration officers' decisions and procedures in case of an error in the decision, which include spousal sponsorships that fall under the "family" category (Carasco et al. 2007). The IAD reviews the request and the documentary proof and decides whether the matter can be handled in writing or requires an oral hearing, where the sponsor can present their case. If the IAD decides to overrule the immigration officer's decision, it will ask the visa official to provide the applicant their spousal visa. If the IAD rejects the appeal or refuses to overrule the immigration officer's decision, then the sponsor can appeal the decision before the High Court of Canada. However, this can take place only after the High Court decides whether it will allow the case to be brought before it. Once the approval is given, the case is filed at the court. These procedures may take months or years (Carasco et al. 2007).

Here, the categories of foreign outsider and insider become blurred because the sponsor, who is the insider, must file the appeal in the case of the spousal visa being refused. The state does not deal directly anymore with the foreign outsider, that is, the spouse applicant (Fuglerud 2005), but with its own citizen/resident, making it a judicial process. The applicant's spouse as foreign insider, who challenges the decision of the immigration officer, passes certain rights to their spouse, who is an outsider. In the case of transnational marriage, the categories of outsider and insider foreigner are so entangled that the state's migration-related practices become illegible to the state itself.

LAWYERS, PARALEGALS, AND CLIENTS

There are many Sri Lankan Tamil paralegal agents running offices in Canada, who will, for a sum of money, work with lawyers to prepare cases and appeals disputing spousal visa rejections and other decisions by immigration officers. These paralegal agents are Sri Lankan Tamils who specialize in immigration cases, and operate as middlemen between Sri Lankan Tamil clients and their English-speaking lawyers in Canada. The client ends up paying a sum of between C$2,000 and C$4,000 to the paralegal agent and the lawyer for presenting their case to the IAD or before the High Court of Canada. Most of the paralegal agents came to Canada as refugees/migrants from Sri Lanka in the 1980s and 1990s. Furthermore, some of them have studied law or practiced as lawyers in Sri Lanka. This gives them added knowledge regarding legal practices in Canada and enables them to better understand the technical issues of Canadian law. However, since they cannot practice as lawyers in Canada without successfully completing the bar exam, they choose to serve as intermediaries between the English-speaking Canadian lawyers and their Sri Lankan Tamil clients. The lawyers are also keen to retain the paralegal agents as their middlemen because they attract the business of Sri Lankan Tamil clients. Since many of the Sri Lankan Tamil refugees do not speak or write English fluently, they prefer to contact the paralegal agents—who come from their community and speak their language—rather than go directly to the English-speaking lawyers. Most of the cases that come to these paralegal agents and the lawyers they work for concern claims for refugee status and visa rejections.

The paralegal agents run their own offices, either in a commercial building or in their homes. The paralegal agents' clients told me that Sri Lankan Tamils preferred to convey their stories to a Tamil paralegal agent rather than having to discuss matters in English with a "Western" lawyer. Today, the situation has changed somewhat, since there are now a number of Sri Lankan Tamil lawyers in Canada who can appear in court to represent their clients' cases directly. There are several paralegal agents in Toronto whose names are well-known within the Sri Lankan Tamil communities there because of their success in winning cases on refugee claims and spousal visa refusals.

When a client consults with a paralegal agent regarding an immigration officer's refusal of a spousal visa, the paralegal agent questions the client in great detail about the marriage—for example, details regarding the history of the marriage, when the visa application was filed, and what questions the immigration officer had asked the spouse during the interview. The agent then examines the refusal letter. After more conversation, they explain to the client the grounds on which the spouse was refused a visa. Most of the filing work for the cases, the collecting of the supporting documents, and the preparing of the clients is handled by the paralegal agent.

Once a paralegal agent and his lawyer accept a case of spousal visa refusal, the lawyer writes to the IAD on behalf of the client, intimating that they wish to appeal the visa officer's decision. Once the appeal is filed at the IAD, the IAD officers inform the immigration officer involved, who then must submit—to the sponsor—copies of all documentary evidence concerning the spousal relationship they received from the applicant, including telephone bills, personal letters, greeting cards, and wedding photos; transcripts of interviews the visa officer had with the applicant; and the reasons for their decision to reject the application. Once the paralegal agent receives all the relevant documents they are sent to the lawyer, who studies the case and asks for further documentary evidence from the client, which is then used to argue against the visa officer's decision. The paralegal agent's technical knowledge on Sri Lankan Tamil marriages is a significant advantage to the lawyer in presenting the case to the IAD or before the court.

During one of my interviews with a paralegal agent, he mentioned that he had to compile documents pertaining to Sri Lankan Tamil marriage customs for one of his cases, which he proceeded to describe to me. A Sri Lankan Tamil marriage had taken place between cross-cousins. Since the client's spouse had been living in India as a Sri Lankan refugee, the marriage was held in India. When the bride applied to the Canadian High Commission in Delhi for a visa to join her spouse in Canada, the immigration officer rejected it. One of the reasons given was that cross-cousin marriage was not permitted in India, where the marriage ceremony was held. This case reveals some ambiguity in the Indian law, which states that marriage with certain degrees of consanguinity is prohibited; nonetheless, exceptions are made for cross-cousin unions, as it is the preferred form of marriage in many communities, including Tamils in South India. The paralegal agent was collecting documentary evidence that would prove it is a common practice among the Jaffna Tamils to marry their cross-cousins. He had attached to the appeal notice articles by several Tamil authors and scholars who have written on Tamil marriage and the customs of Tamil marriage. He had also asked a well-known Sri Lankan Tamil priest to sign an affidavit which explained that according to their customs Sri Lankan Tamils are permitted to marry cross-cousins.

Another service provided by the paralegal agent is that of preparing the client on how to answer the questions they may be asked by the judge, and what should be highlighted in their responses. The client is also briefed on how they must express anticipation about having their respective spouses joining them—the judge must be told how they have rented or bought a new house, along with new furniture and clothes, to set up a family in Toronto. In this, his function is similar to the in-between figure of the wedding photographer (see chapter 3). While the latter intervenes at the upstream level of the marriage process, when it is performed, the paralegal enters the scene at the downstream, when problems emerge as the spouses try to reunite. Moreover, the paralegal agent and the lawyer ask their client to bring more personal letters, greeting cards, and other documents as proof of a continuous relationship between the spouses. These documents are attached to the already-received copies of other documents sent to the visa officer, and all this is sent to the IAD with the appeal letter to reopen the case and prove the genuineness of the marriage.

CANADIAN IMMIGRATION LAW AND PROCEDURES REGARDING MARRIAGE AND SPONSORSHIP

Two Canadian legal texts—the Immigration and Refugee Protection Act (IRPA) and the Immigration and Refugee Protection Regulations (IRPR)—are important in establishing the rules pertaining to family reunification.[4]

Any Canadian citizen or permanent resident should be able to sponsor a foreign national under the "family class category," "on the basis of their relationship as the spouse, common law partner, child, parent, or other prescribed family member of a Canadian citizen or permanent resident" (IRPA 12[1]).[5] Moreover, the sponsor has to demonstrate that they can support the sponsored spouse without letting them become a burden to the public or the Canadian welfare fund (Carasco et al. 2007, 381). This chapter focuses only on the sponsorship of a spouse under the family class category. If the spouses of Canadian citizens and permanent residents want to reunite with their partners, they must apply for a spousal immigration visa at the Canadian embassy in their country of residence (Carasco et al. 2007, 371). The sponsorship applications' processing time varies across regions: from ten to fourteen months for Europe and Americas to twelve to seventeen months for Asia-Pacific, Africa, and the Middle East (Carasco et al. 2007, 372).[6] In order to obtain a spousal visa to Canada under the family class, the sponsor and the applicant must prove that they have contracted a valid marriage.[7]

First, IRPR validates the marriage between a foreign national and a Canadian citizen or permanent resident, based on whether the union is valid under Canadian law as well as the laws of the country where it took place, if outside Canada (IRPR 2; Carasco et al. 2007, 372). "The determination of the validity of a marriage is based on the legal capacity to marry (essential validity) and the technical aspects of the marriage ceremonies (formal validity)" (Carasco et al. 2007, 372). The country where the marriage is celebrated determines the rules for formal validity. Essential validity depends on matters such as the age of consent, the existence of prior marriages, and so forth (Carasco et al. 2007; IRPR 125[1]). There are several application forms to be filled out (e.g., primary application of the spouse, sponsor spouse information, family information, place records, health certificates, and the sponsor's financial evaluation form).

It is important to note that the marriage must be legally valid in both places. This brings out how the migration laws are interwoven with the laws of the particular country where the wedding was held. This intersection of laws opens up the possibility of looking at how the colonial past of legalizing Sri Lankan Tamil marriage traditions unfolds into the present, whereby the legalization of Sri Lankan Tamil marriages is based on the perceptions of the Canadian state. Second, since the marriage must also be valid under Canadian law, it is necessary to consider the Canadian state's values. Third, the marriage must be found to be genuine. In most cases the immigration officers or judges evoke IRPR 4(1), which states that the marriage is deemed invalid if it "was entered into primarily for the purpose of acquiring any status or privilege under the act" and "is not *genuine*."

Interestingly, the immigration regulations and laws do not define or characterize how the genuineness of a marriage is to be determined or measured legally. Therefore, it is left to the immigration officer to assess the genuineness of a union, which is often done by considering personal letters, telephone bills, wedding photographs, gifts, financial transactions, the spouses' personal knowledge of each other, the marriage certificate, or other forms of proof in the case of a common-law partner, in conjunction with a personal interview with the applicant at the embassy (Carasco et al. 2007). Thus, the interpretation of the marriage's genuineness is based on the visa officer's opinion, their personal knowledge of the community's marriage process, and the assemblages of documents provided as proof. Many of the official letters of refusal describe how the particular marriage is not genuine or how it was performed under questionable circumstances. Some applications have been rejected because the ceremony was not performed according to Sri Lankan Tamil marriage customs and immediate family members were not present, while others have failed due to a lack of "sufficient" knowledge of the spouse.

Furthermore, the visa is sometimes refused on the basis that the sponsor does not show adequate income to sponsor another person. IRPA 39 states that the sponsor's demand should be rejected if "they are or will be unable or unwilling to support themselves or any other person who is dependent on them"; they should make "adequate arrangements for care and support, other than those that involve social assistance." Therefore, if a sponsor does not have a viable job or other source of income in Canada, they cannot sponsor a spouse. The immigration officer must ascertain whether the arrival of the spouse of a Canadian citizen or permanent resident will increase the burden on the welfare state.

MARRIAGE VALIDATION IN COLONIAL
VERSUS IMMIGRATION COURTS

In the absence of a civil marriage, the colonial court chose to acknowledge the various customary practices observed by Sri Lankan Tamil communities. However, in the Canadian immigration courts, officers decide whether a marriage is genuine based not only on the civil marriage contract but also on the notion of whether the marriage was performed according to the traditions of a particular ethnic group. What can be seen here is the reversal of a state act with regard to validating a marriage, in that the state has gone back to customary marriage forms as a way of validating a marriage or judging the genuineness of the union. Even though genuineness cannot be equated with validity in a legal sense, the manner in which the immigration officers and judges determine the validity of a marriage (such as looking for other, more personal evidence, in addition to proof of a civil marriage) mirrors the debates in the Sri Lankan colonial courtrooms regarding the validity of customary marriages. According to today's immigration regulations, if a visa is to be granted, the relationship between the spouses should be "genuine," and the marriage should not have been contracted solely to obtain a Canadian permanent residency visa: "The criterion that the relationship be genuine was expressed in terms of an *intention* to reside together permanently. Separating the authenticity of the relationship from the immigration motive implicitly acknowledges that people may have multiple reasons for entering into relationships" (Carasco et al. 2007, 390).

Once again, the weighing of the intentions of the relationship between two individuals plays a crucial role in deciding whether a marriage is genuine, and leads to difficult questions related to credibility for the married couple. The immigration court, the IAD, or the visa officer uses different criteria, knowledge, and documents to decide whether the marriage is valid, on a case-by-case basis:

Inconsistent or contradictory statements regarding matters such as the origin and development of the relationship between the parties, the applicant's history of previous attempts to gain entry into Canada, evidence of a previous marriage for immigration purposes, the parties' knowledge about each other, contact between the parties, family ties, exchange of gifts, and financial support are factors that have *been considered indicators of the existence of a genuine marriage and/or intention to reside with the sponsor.* Arranged marriages are not inherently less credible than the so-called love matches characteristic in Western culture. However lack of a prior acquaintance of the parties poses evident challenges, and decision-makers often attempt to *assess the relationship against customary practices and norms regarding arranged marriages in the community of origin.* (Carasco et al. 2007, 390–91, emphasis added)

Immigration regulations are interpreted by the officers or judges to understand the genuineness of the marriage, measured in terms of the intention of the parties to the relationship. Intention here is enounced in terms of the couple's intention to live together, permanently, as husband and wife or conjugal partners. A similar notion of intention was used to validate customary marriage in the colonial courtrooms. In other words, according to the colonial judges, the carrying out of marriage ceremonies, and community acceptance of that process, is a demonstration of the intention to marry. Therefore, the intention to marry cannot simply be articulated or measured by any single individual's actions: it must be measured through the public display of the marriage ceremonies.

However, in the Canadian context, the intention behind a marriage must be demonstrated not only through validation at the time of the marriage celebration, but also through the establishment of intention about the future as well—that is, the intention to live together permanently in Canada. The future intention is measured and read through the past and present of human action. In other words, yet to be actualized intention must be measured in the actualized and not actualized actions of the married couples and their communities. The Canadian state not only decides the future of the couple, their relationship, and their relatedness in the future, but also judges their future intention of being together. The state does not manage and control the future actions of the couple, but rather imagines the couple's intentions and the future of their relationship. Moreover, the burden of demonstrating intention is placed on the two individuals and their present and past actions, so that the nature of their relationship is subjected to close scrutiny. Thus, aspects such as communications between the two individuals, exchange of gifts and letters, knowledge of each other, and the level of intimacy, are analyzed carefully.

This means that intention is based not simply on the contract at the moment of celebration of the marriage, but must include a commitment to a stable marriage, which brings to mind the Canadian requirement that the marriage comply with both the rules of the place where it is celebrated as well as those of Canada. Hence, the double requirement of intention as social acceptance and intention to stay married should be analyzed as complying to this rule, since the first, developed in the colonial courts, could be read as an expression of the cultural medium of non-Western subjects, and the second, read by the modern state, as an expression of "Western" love and individual choices and actions. The transnational marriage process and the process of validating a marriage based on the scrutiny of couples' intentions through notions of modern love and choices, not only transfigure the relatedness of the couple, but also transfigures the outsider, the other, the non-Western person, into the insider, the future citizen, the Western person.

INTENTION, GENUINENESS, AND
CUSTOMARY MARRIAGE PRACTICES

The following cases (all of which have been abstracted from court cases and decisions gathered from the Federal Court of Canada, the Justice Department, and the Immigration and Refugee Board of Canada)[8] were filed against the immigration officer's refusal to grant a visa to the spouse of a Canadian national or resident. They demonstrate how the genuineness of a marriage is cross-checked against the relationship between the spouses before and after the marriage. The first case shows the importance of customary marriage rituals, which highlights social acceptance over a legal civil marriage contract in measuring the intention of the married couple.

CASE 1: OCTOBER 10, 2001, MA0-02685, IMMIGRATION
AND REFUGEES BOARD (IMMIGRATION APPEAL DIVISION)

Kovalan, a Sri Lankan citizen, filed a sponsored application to reunite with his wife, Sathiya, a Canadian resident. However, the immigration officer at the Canadian High Commission in Colombo decided that the applicant was inadmissible according to IRPR 4(3) ("which excludes from the family class the applicant who entered into the marriage primarily for the purpose of gaining admission to Canada and not with the intention of residing permanently with the other spouse"). The refusal letter states that the applicant's knowledge of his spouse was superficial, especially given that they were cousins. The visa officer's view was that it was "inconsistent with a genuine spousal relationship." According to the refusal letter, the applicant could specify neither his wife's job nor where she lived in Canada. In addition, despite claiming that the marriage was celebrated with a large number of guests, he could not prove it by providing "any photographs of the occasion."

Sathiya filed against the decision at the IAD. The appellant and her mother both testified at the hearing. Sathiya told the board that she had only met her husband—a distant relative—a few times in the past, although they lived in the same village in Jaffna, and that the marriage was arranged by her family. Sathiya, in December 1998, registered a civil marriage with Kovalan in Sri Lanka. They decided to hold the religious ceremony in

Canada after he joined her there. Sathiya postponed the event for many reasons, including the war in Sri Lanka, their financial situation, and the inability of their relatives to attend the wedding during that time. However, after the spousal visa was rejected Sathiya traveled back to Sri Lanka and celebrated a religious marriage in the presence of four hundred guests. They also had a child after a year of marriage. Sathiya claimed that she needed to reunite with her husband to form a family and raise their young son together.

After hearing the case, maître Taya di Pietro acknowledged that there was indeed some inconsistency in the provided evidence. For instance, the appellant stated in her written declaration that they had agreed to tie the thali in Canada after she had sponsored him there. However, in a letter written to her by her husband after the civil marriage, he referred to her proposing to buy a thali in Singapore, and suggested that she do that in Sri Lanka instead. The IRB member explained that, "confronted with the applicant's letter and the reference to Singapore, the appellant had no explanation." Furthermore, the appellant and her mother explained that the spouses were "not first cousins as indicated in the CAIPS [Computer Assisted Immigration Program System] notes but distant relatives who are considered to be 'marriageable cousins'. . . [thus giving] slightly differing accounts as to how exactly the applicant and the appellant are related."

Moreover, the board member agreed with the visa officer's contention that the marriage might not be genuine since the customary marriage practices had not taken place after the civil marriage. It is clear that measuring the genuineness of a marriage is linked with the customary marriage. This is because the credibility of the couple's intention behind the marriage is seen through the performance of the customary marriage. The material and emotional investment put in the marriage, as well as its social acceptance and the effort put into organizing the marriage celebration, serve as the benchmark of measuring the intention of the couple to stay together in the future. Furthermore, the discrepancy in the evidence and the information on the relationship between the two individuals and their knowledge about each other is perceived as a lack of intention to establish a future together. The visa officer noted their lack of knowledge about each other, as well as their minimal effort to change that. In that way, the effort to get to know the other person becomes a site of expression of their future intention to stay together.

However, the board member remarked that even though there were contradictions in certain information given on their whereabouts and knowledge about each other, the marriage appeared to have been "arranged according to custom and tradition." She further pointed out that the appellant justified her spouse's confusion over the differences between love and arranged marriage because he was "unfamiliar with the Western notion of fiancée" and "because he had seen the appellant when they lived in the same area and found her attractive, although the parties were not in any way involved with one another prior to the appellant's arrival in Canada in 1994."

The IAD board member appears to highlight two ways in which a marriage can come about—that is, through an arranged marriage or a love marriage. In the case of a love marriage, it may be expected that the couple know details about the other to a far greater extent than in an arranged marriage. By separating the two forms of marriage, the board member indirectly evoked two ways in which the genuineness of a union can be validated through the couple's intention. Therefore, in the case of an arranged marriage, its validation is based on the acceptance of the marriage by the community, as demonstrated in prior discussion of the colonial courts. On the other hand, the genuineness of a love marriage is established by satisfying certain measurable criteria, including in-depth knowledge of the other person, gift-giving between them, and daily communication. In this case, since the applicants interpreted their union as an arranged marriage, Taya di Pietro evoked the same notions of social acceptance of the marriage and witnessing of the ceremony by family and relatives that were highlighted within the colonial courts of Sri Lanka. In the legal space of the immigration office, intention was read by the confluence of the "love marriage" and the "arranged marriage"; in the immigration court, however, those two forms are separated and intention is read according to the specifics of each of these forms of marriage.

Be it a liberal, "modern" Canadian state or a colonial state from the past, both seem to constantly resort to revising their lawmaking procedures whenever they cannot read their own documents or other state documents or rely on their procedures of assessment of intention. In such instances they have demonstrated a propensity to draw their lawmaking power from other institutions, such as the couple's non-Western community. However, unlike the colonial court cases, the Canadian immigration court cases locate intention within the couple more than in their family members, although they do assign importance to the community's customary practices as way of assessing a marriage's validity. In this case, because traditions were followed, the couple is perceived as having been accepted by their community and having expressed their intention through the appropriate cultural idioms. The IAD member acknowledged the intention behind the act of a genuine marriage: "This commitment to one another appears to be consistent with the couple's cultural norms and traditions and it would appear highly unusual for the parties to have a child together if they did not intend to reside together permanently."

So, finally, the board member returned to the intention of the two individuals to stay together in the future as expressed in the act of having a child. The emergence of the figure of the child within the marriage process transfigures the husband and wife into father and mother, and thus the court sees the relatedness not only as a couple's intention but as the intention of parents, a symbol of the marriage's "sincerity." The certainty of the marriage process and the imagining of a future translate into the figure of the child. Social acceptance and performance of ceremonial rituals may not be enough to convince the Canadian authorities; the couple must prove their intention in the durability of their relation even after the marriage ceremony, and, as shown in case 2, the importance of abiding by the rules of both the country where the marriage is celebrated and Canada can be of the utmost importance.

CASE 2: JUNE 28, 2007, CANLII 52923, IMMIGRATION
AND REFUGEES BOARD (IMMIGRATION APPEAL DIVISION)
The appellant, Mano, thirty-nine years old, came as a refugee to Canada and became a permanent resident. The applicant, Sutharshan, forty-two years old, was born in Sri Lanka. The two families arranged the marriage in August 2004. At that time, Mano's spouse was living in Abu Dhabi. In February 2005, Mano and the applicant were married in a civil ceremony at that city's Sri Lankan embassy. Soon after that, Mano filed an application to sponsor her husband to Canada. The applicant was interviewed, twice, by a visa officer at the Canadian embassy in Abu Dhabi, but the spousal visa was refused. After receiving the decision, Mano went back to Dubai and they celebrated a Hindu customary marriage ceremony in April 2006.

The application for a permanent residency visa was refused pursuant to IRPR 4; the officer concluded that the marriage was not genuine and that the applicant was inadmissible to Canada. The letter stated two grounds for refusal: "(a) the applicant was inadmissible to Canada pursuant to paragraph 36(1)(c) of the *Act* [IRPA], as having committed an act outside of Canada, that if committed in Canada would be punishable by a maximum term of imprisonment of 10 years under 57(1)(b)(i) of the *Canadian Criminal Code*; and, (b) the marriage was not genuine because the parties had neither held a religious ceremony to confirm their marriage nor consummated the marriage." During the appeal, IRB member Renee Miller commented that there were three issues to be determined: (1) the question of the genuineness of the marriage, and if genuine, (2) the question of the inadmissibility of the applicant "pursuant to paragraph 36(1)(c) of the *Act* [IRPA]," and, if again yes, (3) the existence of "sufficient humanitarian and compassionate considerations," notably the "best interests of a minor child affected by this decision, to warrant the granting of special discretionary relief." The first consideration was determining whether the marriage was genuine. The appeal division board member interpreted the facts under its need to

> consider a broad range of factors including: how the couple met, how the relationship evolved, the duration of the relationship, the amount of time spent together prior to the wedding, the nature of the engagement/ wedding ceremony, the intent of the parties to the marriage, the evidence of ongoing contact and communication before and after the marriage, the spouses conduct after the wedding, the depth of knowledge of each other's past, present, and daily lives, the provision of financial support, the partners families' knowledge of and involvement in the relationship, and their plans and arrangements for the future."

The above statement unearths different considerations that surface in validating a marriage as genuine. The notion of genuineness includes many criteria to determine the spouses' intentions. Here, the intention of genuine relationship shifts to an analysis of the individuals who are parties to the marriage, focusing on the nature of the wedding ceremony and the ongoing relationship as revealed in the couple's actions before and after the marriage. The notion of genuineness is placed not only within the language of intention of the marriage event but also highlights the intention of the couple to continue their marriage into the future, getting to know each other, supporting each other in financial matters, and engaging in the daily life of a married couple (despite the borders that separate them). Here, the intention to live together in the future must be acted out, performed to satisfy the officer to validate a marriage as genuine. But the following pages still clarify the importance of customary marriage rituals as part of the proof of a genuine marriage.

The IRB member mentioned that they noted the match was made based on equal caste, education, and ethnic background and through the matching of horoscopes. She further agreed that "all of the ceremonies and rites necessary to affect a legal marriage have occurred between the parties," even though such practices occurred after the first visa refusal. She recognized that "a full religious ceremony" was conducted, "with a number of family members from Canada" and "two Sri Lankan priests were brought from India at the parties' own expense to perform the ceremony according to their cultural religious practices." In the first instance, the visa was refused because only a civil marriage had taken place. Therefore, that first visa officer was not convinced that the marriage was genuine, since it did not show the "real" intention of the marriage. Thus, the couple went to the extent of flying in Sri Lankan priests to conduct a customary marriage. Their relatives and friends traveled to the UAE and took part in the ceremony.

This case further illustrates the ongoing marriage process, with its certainty and uncertainty. The spouses constantly work to express and establish the genuineness of their marriage. By going back and forth within the marriage process and constantly reworking it to express their intention in multiple ways, all to seek the recognition of their intention by the Canadian state and reunite in Canada, the transnational married couples navigate, contest, and plead against their visa refusals. But even within the uncertainty of the prolonged marriage process, the couples imagine a future together and some semblance of certainty by refusing to accept the rejection of their visa and contesting the Canadian state's decision in various legal spaces.

The IRB member pointed out that if the couple had the intention of entering a genuine marriage, they would have had the customary marriage in the first place, after the civil marriage. She explained that after the first refusal, arrangements for a religious ceremony were made "in 6 weeks; again indicating the ability to arrange a religious ceremony once there was sufficient motivation." She therefore judged that "the complete lack of inquiry and effort into arranging a religious ceremony, by both sides of the marriage, *infers a lack of intention to engage in a true, genuine marriage.*" Not only the authority of the community in participating in the marriage ceremonies but also the individual efforts and actions of organizing the marriage ceremonies are scrutinized as a way of measuring the couple's intention.

The modern state here emphasizes the intention of the individual actions and choices. Later, however, the IRB member agreed and accepted the explanation of the couple that because they wanted to have the marriage in Canada where their relatives and friends were living, they did not inquire into the possibility of conducting a Hindu marriage in a temple in Dubai (the closest one). The performance of a customary marriage was sufficient to convince the appeal division to measure and read the intention of the couple and, thus, to decide the marriage was genuine. In the eyes of an immigration officer, a customary marriage shows some degree of intention, and marriage ceremony rituals where the community takes part are perceived as a form of social acceptance. Thus, once again, the authority of the family and community is called on to assess the intention and genuineness of a marriage even by the modern liberal Canadian state. In other words, the immigration officers' and the courts' reliance on proof of customary marriage over civil marriage in order to assess the genuineness of a relationship represents a continuity of the colonial past where validity of marriage is measured through the legal language of intentionality.

However, this is not enough in the case of the immigration authorities. For them, intention in a marriage does not revolve only around the authority of community or family in the form of social acceptance, but around the couple as well. The intention of living together is cross-checked with the relationship between the two individuals. Thus, intention is further validated by other factors—it is not only measured through the actualized and not actualized actions of couples and others around them in the present and past, but their actions are also measured in terms of the couples' intention toward a future. The immigration state together with the couple imagines a future for the couple, which of course includes the would-be future citizen or resident. Imagination of the future reunion of spouses in the marriage process travels through different state institutions, actors, and documents. These assemblages produce mingled notions comprising the futures imagined by individuals, communities, parents, photographers, photos, and states. The future and present of the marriage process also connect within the potential spaces of immigration courtrooms.

Therefore, the appeal division examined the ongoing relationship after the marriage celebration. Upon consideration of the telephone recordings, the tribunal acknowledged that there had been extensive and continuous communication between the parties since 2004. The parties' overall credibility was further assessed based on the consistency of their evidence, both internally and between the two witnesses. The spouses' stories matched on a wide variety of facts: their knowledge of each other's work and living arrangements, their families, their work histories, how they learned about each other, the arrangements of their family, and their plans for the future. Nonetheless, the board member noted some inconsistency on certain points, including the frequency of writing letters to each other and the lack of a proper explanation for other contradictory statements. However, she held that those issues were not sufficient to invalidate the marriage. Rather, she found that "the evidence, in its totality, indicated that there has been a meaningful exchange of information between the parties which is in the nature of a genuine spousal relationship," and therefore "sufficient credible and reliable evidence to conclude that the marriage between the appellant and applicant is genuine."

However, the immigration officer argued that the applicant had committed a crime which was punishable in Canada. The applicant agreed, in his oral testimony, that he had hired an agent who promised to traffic him to Germany and gave him a false passport to enter India from Thailand. From India he was deported back to Thailand. The defense of the applicant was that he had not been charged with or convicted of any offense. The applicant admitted to knowingly using a fraudulent passport to attempt to travel from Thailand, through India, to get to Germany. The IRB member declared it "a serious offense, but added:

> The seriousness of the offense is mitigated by the fact that the applicant was fleeing civil war in his home country. . . . He (applicant) testified that the "LTTE" (Liberation Tigers of Tamil Eelam), the guerrilla fighters opposed to the government, have a policy that all Tamil families must donate one son to their army. Therefore, any family with an unmarried son is targeted and harassed for donation of that son to their army and/or funds. Similarly, a single Tamil man is suspect to the government, as being associated with the LTTE, and subject to more frequent harassment and detention at the government checkpoints. There is a significant danger to him in returning to Sri Lanka.

The board member also took into consideration his family members already living in Canada, his stable work history, and his fluency in English, noting that these will all help him to establish himself in Canada without any problem. The IAD's conclusion was that the visa officer's refusal was not valid. Thus, other factors concerning the applicant—such as his criminal records and his possible adaptability in Canada—were also taken into consideration when granting a visa. The evocation of escaping civil war in Sri Lanka and suffering the effects of displacement shows that appeals arm of the Canadian state could contradict its bureaucratic arm, which tries to protect the nation's borders. Here, the humanitarian face of the state emerges, that of a country sympathetic to refugees of war. At the same time, the Canadian state considers factors which ensure that a possible future citizen is not a criminal or will not become a welfare burden, encompass-ing a state's imaginations of its future citizens. The board pronounced a favorable judgment, aided by the added factor of the presence of a child, which served as proof of the couple's future intentions, as in case 1.

CASE 3: MAY 30, 2002, *VIGNESWARAN KANDIAH V.*
MINISTER OF CITIZENSHIP AND IMMIGRATION (IMM-2055-01)
Vigneswaran was born in Sri Lanka and, in 1992, became a refugee in Canada. He lived in Montreal until 1999 and then moved to Toronto. In Montreal he lived in a house with several others, including Sugantee Makanda. In 1994, Vigneswaran made known his interest in marrying Sugantee's sister, Thevaki. After she informed her family in Sri Lanka, the marriage was arranged and the wedding took place, in Sri Lanka, in 1997. After a month of living together in Sri Lanka, Vigneswaran returned to Canada. In March 1998, Vigneswaran started the process of sponsoring his wife to join him. The wife was called for the visa interview and questioned about her knowledge of her husband's personal background, the timeline of the marriage, and many other subjects. Based on her answers and other documentary proof, the visa officer refused the permanent residence visa application.

The husband made an appeal at the IAD against the visa officer's deci-sion. The hearing took place after a period of two years, in 2001. The IAD dismissed the appeal on the basis that, on the balance of probabilities, "the marriage of the applicant was primarily for the purpose of gaining admis-sion into Canada as the wife of a member of the family class." The applicant further appealed for judicial review to challenge the IAD's decision. The judge found "evidence of the wife's intentions before the Appeal Division," in "the impressions of the visa officer and the refusal letter." She decided that "according to that *evidence, the Appellant's wife lacked knowledge of basic facts about her husband, including his caste, his ethnic background and his salary*" (emphasis added).

The judge shifted from social acceptance of the marriage as the indicator of the marriage's validity, to the individual's knowledge of the other party to the contract as the expression and measure of intention. In other words, the individual who enters into a marriage needs to have comprehensive information about their spouse to legally assert the intention of wanting to stay together. For such reason, the judge dismissed the appeal for judicial review. Despite the long-distance relationship, the Canadian state presumes that a marriage is a relationship where the husband and wife live together soon after the marriage and become intimately familiar with the details of each other's lives. However, in a transnational marriage, such familiarity is limited by the distance between the spouses, although modern conveniences like telephones, webcams, bank transfers, and emails help to reduce that distance.

Even though the modern Canadian state uses a combination of factors to measure the future intention of the couple to establish a family in Canada, it mostly falls back on the crucial category of the couple proving they will continue to have an ongoing, genuine relationship. The future of their reunion is validated through the present of the marriage process, despite the long-distance relationship. Unlike the other two cases, this case failed, as the state did not recognize the marriage, and therefore the couple could not reunite in Canada. The process of reuniting in the marriage process, however protracted, does not always end in the certainty of reunion through the final court proceedings. In the first case, the IAD distinguished between love and arranged marriages to assess the couple's personal knowledge of each other, but in this case such an issue was not evoked by any of the authorities. The marriage process travels through different state spaces and their varying practices. At times, the location of intention rests on the individual interaction, knowledge, and presence of children, and at other times, it rests on social acceptance and family participation in the wedding ceremony. The Canadian state seems to be constantly moving, shifting, and redefining its requirements, trying to capture the uncertainty of the intention of the married couple and to imagine their future, yet to be actualized life together.

STANDARDIZING SRI LANKAN TAMIL MARRIAGES

By validating the genuineness of marriage through customary marriage ceremonies, the Canadian authorities ended up standardizing the multiple varieties of Sri Lankan Tamil marriage practices that had been acknowledged by the colonial courts in Sri Lanka (as explored in the previous chapter). In attempting to legalize certain Sri Lankan Tamil marriage cultural practices, the Canadian state has been attempting to identify specific local ceremonies that will serve to benchmark the "authentic" Tamil marriage.

The popular choice for Canadian immigration officers has been the thali-tying ritual, which has become the standard Tamil customary marriage form they look for in accepting the legal validity of a marriage. As shown in chapter 3's discussion of wedding photographs, the thali-tying ceremony has come to occupy a special place in the wedding album, in anticipation of the future gaze of immigration officers. In the first case discussed in this chapter, the judge contested the immigration officer's decision on the basis that the thali was tied according to Tamil custom; thus, the validity and genuineness of the marriage was not in question. According to the judge, the appellant's intention was shown through the following action: "The appellant returned to Sri Lanka in order to tie the thalie and religiously solemnise her union to the applicant in the presence of numerous family members and friends. The video of the ceremony, which was filed at the hearing, clearly illustrates that the occasion was celebrated in an elaborate fashion and was well attended by numerous guests" (Case 1).

The various Tamil customary marriages here are syncretized into a homogeneous marriage with rituals mostly practiced by the vellalar caste or other privileged castes—such as tying the thali, an elaborate marriage ceremony with a priest chanting the manthras, and the gathering of a large number of people. It seems that such homogenous Tamil customary marriage has become the standard formula for immigration offices to apply and measure the genuineness of all marriages of different Sri Lankan Tamil communities. The legal language of measuring intention within Canadian state spaces (from the immigration office to the courtroom) caused Tamil traditions to be changed, re-created, or even invented, just as they had been in the colonial court. However, the standardization of customary marriage practices in Canadian courtrooms or at embassies has become more rigid than it was in colonial courtrooms. The Canadian state appears more intent on protecting its territories from unwanted subjects than on acknowledging different customary marriage practices within the Sri Lankan Tamil community. Overall, the colonial state, despite its desire to organize an alien culture, was forced to acknowledge and adjust to the diversity of the culture encountered in the marriage practices, while the modern Canadian state, despite promoting multiculturalism, when confronted with the issue of protecting its borders tends to homogenize a diverse alien culture into a syncretic one. However, the movement of the marriage process, along with associations of documents, individuals, and practices, sometimes challenges the standardization of Tamil customary marriages that has emerged at Canadian immigration offices, courtrooms, and IAD hearings.

CASE 4: SEPTEMBER 27, 2004, TA3-17873, IMMIGRATION AND REFUGEES BOARD (IMMIGRATION APPEAL DIVISION)

Kandipan filed an appeal case at the IAD regarding the sponsorship of his wife from Sri Lanka. Kandipan's marriage to Yalini was arranged by his elder sister, his father, and a marriage broker. In November 2002, Kandipan traveled to Sri Lanka and married Yalini. The civil marriage was performed at his sister's house in Colombo. Since his parents could not travel from Jaffna, they did not take part in the wedding. He did not have elaborate ceremonies, as he did not have enough money. Kandipan and Yalini lived in his sister's house for a month before he returned to Canada. Kandipan then made a third trip to Sri Lanka, in July 2004, to see his wife. However, despite having submitted all the details of their marriage, the wife's application for permanent residency in Canada was rejected by the visa officer in Colombo.

The following reasons were given in the letter of rejection (abstracted from the IAD proceedings): (1) the absence of a religious ceremony; (2) the tying of the thali not being performed by "an elderly person" and therefore being "culturally inappropriate for Sri Lankan Tamils"; (3) the absence of the sponsor's parents in "any of the photographs of the civil marriage ceremony"; (4) "insufficient evidence of contact between the applicant and the appellant . . . after their civil marriage"; and (5) "the applicant's lack of knowledge of her sponsor's employment in Canada."

Kandipan informed the IAD that he and Yalini were communicating regularly over the phone, using calling cards. He explained that this method was cheaper than using a landline. However, this method does not produce the same documentary evidence, as the cards are hard to trace back to their users and do not provide detailed information on the calls' duration and their receivers. The IRB member who heard the case declared that although the lack of a religious wedding does not support the appellant's case, it "is not in and of itself decisive as to the issue of the genuineness of the marriage." In this, he disagreed with the immigration officer. The board member further pointed out that the thali was handed over by the sister of the groom and placed around the bride's neck—thus, it was performed in accordance with "Tamil culture and custom." He said that although the visa officer mentioned that the marriage ceremony was not conducted according to Tamil traditions, no expert reports were provided to clarify what constituted proper Tamil cultural wedding ceremonies. The tribunal member held that he was unable to assess the genuineness of the marriage based on the requirements of the cultural marriage ceremony.

The confusion in this case over what constitutes a "proper" Tamil wedding is similar to the confusion experienced in the colonial courts over defining a valid customary marriage and the appropriate rituals. However, the IRB member also took into consideration that a valid reason existed, in this case, for the inability of the groom's parents to participate in the marriage (i.e., they could not travel from Jaffna to Colombo due to the war). As such, he admitted that in this instance the factor of family acceptance or participation in the marriage was not viable. Thus, we see the IAD here taking into consideration social realities of transnational marriages within the Sri Lankan war context. Regarding the lack of knowledge about the other party, the board member commented that since it was an arranged marriage, and "given the distance between them and the fact that the interview was held within four months of the marriage, I am not persuaded that the applicant's lack of precise knowledge of the details of her husband's jobs in Canada is crucial to a determination of the genuineness of the marriage."

The IAD overruled the visa officer's decision. On the one hand, the Canadian state—mostly through its immigration officers—tries to standardize customary Tamil marriages by calling for customary marriage over civil marriage, and to further standardize the evidence of an ongoing relationship between the couple; on the other hand, the same Canadian state takes into consideration the social realities of a long-distance marriage, and the Sri Lankan civil war context, in determining the genuineness of a marriage. As illustrated, the tension about what constitutes a genuine marriage in legal language continues when different state entities have different understandings of the couple's intention. This further substantiates the uncertainty of the marriage process and the difficulty of pinning down the future intention of the couple to live together as husband and wife.

Through the immigration practices of the Canadian state, certain notions that had been defined in the colonial past are continued into the present—namely, validating a marriage as genuine based on the legal language of intention, which spans borders, time, and states. Both court spaces (colonial and Canadian), where the marriage process and couples' intentions within the marriage process, were/are examined or reexamined, have become crucial sites through which the marriage process travels and is measured. For both states, the validity and genuineness of a marriage rest on the idea of the couple's intention. While the colonial court validated the marriage based on the intention of the couple to marry in the past through their conducting of the traditional ceremonies, the Canadian state measures the couple's intention on the basis of their commitment to stay together permanently in the future. The Canadian state has expanded this to include both the notion of social acceptance in arranged marriages and individual commitment to measure the spouses' intention to build a life together. To measure the intention of a married couple, the Canadian state must measure the actions not yet actualized. Intention intrinsically holds both actualized and yet to be actualized actions. In the Canadian marriage immigration cases it becomes more complicated, because the state assesses and acknowledges not only the future intention of the couple but also the possible future citizens or permanent residents of its territory. In that sense, the state needs to predict whether they will fit into the Canadian national imagination and not become a burden to their welfare system. The state imagines not only the future of the applicants and their intentions, but also the future of itself and its citizens.

The marriage process, moving through different legal and administrative spaces, shows that the state's imagination shifts and changes according to the various assemblages of humans, documents, and spaces to prove and measure intention. The uncertainty and certainty of an imagined future by the couple in the present, at the site of the in-between marriage process, is mingled with the state's imagination of a future for its citizens. In these different legal spaces, the transnational marriages get transfigured and re-transfigured, the relatedness made and unmade, the marriage process expanded and shrunk with multiple imaginations of the future. Although the Canadian state tries to control, and institutionalizes through the legal language of intention, the transnational marriage process and marriage migration, such a goal has proven elusive. The readings of intention change and are contradicted from one legal space to another.

These possibilities of multiple readings further foreground the potential of the marriage process—that is, living with the uncertainty of a reunion yet imagining a certain future together. The documents produced by the Canadian state carry the uncertainty and certainty of an imagined future, but they are also undone by the production of new documents and their associations in different legal spaces. The relationship between the couple, which is undone legally by the visa officers' rejection letters, is remade legally in the courts when those officers' decisions are overruled. Thus, the documents, through the possibilities opened by their multiple associations, carry anxieties, hopes, fears, and visions of the future for the married couple. The measure of the intention of the couple, within the courts, as an act of testing the validity of a marriage, deals with the marriage process as a lived and imagined commitment of married couples and their plans to stay together. For those involved in the in-between transnational marriage process, the courts become the potential spaces that transfigure their relationships and futures. Court files and decisions carry a certain future for both the couple and the Canadian state that has yet to be actualized. In these spaces, the intention of the married couples connects to the notion of an enduring relationship, not only as they live it during the marriage process, but also as they anticipate the future. What happens to the couple who reunite after obtaining the spousal visa and how such intentions are actualized and not actualized are questions open for further research.

Conclusion

SRI LANKAN TAMIL MARRIAGE-RELATED MIGRATION AROSE FROM the shifting social–political landscape of Jaffna and of the Tamil diaspora, which heightened during the war. The large Tamil diaspora and the links formed through marriage-related migration endure after the war, as a form of life for Jaffna and diaspora Tamils. A considerable share of marriage migration emerged for labor and economic reasons (Palriwala and Uberoi 2008a), mainly due to "global hypergamy" (Constable 2003), in which women and their families desire foreign grooms, who offer social mobility and a possibility of chain migration for family members. Marriage migration studies problematize the dichotomies between love and instrumental marriages, home and host countries, and victimization and agency (Brettell 2017). For example, transnational/transracial marriages between Filipino brides and American grooms, despite economic elements, also involve love and romance (Constable 2003). Therefore, marriage-related migration should be analyzed in terms of transnational couples, international marriages, and transnational weddings—categories that are not mutually exclusive and may in fact overlap (Charsley 2012, 21).

It is not that marriage has become more mobile with the emergence of "cosmopolitan life" (Appadurai 1988) marked by migration and globalization. Even though mobility has increased in the lives of married couples in the contemporary world, earlier anthropological work on South Asian marriage also documented movements of goods, rights, gifts, and people between households (though not necessarily across borders) (Dumont 1983). Other kinship studies have followed residential patterns after marriage (patrilocal or matrilocal) and the status of spouses in these communities (Tambiah 1973). They have explored the ways a married woman could use her ability to move between the houses of her natal family and her family of procreation to improve her situation in the latter (Grover 2009). Earlier studies on Jaffna kinship show that even before war and displacement, movement (although on a smaller scale) was associated with marriage among the Jaffna Tamils, as fostered by the possibility of finding marriage partners in a larger kinship pool (*sondam*) (Banks 1960).

Mobility within the transnational marriages also affects the temporality of the marriage process (e.g., how its duration is stretched out from the moment a marriage is arranged to the moment the married couple reunites in their adoptive country). Within the context of civil war in Sri Lanka, marriage migration has become both an avenue through which people escape from violence and a process bringing dispersed people together, transfiguring relatedness, rebuilding lives across borders, and enabling the imagination of futures. This is because the marriage process is associated with the futures of rebuilding life, procreating, and living together, as well as the future desires, anxieties, fears, and hopes that are attached to marriage. The practices, ceremonies, and performances during the marriage process hold an imagined future, one entangled with both past and present.

Transnational marriages have been analyzed through the lenses of long-distance relationships, new technologies of communication across borders, and the involvement of different states in the reunion of the couple in a foreign land. Of particular interest have been the future desires, actions, and anticipations that unfold within the present transnational marriage practices and their near and distant imagined futures. The war-related marriage migration of Sri Lanka shifts the lens on transnational marriages from globalization and labor migration to forced migration, experiences of war, dislocations of relatedness, and questions of life and death. However, the war-related marriage migration described in these stories was not devoid of desire for future economic gain, dreams of living in a foreign country, and hopes for a better life with the spouse in another country.

Future desires and needs are mingled with the past context of war, suffering, and loss. The intentions of the marriage migration in this context have multiple meanings and readings. But such intentions can be read in the expression of social relations and sociality as associations of people and things. The Canadian spousal immigration court cases brought out the different intentions of married couples as they were read and reread, measured, and reinterpreted at different points in the Canadian state bureaucracy. At the same time, the wedding photos of these ceremonies aimed both to facilitate the migration process and to create an ideal family within the context of war, loss, and mass migration. The new marriage migration process, immigration laws, and foreign state practices created in light of these disruptions brought a novel set of unfamiliar practices to the Jaffna Tamil marriage. Individuals navigate to rebuild, reconnect, and reimagine life and futures through the marriage process and its associated spaces, documents, and figures: from courtrooms to marriage brokers' offices, from wedding packages to the planting of trees in a temporary place, from wedding photos to court files and verdicts, from marriage brokers to photographers.

The prolonged process of transnational marriage fosters practices in which actualized and not actualized actions and imaginations take place. Within the marriage process, individuals and documents, humans and nonhumans, associate at different moments to create and transfigure relatedness—associations that hold both certainty and uncertainty for the marriage process. This process (and varying associations in the process) enables imagined futures, hopes along with anxieties, despair, and fear that those futures will not be realized. The futures of life and relatedness are entangled with present and past practices as well as memories that are lived and relived, worked out at the site of the marriage process. The transnational marriage process has become a site for people to rebuild their life and imagine a certain future in the time of uncertainty and chaos, and such rebuilding and remaking of life takes place within moments of association between figures, documents, state practices, wedding photos, and temporary places in different temporalities. Of particular interest is the way people travel through these different spaces/documents/figures during the marriage process. These associations take place not only in adoptive and home countries but also sometimes in a third country, a temporary place where the marriage ceremony is held. What becomes known in these temporary times and temporary places is also crucial to the imagination of certain futures.

Three observations emerge in this study of Jaffna Tamil transnational marriage. First, marriage as a process—from arrangement to reunion—is not only about social reproduction and rearrangement of social structure or stability, but also contains uncertainty, desires, and anxieties for a future. During the transnational marriage process and its stretched durability, relationships and relatedness (Carsten 2004) are made, worked out, imagined, and lived.

Second, this marriage process is an in-between and a potential (Deleuze [1968] 1994) that holds different spaces/figures/documents and their assemblages. At times, those figures (marriage brokers, photographers), spaces (courtrooms, marriage brokers' offices, temporary places), and documents (court files, visa refusal letters, marriage brokers' files, photographs) can be seen as an in-between zone between bride and groom, families, desires, and dreams. At other times, their associations become an in-between, singular moment within the marriage process (Latour 2005). Marriage brokers, wedding photographers, and paralegals, along with wedding photos, court-rooms, wedding packages, and temporary celebration places, are some of the figures/spaces/documents through which one may enter to understand the transfigurations and potential of the marriage process. The marriage process as a potential zone holds multiple futures that could be actualized in any form and will have multiple outcomes. These futures are generated not only by "thinking" or "imagining" a possible future, but also by living and imagining such futures in present practices.

When the transnational marriage is arranged in the broker's office, the future is imagined for a migration after the ceremony, connecting with other members of the community, and such futures are entangled with the futures imagined by the broker's matchmaking process. Later, the imagi-nation of the future is entangled with the decisions of the Canadian state on its possible future citizen. Such mingled and multiple futures unfold in fragments of practices, performances, documents, and figures. Spaces/figures/documents within this in-between zone are crucial to transfigure relatedness and constantly make and unmake relationships through their associations. But the potential of imagining the future, living with its uncer-tainty and certainty, constantly shifts and is expressed differently at differ-ent moments of the marriage process. The marriage broker's work of arranging the union or the astrologer's work of calculating the marriage and migration prospect of an individual opens up a potential for certain futures. The potential of the marriage process is expressed in temporary moments in India, when the family members reunite for the marriage cele-bration and imagine a life together in the future as well as remember their life together in the past. The tree planted in a temporary place during the wed-ding ceremony, as an indication of the permanency of their relation, holds an imagination of a future not yet actualized. The documents from mar-riage brokers and court files to wedding photos carry the potential of the couple's migration and reunion, and as such transfigure the relatedness not only with the living but also with the dead. The Canadian courts become a potential space within the marriage process where, at times, the relatedness is re-transfigured through the overruling of a spousal visa rejection. At other times, the refusal is upheld and enforced by the immigration courts, thus breaking again the relatedness. Within the potential of the marriage process, my interlocutors learned to live, rebuild, and reconnect in a time of war and uncertainty.

The documents (in my cases wedding photos, marriage broker's files, court files, love letters, and visa application forms) and their association with humans must be taken seriously as ways of creating both anxieties and hopes for a future: an affective kinship and relatedness. These anxieties unfold not only in the practices of the individuals involved in the marriage process, but also in those of the state authorities and officers who decide on the reunion of a transnational married couple by measuring and reading their intentions. Documents carry both certainty and uncertainty, and affect the process of making, unmaking, and remaking relatedness through their association with humans. Such associations play an important part in creating the sociality of kinship and relatedness.

Third, in the different moments of the marriage process, relatedness, subjectivities, and the collective are transfigured, allowing Jaffna Tamils to rebuild their lives torn apart by war and violence. Those in-between spaces/figures/documents allow the imagining of futures through familiar practices, known categories and figures, without suspending everyday life, both during and in the aftermath of violence. Studies on violence look at the words, performances, and silences through which subjects recover their lives and remake the world and relationships within the everyday through mundane practices (Das 2007; Mulla 2015). But the everyday appears not as complete but as a site of "becoming with differences, newness and surprises" (Biehl and Locke 2010). The marriage process in the Jaffna Tamils' migration stories tells us that recovering life, rebuilding relationships, and reconnecting with community members also takes place in temporary moments and their associations—in transit places where the wedding is held, in the wedding photos that create ideal families, and through the figures of marriage brokers and their documents. In other words, the transnational marriage process not only enables people to imagine futures and bring back memories, but is also a site to rebuild life and connect with others in momentary space and time in the present. Such temporal moments and fragments of familiarities allow the certainty and uncertainty of relatedness to be worked out and imagined. It is in the interstices of "in betweenness" that the ebb and flow of everydayness is enacted anew and remade with the vision of a better, imagined future. The marriage process is one site of potential, an in-between space of creativity and familiarity, carrying both the uncertainty and certainty of the everyday.

The social and political landscape of the Sri Lankan Tamil diaspora and of Jaffna has changed dramatically in the postwar era, and new conditions may render obsolete some steps of the wartime transnational marriage process. For instance, the broker may lose their role as middleman because of the possibilities opened up by easier connectivity. Moreover, now that traveling to Jaffna is a viable option for those of the Sri Lankan Tamil diaspora, India may not remain a transit place for wedding ceremonies. Uncertainty and certainty endure within the Jaffna Tamil transnational marriage process while certain associations between people, space, and documents change with the postwar context. However, though the war may have ended, it casts a long-lasting shadow over the forms of life it generated. Marriage migration has not diminished, nor have the issues associated with obtaining a spousal visa for reunion in a migrant country. The spaces, figures, and documents within the marriage process during a time of war have changed, been reconfigured, or set aside in a postwar context. New and alternative spaces/figures/documents may be crucial within this new world. How notions of kinship, marriage process, and relationships circulate around places, figures, and documents is an important question to engage with in postwar Sri Lanka. Entering the study of marriage as a process, and analyzing relatedness as it is worked out, imagined, and lived while people travel through such process—rather than through assumed perceptions, categories, and rules of kinship and marriage—will tell us a different story of the making, unmaking, and remaking of relatedness.

Notes

Introduction

1   I am not saying that uncertainty only emerges at such extraordinary moments. Of course, uncertainty is associated with everyone's daily life. See Das (2007) and Cavell (1982) for discussion of this. But such moments of violence, war, waiting, and displacement make the uncertainty more visible to the subjects living in it.

2   Lisa Stevenson, in her work on care during the suicide and tuberculosis epidemics among the Canadian Inuit, makes a case for uncertainty: "It also seems that uncertainty, like pain . . . , requires not resolution but acknowledgement, and thus implicates me as an anthropologist in a mutual project of describing a world beset by uncertainty" (2014, 2).

3   See the Human Rights Watch report available at www.hrw.org/en/node/87402.

4   On the 1983 ethnic riots see Kanapathipillai 1990; Daniel 1996; Tambiah 1986; Kapferer 1989; Spencer 1990; McDowell 1996; Fuglerud 1999.

5   The Tamil community is further divided into Malaiyaka Tamils and others. During the British colonial period laborers were brought from South India to work in the tea plantations, and they have since been categorized as Malaiyaka Tamils (Thiranagama 2011; Daniel 1996).

6   See Tambiah 1986; Thiranagama 2011; Spencer 1990; Spencer et al 2015.

7   See UTHR 1994; Thiranagama 2011; Fuglerud 1999, 53. LTTE also started forcefully recruiting members and physically assaulting anyone who stood against its ideology (Thiranagama 2011; Hoole 1997).

8   See Thiranagama 2011; Cheran 2001; Fuglerud 1999; McDowell 1996; Daniel and Thangaraj 1995; Maunaguru 2009.

9   See Daniel and Thangaraj 1995; Cheran 2001; Maunaguru 2009.

10 In Jaffna, caste is based on Hindu religious concepts of purity and pollution, while class is measured through wealth and education. This description necessarily simplifies the complexities of the categories of caste and class, which have been abundantly discussed by scholars on South Asia.

11 See Kanapathipillai 1990; Daniel 1996; Daniel and Thangaraj 1995; Tambiah 1986; Kapferer 1989; Spencer 1990; Thiranagama 2011; Lawrence 2000; Jeganathan 2003, 2004.

12 See Neville 1994, 30; Thiranagama 2011; Maunaguru 2009.

13 See Constable 2003, 2004; Palriwala and Uberoi 2008a; Charsley 2012.

14 Those were the assumptions related to those practices during the time of my study and therefore may have changed since, as the immigration process continues to evolve.

Nowadays, for example, the permanent resident status is usually obtained after a certain amount of time of residence in Canada as a couple.

15 See Perera 1999; Das and Kleinman 2001; Lawrence 2000.

16 See Kanapathipillai 1990; Daniel 1996; Daniel and Thangaraj 1995.

17 See Constable 2004; Charsley 2012; Ong 1999, 2003; Hirsch 2003; Palriwala and Uberoi 2008a.

18 The study was conducted before 2009 and thus reflects the immigration and marriage practices that occurred before then.

19 See Leach 1961; Yalman 1967; Dumont 1983; Tambiah 1973; McGilvray 1982; Kapadia 1995; Clark-Decès 2014.

20 See Clark-Decès 2014; Fuller and Narasimhan 2008; Parry 2001; Kaur and Palriwala 2014.

21 See Yanagisako and Delaney 1995; Ginsburg and Rapp 1995; Meillassoux 1981.

22 See Leach 1961; Tambiah 1973; Banks 1960.

23 See note 2 above.

24 See Ong 1999, 2003; Williams 2010; Werbner 1990; Malkki 1992.

25 See Charsley 2012; Constable 2004; Ballard 1990.

26 See Dumont 1983; Lévi-Strauss 1969; Fuller and Narasimhan 2008; Clark-Decès 2014.

27 I borrow the term "potential" from Gilles Deleuze's (1991, [1968] 1994, 2005) discussion of the virtual, the actual, and the potential. On the actual, virtual, and potential, see also Deleuze 1991, May 2005, Povinelli 2011.

28 Works on violence have generally focused on the place where violence takes place, how it is reinhabited by survivors, or on the place those survivors escape to (Das 2007; Stevenson 2014; Hutchinson 1996; Biehl and Locke 2010).

29 A person's astrological chart is drawn based on their date, time of birth, and corresponding zodiac characteristics. The chart will be read according to the operating astrological methods to describe the person's character, their present and future life, and their suitable marriage partners.

30 See Appadurai 1988; Gell 1994; Henare, Holbraad, and Wastell 2006; Latour 2005; Miller 1987, 2005; Strathern 1999; Hull 2012b.

31 See Stoler 2002, 2009; Navaro-Yashin 2007; Gupta 2012; Lowenkron and Ferreira 2014.

32 See Lowenkron and Ferreira 2014; Latour and Woolgar 1986; Riles 2006; Reed 2006; Hull 2012a, 2012b; Gupta 2012.

Chapter 1: Brokering Marriages in the Shadow of War

1 Palriwala and Uberoi 2008b; Constable 2003; Del Rosario 2008.

2 Lu 2008; Constable 2004; Palriwala and Uberoi 2008a.

3 Lu 2008; Blanchet 2008; Constable 2003, 2004; Palriwala and Uberoi 2008a.

4 Between children of siblings of different gender (e.g., the son of a woman and the daughter of her brother, or the son of a man and the daughter of his sister).

5 Typically, when a marriage is arranged, the families of the prospective spouses contact an astrologer. He "matches" the spouses' astrological charts, in the sense that he

compares both their details and calculates whether they are suitable for each other. Sometimes this task is undertaken by the marriage broker himself.

6   Passes worked as permission cards for northern Tamils who visited the South for medical or other reasons, and were issued for two weeks, one month, or six months. Passes were compulsory, and failure to show one to the police upon request would result in detention.

7   Pusa is a famous prison run by the government, where many suspected LTTE militants and civilians were kept. It was rumored that anyone who ended up in Pusa either would return as a corpse or would not return at all.

8   Lu 2008; Palriwala and Uberoi 2008a; Constable 2003.

9   See David (1973) for discussion on how the caste hierarchy intersects with the notion of pollution and purity regarding marriage among the Jaffna Tamils.

10 Introduced in 2004, the Schengen visa is given to non-Schengen members to enter the Schengen Area as a tourist, worker, spouse, student, and so forth. The Schengen Area comprises twenty-two European Union member states and four nonmember states (Iceland, Liechtenstein, Norway, and Switzerland).

11 Vellalars, the most privileged caste in Jaffna, are the landowning community (Banks 1960; Perinbanayagam 1982).

12 The chidenam can include three types of land (garden, paddy, and house compound) as well as jewelry and cash. Especially among the Jaffna Tamils (i.e., vellalar caste marriage), giving land and a house to the daughter at the time of marriage is significant. On chidenam, see Tambiah 1973, 119–20.

13 On astrology and its importance in the Jaffna Tamils' social life, see Perinbanayagam 1982.

14 Everyday life does, of course, have its uncertainties. For example, even in a place where war has not torn the community apart, there is always uncertainty regarding marriage, and so the matchmaking process continues until a marriage is fixed or takes place—and the marriage may not last. Yet, the uncertainty and chaos of life is accentuated in contexts of prolonged violence and displacement.

Chapter 2: Leaving behind the Trees

1   There are four types of thalis. Most look like the one described above. However, if it is a Christian marriage, the thali is a gold pendant on which the symbol of the cross is engraved. If the horoscopes of the couple do not match, then an *amman* (goddess) is placed on the thali to protect the husband.

2   See Sivathamby 2005; Muthulingam 1996; Meyer 2003.

3   This was drawn from this page of the UN Refugee Agency website, www.unhcr.org /refworld/topic,463af2212,469f2cba2,485f50d82,0.html, which unfortunately is no longer active.

4   Ibid.

5   A decorated canopy under which the couple sits to perform the wedding ceremony.

Chapter 3: Picturing Marriages

1   The virginity test controversy surrounding South Asian wives and British administrative officers between 1979 and 1981 is a notorious example. For further discussion
on this, see Palriwala and Uberoi 2008a; Hall 2002.

2   The discussion on Tamil customary marriage ceremonies, and the debates surrounding the validity of "legal" Tamil marriages according to the Tamil marriage
tradition, took place in Sri Lankan courtrooms during the colonial era. The relationship between the colonial laws of Sri Lanka and the immigration laws of Western
countries will be explored in chapters 4 and 5.

3   The next chapter will explore in more depth the colonial court cases regarding marriages in Sri Lanka.

4   It is important to note that the marriage between a Canadian citizen or permanent
resident and a foreign national must be legally valid in both places (i.e., the country
where it took place and Canada) for the Canadian state to validate it. See chapter 5 for
more details.

5   See Das and Poole 2004b; Hull 2012b; Navaro-Yashin 2007; Maunaguru 2009.

Chapter 4: Framing Tamil Marriages in Colonial Courtrooms

1   See Mody 2008; Chowdhry 1996; Poonacha 1996; Uberoi 1996a; Chatterjee 1993; Dirks
1992, 2003.

2   Tanika Sarkar eloquently states that "the historian cannot afford to view the colonial
past as an unproblematic retrospect where all power was on one side and all protest
on the other" (1993, 1869).

3   Goonesekere 1984; Roberts 1982; Chowdhry 1996; Poonacha 1996; Uberoi 1996b.

4   Goonesekere 1984; Hayley 1923; Risseeuw 1988.

5   For further discussion on this see Goonesekere 1984, 1987; Risseeuw 1988.

6   For further details on colonial authorities' discussions about the introduction of the
law, see Risseeuw 1988, 35–44.

7   The compulsory registration of a marriage has been subjected to various debates. It
emerged in 1847, was repealed in 1867, reemerged in 1895, and was repealed again in
1896. See Goonesekere 1984, 1987.

8   Johnstone sent copies of the translated Thesawalamai to all the courts and magis-
trates. Copies were also given to schools for the schoolmasters to read aloud publicly
(Tambiah 1958, 1954, 2004). Due to such measures, it was during the British period
that the Thesawalamai code became more easily available to the public, even though
the Dutch were the ones who codified it. See Tambiah 1954, 2004.

9   During the kurai ceremony, the groom provides a sari to the bride, which she must
wear before the tying of the thali. See Tambiah 2004.

10 Banks 1960; David 1973; Tambiah 1973.

11 Slavery was practiced among the Jaffna Tamils. The slave caste comprised the caste
attached to the vellalar families, the koviyars, the chandars, the nallavars, and the
pallars. The practice was abolished in 1844 (Tambiah 2004, 75–85).

12 Many cases deal with customary marriages and the validity of marriage according to different castes. See the case of *Wagraver Velaythan v. Amblevaner Wayrawen* (1823, no. 2,260) (Mutukisna, Atherton, and Isaakzoon 1862, 195), which dealt with the marriage ceremonies of the chandar caste in Jaffna.

13 Henry Francis Mutukisna, Robert Atherton, and Class Isaakzoon (1862) combined a number of cases that took place in Jaffna in the nineteenth century. I found the judgment in their collection, but there were no details of the case or why it was contested in court. Thus, I am only working with the judgment that was given in the case.

Chapter 5: Reviewing "Genuine" Marriages in Spousal Migration

1 Petryna 2002; Foucault 1994; Trouillot 2001.

2 Das and Poole 2004a; Gupta 1995, 2012; Riles 2006; Hull 2012b.

3 The right to appeal is limited in certain cases; see http://irb-cisr.gc.ca/en/filing-immigration-appeal/Pages/immapp-a1.aspx.

4 The policies and rules of the Canadian IRPA and the IAD practices along with the spousal immigration procedures discussed in this chapter reflect their rules and regulation until 2009. I have not updated the text with any changes and new processes that may have been implemented after 2009, since the cases I analyze occurred within that time period and therefore were not affected by any subsequent policy amendments. The IRPA can be accessed at http://laws-lois.justice.gc.ca/eng/acts/I-2.5, while the IRPR can be accessed at http://laws-lois.justice.gc.ca/eng/regulations/sor-2002-227.

5 A foreign national can be classified as a family class of a sponsor from Canada if they are their spouse, common-law partner, or conjugal partner (IRPR 117[1]). For further discussion on this, see IRPA 12(1); Carasco et al. 2007, 370–85.

6 The process time has also changed over the years. See Carasco et al. 2007, 369–72.

7 It also concerns common-law and conjugal partners.

8 The names of the people involved in the IRB cases have been modified to preserve their anonymity.

Bibliography

Abrams, Philip. 2006. "Notes on the Difficulties of Studying the State." In *The Anthropology of the State: A Reader*, edited by Aradhana Sharma and Akhil Gupta, 112–30. Oxford, UK: Blackwell.

Adrian, Bonnie. 2003. *Framing the Bride: Globalizing Beauty and Romance in Taiwan's Bridal Industry*. Berkeley: University of California Press.

Agamben, Giorgio. 1998. *Homo Sacer: Sovereign Power and Bare Life*. Translated by Daniel Heller-Roazen. Stanford, CA: Stanford University Press.

Agarwal, Bina. 1988. "Patriarchy and the 'Modernizing' State: An Introduction." In *Structure of Patriarchy: State, Community and Household in Modernizing Asia*, edited by Bina Agarwal, 1–28. New Delhi: Kali for Women.

Anderson, Benedict. 1983. *Imagined Communities*. London: Verso.

Appadurai, Arjun. 1986a. "Introduction: Commodities and the Politics of Value." In *The Social Life of Things*, edited by Arjun Appadurai, 3–63. Cambridge, UK: Cambridge University Press.

———. 1986b. "Putting Hierarchy in Its Place." *Cultural Anthropology* 3 (1): 36–49.

———. 1988. "Introduction: Place and Voice in Anthropological Theory." *Cultural Anthropology* 3 (1): 16–20.

Arasaratnam, Sinnappah. 1961. "Trade and Agricultural Economy of the Tamils of Jaffna during the Latter Half of the Seventeenth Century." *Tamil Culture* 9 (4): 21–34.

———. 1981. "Social History of a Dominant Caste Society: The Vellalar of North Ceylon in the 18th Century." *Indian Economic and Social History Review* 18 (3–4): 377–91.

Ballard, Roger. 1990. "Migration and Kinship: The Differential Effect of Marriage Rules on the Processes of Punjabi Migration to Britain." In *South Asians Overseas: Migration and Ethnicity*, edited by Colin Clarke, Ceri Peach, and Steven Vertovec, 219–49. Cambridge, UK: Cambridge University Press.

Balsutharam, E. 2003. *Thamilar Thirumana Marapukal*. Toronto: Thamilar Senthamarai.

Banks, Michael. 1960. "Caste in Jaffna." In *Aspects of Caste in South India, Ceylon and North Pakistan*, edited by E. R. Leach, 61–78. Cambridge, UK: Cambridge University Press.

Barthes, Roland. 1981. *Camera Lucida: Reflections on Photography*. Translated by Richard Howard. New York: Hill and Wang.

Basso, Keith H. 1996. "Wisdom Sits in Place: Notes on a Western Apache Landscape." In *Senses of Place*, edited by Steven Feld and Keith H. Basso, 53–90. Santa Fe, NM: School of American Research Press.

Bhabha, Homi. 1994. *The Location of Culture*. New York: Routledge.

Biehl, João, and Peter Locke. 2010. "Deleuze and the Anthropology of Becoming." *Current Anthropology* 51 (3): 317–51.

Blanchet, Thérèse. 2008. "Bangladeshi Girls Sold as Wives in North India." In *Marriage, Migration and Gender*, edited by Rajni Palriwala and Patricia Uberoi, 152–79. London: Sage Publications.

Bohannan, Paul. 1960. "The Different Realms of the Law." *American Anthropologist* 67 (6): 33–42.

Borneman, John. 1996. "Until Death Do Us Part: Marriage/Death in Anthropological Discourse." *American Ethnologist* 23 (2): 215–38.

Bourdieu, Pierre. 1990a. *Logic of Practice*. Translated by Richard Nice. Stanford and California: California University Press.

———. 1990b. *Photography: A Middle-Brow Art*. Translated by Shaun Whiteside. Stanford, CA: Stanford University Press.

Braziel, Jana Evans, and Anita Mannur, eds. 2003. *Theorizing Diaspora: A Reader*. Oxford, UK: Wiley-Blackwell.

Brettell, Caroline B. 2017. "Marriage and Migration." *Annual Review of Anthropology* 46 (1): 81–97.

Busby, Cecilia. 2000. *The Performance of Gender: An Anthropology of Everyday Life in a South Indian Fishing Village*. London: Athlone Press.

Carasco, Emily F., et al. 2007. *Immigration and Refugee Law: Cases, Materials and Commentary*. Toronto: Emond Publishing.

Carsten, Janet. 2000. "Introduction: Cultures of Relatedness." In *Cultures of Relatedness: New Approaches to the Study of Kinship*, edited by Janet Carsten, 1–36. Cambridge, UK: Cambridge University Press.

———. 2004. *After Kinship*. Cambridge, UK: Cambridge University Press.

Casey, Edward S. 1996. "How to Get from Space to Place in a Fairly Short Stretch of Time: Phenomenological Prolegomena." In *Senses of Place*, edited by Steven Feld and Keith H. Basso, 14–52. Santa Fe, NM: School of American Research Press.

Cavell, Stanley. 1982. "Politics as Opposed to What?" *Critical Inquiry* 9 (1): 157–78.

———. 1999. *The Claim of Reason: Wittgenstein, Skepticism, Morality, and Tragedy*. New: Oxford University Press.

Charsley, Katharine, ed. 2012. *Transnational Marriage: New Perspectives from Europe and Beyond*. New York: Routledge.

Chatterjee, Partha. 1993. *The Nation and Its Fragments: Colonial and Post-Colonial Histories*. Princeton, NJ: Princeton University Press.

Cheran, R. 2001. *The Six Genres: Memory, History and the Tamil Diaspora Imagination*. Colombo: Marga Institute.

———. 2006. "Multiple Homes and Parallel Civil Societies: Refugee Diasporas and Transnationalism." *Refuge: Canada's Journal on Refugees* 23 (1): 4–28.

———, ed. 2009. *Pathways of Dissent: Tamil Nationalism in Sri Lanka*. Los Angeles: Sage Publications.

Chitty, Simon Casie. 1992. *The Customs Manners and Literature of the Tamils*. New Delhi: Asian Educational Services.

Chowdhry, Prem. 1996. "Contesting Claims and Counter-Claims: Questions of the Inheritance and Sexuality of Widows in a Colonial State." In *Social Reforms, Sexuality and the State*, edited by Patricia Uberoi, 65–82. New Delhi: Sage Publications.

Clark-Decès, Isabelle. 2014. *The Right Spouse: Preferential Marriages in Tamil Nadu*. Stanford, CA: Stanford University Press.

Cohen, Steve. 2001. *Immigration Controls the Family and the Welfare State: A Handbook of Law, Theory, Politics and Practice for Local Authority, Voluntary Sector and Welfare State Workers and Legal Advisors*. London: Jessica Kingsley Publishers.

Comaroff, John, and Jean Comaroff. 2004. "Policing Culture, Cultural Policing: Law and Social Order in Postcolonial South Africa." *Law and Social Inquiry* 29 (3): 513–45.

Constable, Nicole, ed. 2003. *Romance on Global Stage: Pen Pals, Virtual Ethnography, and "Mail-Order" Marriage*. Berkeley: University of California Press.

———. 2004. *Cross-Border Marriages: Gender and Mobility in Traditional Asia*. Philadelphia: University of Pennsylvania Press.

Crawford, J. M. B., and John F. Quinn. 1983. "The Limits of Intention in the Common Law." *University of Dayton Law Review* 8: 275–306.

Daniel, Valentine E. 1987. *Fluid Signs: Being a Person the Tamil Way*. Berkeley: University of California Press.

———. 1996. *Charred Lullabies: Chapters in an Anthropography of Violence*. Princeton, NJ: Princeton University Press.

Daniel, Valentine E., and Yuvaraj Thangaraj. 1995. "Forms, Formations, and Transformations of the Tamil Refugee." In *Mistrusting Refugees*, edited by E. Valentine Daniel and John Chr. Knudsen, 225–56. Berkeley: University of California Press.

Das, Veena. 1995. *Critical Events: An Anthropological Perspective on Contemporary India*. New Delhi: Oxford University Press.

———. 2007. *Life and Words: Violence and the Descent into the Ordinary*. Berkeley: University of California Press.

Das, Veena, and Arthur Kleinman. 2001. "Introduction." In *Remaking a World: Violence, Social Suffering, and Recovery*, edited by Veena Das, Arthur Kleinman, Margaret Lock, Mamphela Ramphele, and Pamela Reynolds, 1–30. Berkeley: University of California Press.

Das, Veena, and Deborah Poole. 2004a. "State and its Margins: Comparative Ethnographies." In *Anthropology in the Margin of State*, edited by Veena Das and Deborah Poole, 3–33. Santa Fe, NM: School of American Research Press.

———, eds. 2004b. *Anthropology in the Margin of State*. Santa Fe, NM: School of American Research Press.

David, Kenneth. 1973. "Until Marriage Do Us Apart: A Cultural Account of Jaffna Tamil Categories from Kinsman." *Man* 8 (4): 521–35.

De Alwis, Malathi. 1998. "Motherhood as a Space of Protest." In *Appropriating Gender: Women's Activism and Politicized Religion in South Asia*, edited by Patricia Jeffery and Amrita Basu, 185–202. New York: New York University Press.

De Munck, Victor C. 1996. "Love and Marriage in a Sri Lankan Muslim Community: Towards a Re-evaluation of Dravidian Marriage Practices." *American Ethnologist* 23 (4): 698–716.

De Silva, K. M. 1981. *A History of Sri Lanka*. Berkeley: University of California Press.

Del Rosario, Teresita C. 2008. "Bridal Diaspora: Migration and Marriage among Filipino Women." In *Marriage, Migration and Gender,* edited by Rajni Palriwala and Patricia Uberoi, 78–97. London: Sage Publications.

Delaney, Carol. 1995. "Father State, Motherland, and the Birth of Modern Turkey." In *Naturalizing Power: Essays in Feminist Cultural Analysis,* edited by Sylvia Yanagisako and Carol Delaney, 177–99. New York: Routledge.

Deleuze, Gilles. (1968) 1994. *Differences and Repetition.* Translated by Paul Patton. New York: Columbia University Press.

———. 1991. *Bergsonism.* Translated by Hugh Tomlinson and Barbara Habberjam. New York: Zone Books.

———. 2005. *Pure Immanence: Essays on a Life.* Translated by Anne Boyman. New York: Zone Books.

Dirks, Nicholas B. 1992. "Introduction: Colonialism and Culture." In *Colonialism and Culture,* edited by Nicholas B. Dirks, 1–26. Ann Arbor: University of Michigan Press.

———. 2003. *Castes of Mind: Colonialism and the Making of Modern India.* New Delhi: Permanent Black.

Dumont, Louis. 1961. "Marriage in India: The Present State of the Question I: Marriage Alliance in South-East Asia and Ceylon." *Contributions to Indian Sociology* 5: 75–95.

———. 1964. "Marriage in India: The Present State of the Question II." *Contributions to Indian Sociology* 7: 77–98.

———. 1966. "Marriage in India: The Present State of the Question III: North India in Relation to South India." *Contributions to Indian Sociology* 9: 90–114.

———. 1983. *Affinity as a Value: Marriage Alliance in South India, with Comparative Essays on Australia.* Chicago: University of Chicago Press.

Duranti, Alessandro. 2015. *The Anthropology of Intentions: Language in a World of Others.* Cambridge, UK: Cambridge University Press.

Feld, Steven, and Keith H. Basso. 1996a. "Introduction." In *Senses of Place,* edited by Steven Feld and Keith H. Basso, 3–12. Santa Fe, NM: School of American Research Press.

———, eds. 1996b. *Senses of Place.* Santa Fe, NM: School of American Research Press.

Ferguson, James, and Akhil Gupta. 2002. "Spatializing State: Towards an Ethnography of Neoliberal Governmentality." *American Ethnologist* 29 (4): 981–1002.

Ferme, Mariane C. 2004. "Deterritorialized Citizenship and the Resonances of the Sierra Leonean State." In *Anthropology in the Margin of State,* edited by Veena Das and Deborah Poole, 81–115. Santa Fe, NM: School of American Research Press.

Foucault, Michel. 1994. "About the Concept of the 'Dangerous Individual' in Nineteenth-Century Legal Psychiatry." In *Power: Essential Works of Michel Foucault, 1954–1984,* edited by Paul Rabinow, translated by Robert Hurley, 176–200. New York: New Press.

Frake, Charles O. 1996. "Pleasant Places, Past Times, and Sheltered Identity in Rural East Anglia." In *Senses of Place,* edited by Steven Feld and Keith H. Basso, 229–57. Santa Fe, NM: School of American Research Press.

Franklin, Sarah, and Susan McKinnon. 2001. *Relative Values: Re-configuring Kinship Studies.* Durham, NC: Duke University Press.

Fuglerud, Øivind. 1999. *Life on the Outside: The Tamil Diaspora and Long-Distance Nationalism.* London: Pluto Press.

———. 2004. "Constructing Exclusion: The Micro-Sociology of an Immigration Depart-
    ment." *Social Anthropology* 12 (1): 25–40.
———. 2005. "Inside Out: The Reorganization of National Identity in Norway." In *Sov-
    ereign Bodies: Citizens, Migrants, and States in the Postcolonial*, edited by Thomas
    Blom Hansen and Finn Stepputat, 291–311. Princeton, NJ: Princeton University Press.
Fuller, Christopher J., and Haripriya Narasimhan. 2008. "Companionate Marriage in
    India: The Changing Marriage System in a Middle-Class Brahman Sub Caste." *Jour-
    nal of Royal Anthropological Institute* 14 (4): 736–54.
Gallo, Ester. 2008. "Unorthodox Sisters: Relationship and Generational Changes among
    Malayali Migrants in Italy." In *Marriage, Migration and Gender*, edited by Rajni Pal-
    riwala and Patricia Uberoi, 180–212. London: Sage Publications.
Gardner, Katy. 1995. *Global Migrants, Local Lives: Travel and Transformation in Rural
    Bangladesh*. Oxford, UK: Clarendon Press.
Gell, Alfred. 1998. *Art and Agency: An Anthropological Theory*. Oxford, UK: Clarendon
    Press.
Gell, Simeran Man Singh. 1994. "Legality and Ethnicity: Marriage among the South
    Asians of Bedford." *Critique of Anthropology* 14 (4): 335–92.
Gennep, Arnold van. (1909) 1960. *The Rites of Passage*. Translated by Monika B. Vizedom
    and Gabrielle L. Caffee. Chicago: University of Chicago Press.
Ginsburg, Fay D., and Rayna Rapp. 1995. *Conceiving the New World Order: The Global
    Politics of Reproduction*. Berkeley: University of California Press.
Goonesekere, Savitri. 1984. "Some Reflection of Solemnization of Marriage in the Gen-
    eral Law of Sri Lanka." *Mooter: Journal of the Moot Society*, 24–37.
———. 1987. *The Sri Lankan Law on Parent and Child*. Colombo: M. D. Gunasena.
Grover, Shalin. 2009. "Lived Experienced: Marriages, Notions of Love, and Kinship
    Support amongst the Poor Women in Delhi." *Contributions to Indian Sociology* 43(1):
    1–33.
Gupta, Akhil. 1995. "Blurred Boundaries: The Discourse of Corruption, the Culture of
    Politics, and the Imagined State." *American Ethnologist* 22 (2): 375–402.
———. 1997. *Culture, Power, Place: Explorations in Critical Anthropology*. Durham, NC:
    Duke University Press.
———. 2012. *Red Tape: Bureaucracy, Structural Violence, and Poverty in India*. Durham,
    NC: Duke University Press.
Gupta, Akhil, and James Ferguson. 1992. "Beyond 'Culture': Space, Identity, and the Pol-
    itics of Differences." *Cultural Anthropology* 7 (1): 6–23.
Hall, Rachel A. 2002. "When Is a Wife Not a Wife? Some Observations on the Immigra-
    tion Experiences of South Asian Women in West Yorkshire." *Contemporary Politics*
    8 (1): 55–68.
Hansen, Blom Thomas, and Finn Stepputat. 2005a. "Introduction." In *Sovereign Bodies:
    Citizens, Migrants, and States in the Postcolonial*, edited by Thomas Blom Hansen
    and Finn Stepputat, 1–38. Princeton, NJ: Princeton University Press.
———, eds. 2005b. *Sovereign Bodies: Citizens, Migrants, and States in the Postcolonial
    World*. Princeton, NJ: Princeton University Press.
Hayley, F. A. 1923. *A Treatise on the Laws and Customs of the Sinhalese, including Portions
    still Surviving under the Name of Kandyan Law*. Colombo: Cave and Company.

Henare, Amiria, Martin Holbraad, and Sari Wastell, eds. 2006. *Thinking through Things: Theorising Artefacts Ethnographically*. London: Routledge.

Hirsch, J .S. 2003. *A Courtship after Marriage: Sexuality and Love in Mexican Transnational Families*. Berkeley: University of California Press.

Hirsch, Marianne. 1997. *Family Frames: Photography, Narratives, and Postmemory*. Cambridge, MA: Harvard University Press.

Holmes, Robert W. 1982. *Jaffna, Sri Lanka, 1980*. Jaffna: Christian Institute for the Study of Religion and Society of Jaffna College.

Hoole, Ratnajeevan H. 1997. *The Exile Returned: Self-Portrait of the Tamil Vellahlahs of Jaffna, Sri Lanka*. Colombo: Aruvi Publishers.

Hull, Matthew S. 2008. "Ruled by Records: The Expropriation of Land and the Misappropriation of Lists in Islamabad." *American Ethnologist* 35 (4): 501–18.

———. 2012a. "Documents and Bureaucracy." *Annual Review of Anthropology* 41 (1): 251–67.

———. 2012b. *Government of Paper: The Materiality of Bureaucracy in Urban Pakistan*. Berkeley: University of California Press.

Hutchinson, Sharon E. 1996. *Nuer Dilemmas: Coping with Money, War, and the State*. Berkeley: University of California Press.

Jeganathan, Pradeep. 2003. "Violence as an Analytical Problem: Sri Lankanist Anthropology after 1983." *Nethira: Journal of the International Center for Ethnic Studies Colombo* 6 (1–2): 7–47.

———. 2004. "Check Points: Anthropology Identity and State." In *Anthropology in the Margin of State*, edited by Veena Das and Deborah Poole, 67–80. Oxford, UK: James Currey.

Kalpagam, U. 2008. "American Varan Marriage among the Tamil Brahmans: Preferences, Strategies and Outcomes." In *Marriage, Migration and Gender*, edited by Rajni Palriwala and Patricia Uberoi, 98–124. London: Sage Publications.

Kanapathipillai, Valli. 1990. "July 1983: The Survivor's Experience." In *Mirrors of Violence: Communities, Riots and Survivors in South Asia*, edited by Veena Das, 321–44. New Delhi: Oxford University Press.

Kapadia, Karin. 1995. *Siva and Her Sister: Gender, Caste and Class in Rural South Asia*. Oxford, UK: Westview Press.

Kapferer, Bruce. 1989. "Nationalist Ideology and a Comparative Anthropology." *Ethnos* 54 (3–4): 161–99.

———. 2012. *Legends of People, Myths of State: Violence, Intolerance, and Political Culture in Sri Lanka and Australia*. New York: Berghahn Books.

Kaur, Ravinder, and Rajni Palriwala, eds. 2014. *Marrying in South Asia: Shifting Concepts, Changing Practices in a Globalizing World*. New Delhi: Orient Black Swan.

Kukaplan, K. 1996. *Yalpana Edapivu*. Jaffna: Jaffna University.

Latour, Bruno. 2005. *Reassembling the Social*. Oxford, UK: Oxford University Press.

Latour, Bruno, and Steve Woolgar, eds. 1986. *Laboratory Life: The Construction of Scientific Facts*. 2nd ed. Princeton, NJ: Princeton University Press.

Lawrence, Patricia. 2000. "Violence, Suffering, Amman: The Work of Oracles in Sri Lanka's Eastern War Zone." In *Violence and Subjectivity*, edited by Veena Das et al., 171–204. New Delhi: Oxford University Press.

Leach, E. R. 1961. *Pul Eliya: A Village in Ceylon.* Cambridge, UK: Cambridge University Press.

Lévi-Strauss, Claude. 1969. *The Elementary Structures of Kinship.* Translated by John Richard von Sturmer, James Harle Bell, and Rodney Needham. Boston: Beacon Press.

Low, Setha M., and Denise Lawrence-Zúñiga. 2003. *The Anthropology of Space and Place: Locating Culture.* Malden, MA: Blackwell.

Lowenkron, Laura, and Letícia Ferreira. 2014. "Anthropological Perspectives on Documents: Ethnographic Dialogues on the Trail of Police Papers". *Vibrant: Virtual Brazilian Anthropology* 11 (20): 76–112.

Lu, Melody Chia-Wen. 2008. "Commercially Arranged Marriage Migration: Case Studies of Cross-Border Marriages in Taiwan." In *Marriage, Migration and Gender*, edited by Rajni Palriwala and Patricia Uberoi, 125–51. London: Sage Publications.

Lubkemann, Stephen C. 2007. *Culture in Chaos: An Anthropology of the Social Condition of War.* Chicago: University of Chicago Press.

Majumdar, Rochona. 2004. "Looking for Brides and Grooms: Ghataks, Matrimonials, and the Marriage Market in Colonial Calcutta, circa 1875–1940." *Journal of Asian Studies* 63 (4): 911–35.

Malkki, Liisa. 1992. "National Geographic: The Rooting of Peoples and the Territorialization of National Identity among Scholars and Refugees." *Cultural Anthropology* 7 (1): 24–44.

Marcus, George A. 1995. "Ethnography in/of the World System: The Emergence of Multisited Ethnography." *Annual Review of Anthropology* 24 (1): 95–117.

Maunaguru, Sidharthan. 2009. "Brides as Bridges? Tamilness through Movements, Documents and Anticipations." In *Pathways of Dissent: Tamil Nationalism in Sri Lanka*, edited by R. Cheran, 55–80. London: Sage Publications.

———. 2013. "Transnational Sri Lankan Tamil Marriages." In *Encyclopedia of Sri Lankan Diaspora*, edited by Peter Reeves, 61–62. Singapore: Editions Didier Millet in association with Institute of South Asian Studies, National University of Singapore.

Maunaguru, Sidharthan, and Nicholas Van Hear. 2012. "Transnational Marriages in Conflict Settings: War, Dispersal, and Sri Lankan Tamil Marriages." In *Transnational Marriage: New Perspectives from Europe and Beyond*, edited by Katharine Charsley, 127–41. New York: Routledge.

May, Todd. 2005. *Gilles Deleuze: An Introduction.* Cambridge, UK: Cambridge University Press.

McDowell, Christopher. 1996. *A Tamil Asylum Diaspora: Sri Lanka Migration, Settlement and Politics in Switzerland.* Oxford, UK: Berghahn Books.

McGilvray, Dennis B. 1982. "Mukkuvar Vannimai: Tamil Caste and Matriclan Ideology in Batticaloa, Sri Lanka." In *Caste Ideology and Interaction*, edited by Dennis B. McGilvray, 34–97. Cambridge, UK: Cambridge University Press.

———. 2008. *Crucible of Conflict.* Durham, NC: Duke University Press.

Meillassoux, Claude. 1981. *Maidens, Meal, and Money: Capitalism and the Domestic Community.* New York: Cambridge University Press.

Meyer, Eric. 2003. "Labour Circulation between Sri Lanka and South Asia in Historical Perspective." In *Society and Circulation: Mobile People and Itinerant Cultures in*

South Asia 1750–1950, edited by Claude Markovits, Jacques Pouchepasass, and Sanjay Subrahmanyam, 56–58. New Delhi: Permanent Black.

Miller, Daniel. 1987. *Material Culture and Mass Consumption*. Cambridge, MA: Basil Blackwell.

———, ed. 2005. *Materiality*. Durham, NC: Duke University Press.

Mitchell, T. J. W. 2005. *What Do Pictures Want? The Lives and Loves of Images*. Chicago: University of Chicago Press.

Mitchell, Timothy, and George Steinmetz. 1999. "Society, Economy, and the State Effect." In *State/Culture: State Formation after the Cultural Turn*, edited by George Steinmetz, 169–86. Ithaca, NY: Cornell University Press.

Mody, Perveez. 2008. *Intimate State: Love-Marriage and the Law in Delhi*. London: Routledge.

Mulla, Sameena. 2015. "Sexual Violence, Law, and Qualities of Affiliation." In *Wording the World: Veena Das and Scenes of Inheritance*, edited by Roma Chatterji, 172–90. New York: Fordham University Press.

Mutukisna, Francis Henry, Robert Atherton, and Class Isaakzoon. 1862. *A New Edition of the Thesawaleme; or, The Laws and Customs of Jaffna*. Ceylon: Ceylon Time Office.

Muthulingam, N. 1996. *Elangail thiravida kalagam*. Colombo: South Asian Press.

Navaro-Yashin, Yael. 2007. "Make-Believe Papers, Legal Forms and the Counterfeit: Affective Interactions between Documents and People in Britain and Cyprus." *Anthropological Theory* 7 (1): 79–98.

Neville, S. Arachchige Don. 1994. *Patterns of Community Structure in Colombo Sri Lanka: An Investigation of Contemporary Urban Life in South Asia*. New York: University Press of America.

Obeyesekere, Gananath. 1967. *Land Tenure in Village Ceylon: A Sociological and Historical Study*. Cambridge, UK: Cambridge University Press.

Olwig, Karen Fog. 2007. *Caribbean Journey: An Ethnography of Migration and Home in Three Family Networks*. Durham, NC: Duke University Press.

Ong, Aihwa. 1999. *Flexible Citizenship: The Cultural Logics of Transnationality*. Durham, NC: Duke University Press.

———. 2003. *Buddha Is Hiding: Refugee, Citizenship, and New America*. Berkeley: University of California Press.

Oxfeld, Ellen. 2005. "Cross-Border Hypergamy? Marriage Exchanges in a Transnational Hakka Community." In *Cross-Border Marriages: Gender and Mobility in Traditional Asia*, edited by Nicole Constable, 17–33. Philadelphia: University of Pennsylvania Press.

Palriwala, Rajni, and Patricia Uberoi. 2008a. "Exploring the Links: Gender Issues in Marriage and Migration." In *Marriage, Migration and Gender*, edited by Rajni Palriwala and Patricia Uberoi, 23–60. London: Sage Publications.

———, eds. 2008b. *Marriage, Migration and Gender*. London: Sage Publications.

Parkin, Robert, and Linda Stone. 2004. "General Introduction." In *Kinship and Family: An Anthropological Reader*, edited by Robert Parkin and Linda Stone, 1–24. Oxford, UK: Blackwell Press.

Parry, Jonathan. 2001. "Ankalu's Errant Wife: Sex, Marriage and Industry in Contemporary Chhattisgarh." *Modern Asian Studies* 35 (4): 783–820.

Perera, S. 1999. *Stories of Survivors: Socio-Political Contexts of Female-Headed House-holds in Post-Terror Southern Sri Lanka*. New Delhi: Vikas Publishing.

Perinbanayagam, R. S. 1982. *The Karmic Theater: Self, Society, and Astrology in Jaffna*. Amherst: University of Massachusetts Press.

Petryna, Adriana. 2002. *Life Exposed: Biological Citizenship after Chernobyl*. Princeton, NJ: Princeton University Press.

Pfaffenberger, Bryan. 1982. *Caste in Tamil Culture: The Religious Foundation of Sudra Domination in Tamil Sri Lanka*. New Delhi: Vikas Publishing.

Philips, Amali. 2005. "The Kinship Marriage and Gender Experiences of Tamil Women in Sri Lankan's Tea Plantations." *Contributions to Indian Sociology* 39 (1): 107–42.

Pinney, Christopher. 1997. *Camera Indica: The Social Life of Indian Photographs*. Chicago: University of Chicago Press.

Ponnambalam, Shirani. 2003. *Law and the Marriage Relationship in Sri Lanka*. Pannipi-tiya: Stamford Lake.

Poole, Deborah. 2004. "Between Threat and Guarantee: Justice and Community in the Margin of the Peruvian State." In *Anthropology in the Margin of State*, edited by Veena Das and Deborah Poole, 35–65. Santa Fe, NM: School of American Research Press.

Poonacha, Veena. 1996. "Redefining Gender Relationships: The Imprint of the Colonial State on the Coorg/Kodava Norms of Marriage and Sexuality." In *Social Reforms, Sexuality and the State*, edited by Patricia Uberoi, 39–64. New Delhi: Sage Publications.

Povinelli, Elizabeth A. 2011. *Economies of Abandonment: Social Belonging and Endurance in Late Liberalism*. Durham, NC: Duke University Press.

Raghavan, M. D. 1971. *Tamil Culture in Ceylon: A General Introduction*. Colombo: Kalani Nilayam.

Ramanathan, T. 1972. *Thesawaleme: The Laws and Customs of the Inhabitants of Province of Jaffna*. Colombo: Nadaraja Press.

Reed, Adam. 2006. "Documents Unfolding." In *Documents: Artifacts of Modern Knowledge*, edited by Annelise Riles, 158–77. Ann Arbor: University of Michigan Press.

Riles, Annelise, ed. 2006. *Documents: Artifacts of Modern Knowledge*. Ann Arbor: University of Michigan Press.

Risseeuw, Carla. 1988. *The Fish Don't Talk about the Water: Gender Transformation, Power, and Resistance among the Women in Sri Lanka*. New York: E. J. Brill.

Roberts, Michael. 1982. *Caste Conflict and Elite Formation: The Rise of a Karava Elite in Sri Lanka, 1500–1931*. Cambridge, UK: Cambridge University Press.

Rosen, Lawrence, ed. 1995. *Other Intentions: Cultural Contexts and the Attribution of Inner States*. Santa Fe, NM: School of American Research Press.

Sanpukathas, A., and Manonmani Sanpukathas.1984. *Thamilar Thrimana Nadamurai-kal*. Jaffna: Muthamil veliyidu Kalakam.

Sarkar, Tanika. 1993. "Rhetoric against Age of Consent: Resisting Colonial Reason and Death of a Child-Wife." *Economic and Political Weekly* 28 (36): 1869–78.

Sasivalli, S. 1984. *Thamilar Thirumanam*. Chennai: International Institute for Tamil Studies.

Sathiyaselan, K. 2004. *Malay kutipayavu*. Colombo: Kumaran Book House.

Schneider, David M. 2004. "What Is Kinship All About?" In *Kinship and Family: An Anthropological Reader*, edited by Robert Parkin and Linda Stone, 257–74. Oxford, UK: Blackwell Press.

Scott, James C. 1998. *Seeing Like a State*. New Haven, CT: Yale University Press.

Shanmugampillai, M, ed. 2006. *Tholkaapiyam Porulathikaram Ellampuranam*. Chennai: Mullai Nilayam.

Sharma, Aradhana, and Akhil Gupta, eds. 2006. *The Anthropology of the State: A Reader*. Oxford, UK: Blackwell.

Sheel, Ranjana. 2008. "Marriage, Money and Gender: A Case Study of the Migrant Indian Community in Canada." In *Marriage, Migration and Gender*, edited by Rajni Palriwala and Patricia Uberoi, 215–34. London: Sage Publications.

Sivathamby, Karthigesu. 1984. "Some Aspects of the Social Composition of the Tamils of Sri Lanka." In *Ethnicity and Social Changes in Sri Lanka: Papers Presented at a Seminar Organised by the Social Scientists Association*, 175–99. Colombo: Social Scientist Association.

———. 2000. *Yalpana Samukam (Jaffna Society)*. Jaffna: Karthikasu Press.

———. 2005. *Being a Tamil and Sri Lankan*. Colombo: Aivakam.

Spencer, J., J. Goodhand, S. Hasbullah, B. Klem, B. Korf, and K. T. Silva. 2015. *Checkpoint, Temple, Church and Mosque: A Collaborative Ethnography of War and Peace*. London: Pluto Press.

Spencer, Jonathan. 1990. "Collective Violence and Everyday Practice in Sri Lanka." *Modern Asian Studies* 24 (3): 603–23.

———. 2003. "A Nation 'Living in Different Places': Notes on the Impossible Work of Purification in Post-Colonial Sri Lanka." *Contributions to Indian Sociology* 37 (1–2): 1–23.

Sriskandarajah, Dhananjayan. 2002. "The Migration–Development Nexus: Sri Lanka Case Study." *International Migration* 40 (5): 283–307.

Stevenson, Lisa. 2014. *Life beside Itself: Imagining Care in the Canadian Arctic*. Berkeley: University of California Press.

Stoler, Ann Laura. 2002. "Colonial Archives and the Art of Governance." *Archival Science* 2 (1–2): 87–109.

———. 2009. *Along the Archival Grain: Epistemic Anxieties and Colonial Common Sense*. Princeton, NJ: Princeton University Press.

Strathern, Marilyn. 1992a. *After Nature: English Kinship in the Late Twentieth Century*. Cambridge, UK: Cambridge University Press.

———. 1992b. *Reproducing the Future: Essays on Anthropology, Kinship, and the New Reproductive Technologies*. New York: Routledge.

———. 1995. "Disembodied Choice." In *Other Intentions: Cultural Contexts and the Attribution of Inner States*, edited by Lawrence Rosen, 69–90. Santa Fe, NM: School of American Research Press.

———. 1999. *Property, Substance, Effect: Anthropological Essays on Persons and Things*. London: Athlone Press.

Suryanarayan, V., and V. Sudarshan. 2000. *Between Fear and Hope: Sri Lankan Refugees in Tamil Nadu*. Chennai: T. R. Publications.

Tambiah, Henry W. 1954. *The Laws and Customs of the Tamils of Ceylon*. Colombo: Tamil Cultural Society of Ceylon.

———. 1958. "The Law of Thesawalamai." *Tamil Culture* 7 (4): 386–408.

———. 2004. *The Law and Customs of the Tamils of Jaffna*. Colombo: Women's Education and Research Center.

Tambiah, Stanley J. 1973. "Dowry and Bridewealth, and the Property Rights of Women in South Asia." In *Bridewealth and Dowry*, by Jack Goody and Stanley J. Tambiah, 59–160. Cambridge, UK: Cambridge University Press.

———. 1986. *Sri Lanka: Ethnic Fratricide and the Dismantling of Democracy*. Chicago: University of Chicago Press.

Thashanamurthi, A. 2001. *Sanka elakiyankal unarthum manitha uravukal*. Chennai: Makayarkarasi Pathipakam.

Thiranagama, Sharika. 2011. *In My Mother's House: Civil War in Sri Lanka*. Philadelphia: University of Pennsylvania Press.

———. 2007. "Moving On? Generating Homes in the Future for Displaced Northern Muslims in Sri Lanka." In *Ghosts of Memory: Essays on Remembrance and Relatedness*, edited by Janet Castern, 126–49. Malden, MA: Wiley-Blackwell.

Thiruchandran, Selvy. 1999. *The Other Victims of War: Emergence of Female-Headed Households in Eastern Sri Lanka*. New Delhi: Vikas Publishing.

Trautmann, Thomas R. 1981. *Dravidian Kinship*. New York: Cambridge University Press.

Trawick, Margaret. 1992. *Notes on Love in a Tamil Family*. Berkeley: University of California Press.

Trouillot, Michel-Rolph. 2001. "The Anthropology of the State in the Age of Globalization: Close Encounters of the Deceptive Kind." *Current Anthropology* 42 (1): 125–38.

Turner, Victor W. 1969. *The Ritual Process: Structure and Anti-Structure*. London: Routledge and Kegan Paul.

Uberoi, Patricia, ed. 1994. *Family Kinship and Marriage in India*. New Delhi: Oxford University Press.

———. 1996a. "Introduction: Problematising Social Reform, Engaging Sexuality, Interrogating the State." In *Social Reform, Sexuality and the State*, edited by Patricia Uberoi, ix–xxvi. New Delhi: Sage Publications.

———. 1996b. "When Is a Marriage Not a Marriage? Sex, Sacrament and Contract in Hindu Marriage." In *Social Reform, Sexuality and the State*, edited by Patricia Uberoi, 319–46. New Delhi: Sage Publications.

Velupillai, K. 2004. *Yalapana vaibhava kaumudi*. New Delhi: Asian Educational Service.

Werbner, Pnina. 1990. *The Migration Process: Capital, Gifts and Offering among the British Pakistanis*. Oxford, UK: Berg.

Williams, Lucy. 2010. *Global Marriage: Cross-Border Marriage Migration in Global Context*. New York: Palgrave Macmillan.

Yalman, Nur. 1967. *Under the Bo Tree: Studies in Caste Kinship and Marriage in the Interior of Ceylon*. Berkeley: University of California Press.

Yanagisako, Sylvia, and Carol Delaney. 1995. *Naturalizing Power: Essays in Feminist Cultural Analysis*. New York: Routledge.

Zutshi Trakroo, Ragini. 2008. *Refugees and the Law*. New Delhi: Human Rights Law Network.

Index

actualization, 19

adoptive country, 10, 12, 19, 40, 51, 62, 84, 95, 130, 157

agency, 156, 165n3

agent: compared to marriage broker, 26; paralegals in Canada, 134–36; and the Sri Lankan state, 83; trafficking, 3, 25, 76, 148; and wedding packages, 63

alliance, 15, 17, 43, 73

anxiety, 21, 55, 105, 108

archives, 12

army, 30, 32–33, 54, 66, 75, 148

artifacts, 12, 19, 21–22

assemblages: of documents, 43, 138; and legal matters/actors, 111, 127–28, 154; in producing sociality, 21

association: between documents and humans, 21–22, 56–58, 88, 105, 132; of different materiality, 52, 157; kinship and relatedness, 160; and photos, 106–8

astrologer, 29, 44, 49, 50, 159, 164n5

astrological charts, 20, 33, 36, 38–39, 43–44, 47–50, 52, 76, 164n29, 164n5

asylum, 7, 24, 68, 76, 131–32

asylum seekers, 7, 68

Australia, 4, 8–10, 39, 51

borders: geopolitical, 10; international, 3, 49; national, 4, 148; protection/restriction, 131, 151

bride: acceptance of, 79; astrological charts, 49; brokers' files, 12, 20–21, 158; and caste associations, 86, 93, 115, 121; and domestic violence, 25; dowry value of, 52; role of brother, 73; Sri Lankan, 46, 51; and thali, 61, 103, 115–16, 121, 152, 166n9

bridegroom, 115, 123, 126. *See also* grooms

Canada: immigration, visa, and citizenship processes in, 9, 10, 13, 22, 39, 75, 80, 89, 129, 133–39, 166n4; marriage brokering in, 39, 45, 47, 48, 55–56; marriage genuineness in, 130–33, 140, 141–55; refugee migration to, 7–8, 9, 71, 88; reunited in, 20, 88; spouse from, 12, 33, 40, 51–52, 55, 63, 167n5

capital, 3, 6, 9, 131

caste: and community connections, 21–22; and endogamous marriage, 28, 43; and Jaffna society, 37, 40, 163n10; koviyar, 123, 166n11; marginalized, 8, 115, 122; pallar, 166n11; privileged and middle, 8, 24, 28, 41–44, 51, 112, 114–15, 121–22; and region, 116–17, 119, 124; and the right spouse, 16, 42; service, 27, 93–94, 123; slave, 122, 166n11; sondakara, 41–42; subcaste, 40–41, 43; vellalar, 41–43, 45, 93, 115, 121, 123, 151, 165n11–12, 166n11

ceremony: civil, 82; kurai, 166n9; marriage, 10, 44, 47, 86; and photographs, 87–89, 94, 99; and priest, 63, 96–98; ponnuruku, 61; religious, 81, 90, 141, 145–46, 152; and thali ritual, 61, 93, 103, 126, 151; and *ur* traditions, 86; and visual documents, 107; wedding, 36, 49, 60–63, 83–85, 88, 104, 107, 123, 145, 150, 159, 165n5 certainty: and documents, 17, 50, 55, 160; and the future, 14, 19, 55, 59, 71, 133, 154, 159; and marriage, 15, 18, 24, 38, 49, 57, 59, 63, 111, 127–28, 144, 146, 158, 161; and uncertainty, 15, 17–20, 24, 28, 43, 50, 55, 71, 106, 117, 133

Chennai, 12, 33, 48, 62–63, 77, 80–82, 84, 86, 89, 95

chidenam, 44–45, 165n12. *See also* dowry

children: and citizenship, 69; clients like, 33, 38; legitimate, 25, 112, 115–16; parents brokering marriages for, 27, 31, 58, 83; separated from, 77–78; supporting family financially, 33, 58, 67

circulation, 21; of documents, 20, 57, 132; of photographs, 95, 102, 106–8

citizen, 4, 9, 22, 25, 33, 36, 40, 81; and future, 141, 147, 149, 154, 159; and insider/outsider, 134; and legal status, 69; and migration, 45; spouse of, 109, 137–38, 159

citizenship, 68, 88; in adoptive country, 10, 24, 40, 51, 62; and different statuses, 39, 58; and documents, 81; possibility of attaining, 9, 71; and refugees, 25, 69

class, 102, 137, 141, 149, 163n10, 167n5; lower, 8; middle, 8–9, 12, 14, 28–29, 42, 44; upper, 24

Colombo, 3, 9, 11–12, 30–32, 36, 42, 45, 55, 76–77, 79–81, 141, 152–53

colonialism, 28, 52, 110–11

complexion, 36, 51. *See also* skin color

community, 74, 79, 87, 126–27, 163n5; association with war and violence, 5–6, 8, 16, 56, 58, 83, 165n14; and fragmented practices, 57, 64, 71, 83; and marriage brokering, 35, 56; Muslim, 6; and potential zones, 17, 18, 71; rebuilding and reconnecting, 19, 21–2, 23, 56, 58, 60, 62–64, 69, 75, 83–86, 108, 160; Sinhala, 6; and transnational marriages, 10–11, 15, 24, 28, 29, 31, 94, 109, 119, 124–25, 147, 151

contract, 101, 107, 120, 126, 130–31, 138, 140–41, 149

court cases, 20–21, 111, 115, 141; in the Canadian context, 133, 141, 143, 157; colonial, 13, 92–93, 114, 125, 143, 166n3; immigration, 12–13

courtrooms: colonial, 109–11, 116, 119, 124, 126, 128, 130, 140, 151, 166n2; immigration, 11, 15, 19, 132, 133, 147, 151; as in-between space, 110, 111, 127, 158, 159

cross-cousin, 28, 72–73, 88, 135–36

culture, 17, 65, 70, 92, 107, 110–11, 119, 139, 151–52

custom, 17, 56, 84–86, 89–90, 118, 121–22, 129, 151–52; continuity and discontinuity of, 59, 105, 110–12; marriage and, 117, 119–20, 123–24, 128, 130, 135–36, 138, 143

desire, 5, 28, 49, 53, 59, 117, 151, 156; and anxieties, 14, 16–17; for the future, 37, 52, 157–58; imagined, 15, 103

diaspora, 15, 19, 84; Jaffna, 12; and marriage, 17, 62–63; Sri Lankan Tamil, 6–7, 9–10, 15, 22, 42, 60, 62–63, 69, 71, 156, 160–61

discourse, 14, 90, 113

displacement, 23, 27, 42–43, 46, 59, 68, 148, 165n14; due to war and dispersion, 5–6, 10, 13, 31, 54, 57, 75, 83, 156, 163n1; internal, 7, 16

divorce, 14, 18, 34, 112

documents: circulation of, 22, 107; and citizenship, 81; and court files, 21, 127–29, 132, 155, 158–59; as in-between moments, 16–22, 50, 56–57, 95; legal, 5, 49, 90, 94, 111, 127, 132, 135, 143; and marriage broker's file, 12, 20, 23, 37–38, 43, 46–47, 55, 57–59, 158–59; and materials, 20–21, 38; permanent resident, 4; to prove genuineness of marriage, 4, 10, 12, 82, 87–89, 92, 123, 130–32, 136, 138–39; state and marriage processes, 24, 30, 126, 133, 147; travel, 4, 8, 63, 81; visual, 106–8, 151, 154, 160–61

dowry, 36, 44–45, 48, 52, 110, 121, 123, 125. *See also* chidenam

certificate, 12, 80, 89, 92, 138; civil, 11, 19, 80–82, 89–94, 111, 115–16, 126–27, 130–31, 138–39, 141–42, 146–47, 152–53; customary, 11–13, 91, 93–94, 109–11, 113–22, 124–28, 130–31, 139–42, 144–47, 150–51, 153, 166n2, 167n12; customs, 85, 89, 117–21, 123, 135, 138; institution of, 5, 13–14, 23, 43; law, 13, 109, 111–13, 128; monogamous, 112–13; ordinance, 112, 114–15, 127; packages, 38–39, 47–48, 80, 83; process, 5, 13–15, 17–20, 24, 38, 46–47, 49, 54–59, 63, 106–8, 111, 120, 127–28, 130, 133, 136, 138, 140, 144, 146–47, 150–51, 153–55, 157–61; rituals, 74–75, 78–79, 92–93, 95, 107, 117, 119–22, 125, 128, 141, 145; validity of, 119

marriage broker: as in-between, 5, 9–10, 19, 38; as matchmaker, 28, 30, 40, 47, 53; and matchmaking, 19, 23–24, 27, 29, 35, 40, 43, 46–47, 49–50, 52–53, 55–59, 159, 165n14; Nimal, 33–34, 38–39; process, 12, 15, 20–21, 23; as profession, 23–30; Rajan, 30–32, 35, 38, 39; Vikram, 32–33, 39–40

matchmaking. *See* marriage broker

materiality, 18, 21, 52, 123

Middle East, 7, 137

migrants: forced, 31, 84; marriage, 16; and refugees, 7, 9, 11, 15, 134; temporary, 8

migration; chain, 7, 25, 156; forced, 7, 9, 23, 66, 157; labor, 7, 131, 157

militant movements, 3, 6, 56, 65

mobility, 16–17, 21, 23, 29, 42, 70, 131, 156–57

modernity, 13–14, 23, 102

monogamy, 116

movement: and displacement, 5, 8; militant, 3, 6, 56, 65; political, 65–66; reformer, 113; temporary, 17, 32

multiculturalism, 151

narrative, 5, 12, 16–17, 91, 95

nation, 65

negotiation, 13, 29, 39, 46–47, 49–50, 52, 54, 110

networks: global, 25; personal, 10, 12, 23, 29, 31–32, 42–43, 46, 49

norms, 87, 139, 144

paralegal, 19, 134–36, 159

photographs: Barthes' discussion of, 91; editing, 88; as evidence, 104; for matchmaking, 35, 52; power of, 103, 105–6; in recognizing marriage as genuine, 21, 26, 87–89, 95, 131, 141; as supporting documents, 87; of the 1940s–70s, 101; wedding, 5, 11, 19, 22, 26, 88, 90–92, 94–95, 102, 105, 107, 138, 151; as witness, 90, 95, 105

photographer: and the capturing of couples' intimacy, 95–96; and conduct of wedding rituals, 85–86, 100; and imagination of futures, 147, 158; as in-between figure, 19, 106, 108, 136, 158–59; as a job, 67; as part of wedding package, 63, 73; and recreating Sri Lankan traditions, 74–75, 79, 97–98, 100, 104, 107; as witness, 81–82, 103, 105

photography, 90–91, 95, 103–7

place-making, 69

politics, 13, 52, 65

pollution, 43, 163n10, 165n9

polygamy, 115–16

potential: future, 50, 55, 71, 86; life of documents, 22, 38, 88, 101–2, 105–11; of the marriage process, 154–55, 158–60, 164n27; spouse, 10, 29, 36–38, 42–43, 48, 50, 57–59; zones, 18–20, 22, 50, 64, 127–28, 132, 147

potentiality, 18, 21–22, 128

power: and documents, 21; and the law, 143; in relation to marriage union, 19, 49; in relation to restricting refugees, 68; technologies of, 132; and wedding photos, 52, 88, 103, 105; over women's labor, 14

priest: absence of, 126; in ascertaining a wedding match, 29; Brahmin, 123; and the conduct of wedding ceremonies, 75, 78, 85, 96–97, 105, 119, 121, 151;